*T*his book is dedicated to the fond memory
of my mother, Tran-Thi-Cuc.

Published in 1989 by
Stewart, Tabori & Chang
A division of U.S. Media Holdings, Inc.
115 West 18th Street
New York, NY 10011

Distributed in Canada by
General Publishing Company Ltd.
30 Lesmill Road
Don Mills, Ontario, Canada M3B 2T6

Library of Congress has cataloged the original edition as follows:
Routhier, Nicole.
    Foods of Vietnam/Nicole Routhier; photographs by
    Martin Jacobs.
        p.   cm.
    Includes index.
    ISBN 1-55670-095-4 (hardcover)
    ISBN 1-55670-959-5 (paperback)
    1. Cookery, Vietnamese.   I. Title
TX724.5.V5R68   1989
641.59597–dc20   89-11320
                                                  CIP

Printed in Japan

10 9 8 7 6 5 4 3 2 1

First Printing

THE
foods of
VIETNAM

NICOLE ROUTHIER

PHOTOGRAPHS BY
MARTIN JACOBS

FOREWORD BY CRAIG CLAIBORNE

STEWART, TABORI & CHANG
NEW YORK

FOREWORD

Although I have travelled around the world many times to such outposts as Singapore, Ethiopia, China, Japan, Kenya and the North Pole, always in pursuit of tasting and reporting on the foods of the universe, my most curious motivation along these lines came about in 1974, seven months before the end of the Vietnam conflict.

Truth to tell, prior to that terrible involvement on America's part, I had only the vaguest notion of where the nation existed. Somewhere in the direction of China and Thailand, I knew, but precisely where, I could not pin-point on my mental map.

My interest in the country was not inspired by the conflict there but by a visit to a Vietnamese restaurant in Paris during the 1960s. It was a cuisine hitherto unknown to me. There were, in fact, far more Vietnamese restaurants in Paris at that time than there were Chinese or Japanese. The name of the restaurant I visited was La P'tite Tonkinoise on the Rue Faubourg. I sampled, for the first time, the Vietnamese version of a spring roll, called *cha gio* (pronounced zhah-zhaw). It was one of the most captivating food experiences of my life. It is a deep-fried dish made with crabmeat, shrimp and ground pork and served with an irresistible dip made with the widely available Vietnamese fish sauce called *nuoc mam* (nook-mahm). The memory of the taste and texture of that dish became indelible in my mind and I determined that somehow, despite the wartime upheaval in Vietnam, I must travel to that country to sample *cha gio* in its own atmosphere.

A few months later I discussed the possibility of writing about the food of that nation with my editors at the *New York Times*. I did not mention the fact that my desire to go was based almost solely on sampling one appetizer. They agreed, however, and I arrived in Saigon during the first week of December. There were, of course, armed soldiers, rolls of barbed wire on the sidewalks and the sound of artillery fire somewhere to the north. I interviewed home cooks and dined in fine restaurants—both French and Vietnamese—and returned to New York, my gustatory mission accomplished.

Approximately five years ago, I began hearing a good deal of the cooking talents of a young Vietnamese woman living in New York named Nicole Routhier. I invited her to come to my home in East Hampton for an interview. She masterfully prepared dishes of her native land, including a bright and tangy shrimp soup, barbecued pork in a caramel sauce, chicken wings with ginger and, of course, that formidable appetizer, *cha gio,* which had introduced me to a life-long love of the Vietnamese table. I learned that such dishes are easily translated into the American kitchen.

I was not wrong in my enthusiasm for Nicole's extraordinary techniques at the cookstove. She was, when I first met her, a student at the Culinary Institute of America in Hyde Park. She subsequently became a professional chef and cooking school teacher.

To my great delight I learned that she was preparing a book about Vietnamese cooking. And now it is in print, a glorious compendium of the foods I love. And food we can all make in our homes. It is brilliantly illustrated and the recipes are skillfully outlined. It is, to my mind, the definitive work on the subject yet to be published in the English language.

Craig Claiborne
East Hampton, New York
May 1989

PREFACE

I am often asked where I learned Vietnamese cooking. I was born in Saigon (now Ho-Chi-Minh City) of a Vietnamese mother and a French father. As I grew up in Vietnam and Laos, my mother insisted upon her children learning about their Vietnamese culture. Although my sister and I had a formal French education, we spoke only Vietnamese to our mother and nanny at home. I learned about cooking from my nanny, a native of Hue, and my mother, from Haiphong; both were home cooks of the first order. Later, my mother owned a small French-Vietnamese restaurant in Laos. When the chef let me help in the kitchen and showed me a few tricks, I knew what my true calling would be.

Although I wasn't fully aware of it, my obsession with food started when I was much younger. There were many times of hardship while I was growing up in Asia, especially after my father left home. During the war, food was scarce and we ate what we could. Sometimes we had to hide in the village bomb shelter for days if not weeks on end, and rice was often the only food available. Our nanny fed us a sort of pressed mashed rice. Each of us was allotted a few sticks of that rice at a time. Unlike my sister, I would never eat my entire ration, but instead I hid it in a very safe place where nobody could find it. Every now and then I would sneak away from my nanny and take a small bite from my treasured food. Although my young, innocent eyes viewed the episode as a game, there was also fear; I was hungry and terrified at the idea of lacking food. That childhood fear never abandoned me.

I also knew better times. I was very fortunate in being able to do a lot of traveling with my family during my teenage years. Those trips throughout Europe and Asia helped shape my ideas about food.

In Vietnamese tradition (as in most of Southeast Asia), recipes are never written but simply taught to the children by letting them help in the family kitchen.

I consider it a great honor when somebody requests certain dishes from my country, and giving a recipe is a very personal gesture of friendship and respect. I have always had a secret desire to write a cookbook which would bring the wonderful tastes of Vietnam to as many people as possible. This dream became a reality through an unusual sequence of events.

Ever since I started reading food columns in the *New York Times,* Craig Claiborne has been my culinary hero. One day, taking up a challenge from my husband, I wrote Mr. Claiborne a short letter asking whether he was interested in sampling true Vietnamese food, the kind he used to have in Saigon, as I would be very honored to prepare a few of my native dishes for him. After mailing the letter, I couldn't sleep that night; I could not stop thinking about how presumptuous it was for me to write such a letter, much less to expect a response. A few days later, I was stunned to receive a brief but warm and very encouraging note from Mr. Claiborne. He welcomed the idea that I cook a Vietnamese meal and said he might even write about it in one of his articles. I was thrilled—and a little nervous—when he asked me to come cook at his house (which he liked to call his "laboratory") in East Hampton, New York. As I was preparing and cooking the food, he sat at the kitchen counter and took notes at his typewriter. Fortunately, I was encouraged by the presence of my husband Tony, but Mr. Claiborne also made me feel at ease and everything went smoothly. The results were a delicious meal that Mr. Claiborne described in the *New York Times* of February 27, 1985.

Based on the interest in Vietnamese cuisine stimulated by that article, and further advice from Mr. Claiborne, I decided to write this cookbook. My hope is that with *The Foods of Vietnam* I can share my love for the tastes of my homeland with you.

ACKNOWLEDGMENTS

I'm deeply grateful to Craig Claiborne, who is responsible for this book more than he will ever know. I would like to particularly thank Barney Karpfinger, my agent, and Leslie Stoker, my editor, for believing in this book enough to make it possible and for supporting my efforts with their great enthusiasm. Many thanks also to the Stewart, Tabori & Chang staff for their hard work and friendliness.

Special thanks to Martin Jacobs for his delectable food photography; to the assistant to the photographer, Francis Hesse; to Linda Johnson for always finding just the right backgrounds, flowers and props; to Beverly Cox for her expert food styling help; and to Rita Marshall for her superb and imaginative design for this book.

I'm especially grateful to Mr. Nguyen-Dang-Trinh for his noble, nostalgic and unique photographs of Vietnam which grace the beginning of this book.

My love and appreciation go to my nanny, Nguyen-Thi-Cuc, who nurtured in me a love for food; to my sister, Alice Dezier, who helped me sort through our mother's piles of recipes and, finally, to my wonderful husband, Anthony Laudin, without whose help and support I could not have completed this book.

CONTENTS

Ground Pork in Tomato Sauce

INTRODUCTION

The knowledge and impressions most Westerners have of Vietnam are based on the political events that have shaped that country's history during the twentieth century. Unfortunately, this has left the rich and diverse culture of the Vietnamese people relatively unexplored. The Vietnamese are proud of their long-lived civilization and traditions. This is especially true of their culinary heritage.

Vietnam's land area of approximately 127,000 square miles is slightly smaller than that of Japan or about three-fourths the size of California. The country is shaped like an elongated letter *S,* with two wide river deltas, the Red River delta in the north and the Mekong River delta in the south, separated from each other by a long, narrow stretch of mountainous coastal land. This natural geographic formation divides the country into three distinct regions: the north, the center and the south. Vietnamese people like to describe their country as a bamboo pole holding a bucket of rice on each end. The buckets represent the lush rice lands found in both deltas, the country's most fertile and populous regions. The pole is the long and narrow (no wider than 45 miles) central region of the country.

Vietnam has a tropical climate governed by the monsoons (seasonal winds of the Indian Ocean and Southeast Asia), which produce a dry season that co-incides with winter and a wet summer season. There is little variation of temperature year-round in the south, while the north experiences a mild cooling during the winter months.

Despite decades of ravaging wars, Vietnam still has some of Southeast Asia's most beautiful and diverse terrain. About 80 percent of the country is covered with trees, bush, mountains and hills, and about half of that is jungle. The remainder consists of open plains in the rice-bearing deltas, alternating with deep valleys, savannas and even deserts.

Vietnam is bordered by Laos and Cambodia on the west, by China on the north and by the South China Sea and Gulf of Thailand on its eastern and southern coastline. Across the South China Sea, it faces the Philippines to the east, and across the Gulf of Thailand, Malaysia and Indonesia to the southeast.

Its geographic location places Vietnam at one of the crossroads of the Asian world. The Vietnamese people can trace their origins to immigrants from southern China, Indonesia, Mongolia, Thailand and elsewhere who settled in the Red River area more than 2,000 years ago.

From its beginnings as a distinct nation, Vietnam has been strongly influenced by China. Ten centuries of Chinese rule introduced such things as Confucianism, writing, methods of administration, art and architecture. The Chinese also contributed the custom of eating with chopsticks, the art of stir-frying and deep-frying in a wok, and food staples such as soy sauce, bean curd and noodles, among others. However, the Vietnamese, ever-conscious of retaining the native character of their culture, assimilated rather than adopted Chinese cooking, leading to a distinctly different cuisine.

Perhaps the most profound and long lasting of the Chinese influences on Vietnam was the introduction of Buddhism. The practice of Buddhism led to the development of a vegetarian cuisine that is incredible in its variety, complexity and taste.

Mongolian invasions of Vietnam during the thirteenth century also left a lasting imprint on Vietnamese food. This is evident in the prominence of beef in northern specialties such as *Pho* (a beef and noodle soup), *Bo Bay Mon* ("beef in seven ways") and *Lau* (Mongolian hot pot).

Contacts with Vietnam's Southeast Asian neighbors —Laos, Cambodia and Thailand—all of which had been under the cultural influence of India, introduced curried dishes and Indian spices into Vietnamese cuisine.

In the sixteenth century, European explorers brought food staples from the New World: watercress, corn, tomatoes, potatoes and peanuts, among others. Snow peas from Holland are now called "Holland peas" and asparagus from France is known as "Western bamboo shoots." In return, the Vietnamese traded rare spices such as cinnamon and pepper.

Vietnamese gastronomy also owes a great deal to the example of France, which ruled the country for almost a century (1859–1954). In the old trading port of Cholon the French built a new city as the central market for all Indochina, and Saigon (now Ho Chi Minh City) was dubbed "the Paris of the Orient." The French implanted a passion for café au lait, French bread, milk, butter, yogurt and even ice creams. Custard tarts and French pastries were de rigueur in Saigon and Hanoi teahouses. Tea served with milk and sugar became fashionable in big-city cafés despite purist disapproval. In the south, the French technique of sautéing in a skillet was preferred to China's speedier stir-frying in a wok.

As much as Vietnamese cuisine has borrowed from or been influenced by various cultures, it has succeeded in retaining its unique character.

What are the characteristics of Vietnamese cuisine? A first look at the flavors and textures reveals many techniques and ingredients adopted from the Thai and the Chinese kitchens. However, it is apparent from the first bite that the Vietnamese have developed a novel cuisine with a unique delicacy and subtlety of taste. A spicy Vietnamese dish will generally be less intense than a Thai dish even though both cuisines use fish sauce, shrimp paste, lemon grass, mint, basil, fiery chile peppers and curry. The Vietnamese *cha gio* may look like the Chinese egg roll but is totally different, from the filling inside to the outside wrapping, and even to the manner in which it is eaten.

The one most characteristic element in virtually every Vietnamese dish is *nuoc mam,* a salty, pungent sauce derived from fermented tiny anchovies. *Nuoc mam* is to the Vietnamese what soy sauce is to the Chinese; it is used as a flavoring in cooking and takes the place of salt at the table. It enhances and blends so subtly with other flavors that one can barely detect its presence.

When mixed with lime juice, chiles, sugar, garlic and vinegar, *nuoc mam* becomes *Nuoc Cham,* an exciting hot sauce that can also be used to spice up almost any cooked dish or as a dressing for salads. Every cook has his own formula for *Nuoc Cham,* and the versions vary according to the foods with which they are to be eaten. For the simplest possible meal, the equivalent of bread and butter, a Vietnamese peasant might eat a bowl of rice accompanied by a few spoonfuls of *Nuoc Cham.*

Nuoc mam is commercially prepared by layering tiny fresh anchovies *(ca com)* alternately with salt, and allowing them to ferment in huge wooden barrels with

open spigots. After three months, liquid drips from the open spigot; it is then poured back into the top of the barrel and left to ferment for an additional three months. When the six-month period is up, the fish sauce is drained off, processed and bottled.

Like olive oil and good wine, there are different grades of fish sauce. The very best fish sauce is obtained from the first drainage. The resulting liquid is amber in color, very dark and usually expensive. If you see the words *nhi* or *thuong hang* on a label, it means that the fish sauce is of the highest quality. This type of fish sauce is usually reserved for table use. Second-grade *nuoc mam,* cheaper and intended for all-purpose cooking, is made by adding water and pressing the fish after the first-quality sauce has been extracted. The resulting liquid is light and very clear.

Another characteristic of Vietnamese cuisine is the combination of complementary ingredients to form new and unique flavors with contrasting textures. The selection of different textures in one single dish is as important as the blending of different flavors and the contrast of complementary colors. Many dishes combine cooked food with fresh greens. In *Bun Bo,* for example, crunchy roasted peanuts contrast with the softness of cooked noodles and sautéed beef, and the crispness of shredded lettuce, cucumber, bean sprouts and herbs.

Vietnamese dishes are generally light in nature, using little fat, even in stir-fried foods. Oil- and corn-starch-laden sauces are virtually unseen. Indeed, the Vietnamese like their foods as fat-free as possible, and use vegetable oil instead of lard for frying. Vietnamese food, therefore, is well suited to today's health- and diet-conscious diners.

The Vietnamese are quick to point out that their cuisine, like their country, is divided into three regions, each with a distinct culinary tradition. However, regional differences are less pronounced than in Chinese cooking. In the Vietnamese repertoire, all three cuisines include many barbecued dishes, fish, seafood and fresh uncooked vegetables.

In the north, the influence of China is most evident. Stir-fries, stews, congees and soups are popular in this part of the country where the climate is cooler and drier. The food tends to be mild because fewer spices are naturally available. During the winter, people like to gather around a charcoal-fired table brazier to cook portions of meat and vegetables by swishing them around with chopsticks in a seasoned broth—just like Chinese hot pot cookery.

The most popular northern dish is the famed Hanoi soup, *Pho Bac. Pho* begins with boiling-hot beef stock poured over fresh rice noodles and paper-thin slices of raw beef in a bowl. When the meat is partially cooked, fresh raw bean sprouts, onion, green chile peppers, lemon juice and the ever-present coriander and mint leaves are added just before eating. The soup may be eaten at breakfast, lunch, dinner and anytime in between. Other northern specialties are a delectable soup of crab and asparagus *(Mang Tay Nau Cua)* and flavorful stuffed bean curd *(Dau Hu Nhoi)*.

In the center of the country, around Hue, the ancient imperial capital of Vietnam, food was brought to a high degree of sophistication. Gastronomy was viewed as an essential element to the art of good living. Special attention was paid to food presentation and styling, intended to reflect the pleasures of the royal palate. Spicy concoctions of fried tomato concentrate, chile peppers and shrimp sauce are often added to soups for a fresh zing. Hue cooks are famed for their pork sausages *(nems)*, vermicelli soups with exceptional flavors and sweet or salty rice cakes. The cooking of this region also incorporates Western-style vegetables, such as potatoes, asparagus, artichokes and cauliflowers, which are grown locally.

The cuisine of the tropical south is simpler than that

of the north and center, but also spicier. The fertile soil yields an abundance of high-quality exotic fruits and vegetables that are added raw to many dishes to contribute their natural flavors. Brief stir-frying is preferred to deep-frying or stewing, and highly spiced curries are common. The French influence is best seen here in the use of asparagus, tomatoes and white potatoes, but preparation is with a definite Vietnamese touch. Barbecued dishes are popular, such as *Chao Tom,* a shrimp paste and sugar cane delicacy. A traditional custom indigenous to the south is for each diner to assemble a little packet by wrapping a morsel of grilled food in a lettuce leaf along with fresh herbs and vegetables. The packet is then dipped in a special hot sauce, often containing peanuts, as in the *saté* sauces of Indonesia.

Breakfast *(bua an sang)*

Vietnamese breakfasts are usually big meals consisting of one hearty dish eaten quite early in the morning. A typical breakfast might be *chao* (a rice gruel or congee served with meat or seafood) and Chinese-style crullers *(dau chao kuai).* Noodle soups are also common breakfast dishes, such as *pho* (a beef and rice noodle soup) or *chao canh* (a rice noodle soup with pork or chicken). *Xoi* (sticky rice) may be mixed with cooked beans and sprinkled with sugar, ground peanuts and shredded coconut. On the way to work, people might stop at a street vendor for *banh cuon* (steamed rolled ravioli) Children like to eat *banh mi gio* (French bread with Vietnamese sausage).

Lunch *(bua com trua)*

Lunch is usually a light meal. If eating out, typical fare is noodle soup, cold noodle salad, or *com dia,* barbecued meats and pickled vegetables served on a bed of rice.

Lunch at home with the family may consist of a bowl of rice, a clear soup with vegetables and a seafood or meat and vegetable stir-fry. Lunch may be followed by a siesta.

At about four o'clock, people enjoy tea or French coffee with snacks, such as sweet puddings *(che)* or French cakes purchased from street vendors.

Dinner *(bua com chieu)*

For dinner, the family gathers together around a low table, everyone sitting cross-legged on mats. A bowl of rice, bamboo chopsticks and a porcelain soup spoon are placed in front of each diner. Ever-present at the table is a small bottle of *nuoc mam* or a saucer of *Nuoc Cham.*

A typical dinner would include a soup and three or four dishes, such as a fried, grilled or simmered fish or meat, a boiled or stir-fried vegetable and pickled or fresh vegetables.

All the dishes are presented together on the table and there is no special order in which they are eaten. Each diner helps himself to a small amount of food and places it on top of his bowl of rice, perhaps dipping a morsel in the *Nuoc Cham* en route. He then brings the bowl to his mouth and shovels the rice in with chopsticks. When taking food from a communal serving dish, the blunt ends of the chopsticks are used in order not to contaminate the food.

Each diner refills his rice bowl until he is satisfied. Then, the remaining soup is poured over the rice to end the meal. Dessert, if any, usually consists of fresh fruits.

Beverages

Of all beverages, tea *(che/tra)* is the most commonly consumed in Vietnam. Like the Chinese, the Vietnamese drink tea all day long. Customarily, tea is prepared very early each morning, then kept in a padded tea cozy for the day's consumption. Visitors are automatically offered tea on arrival, accompanied by cakes, nuts, dried fruits or watermelon seeds. A small amount of tea is poured in a cup and diluted with hot water from a thermos. To the Vietnamese, tea drinking is an important aspect of daily life.

Although there are many varieties of tea, there are only two basic categories: green and black. The main difference lies in the treatment of the leaves. Green tea comes from leaves that have been roasted immediately after harvesting, and is unfermented. Black tea comes from partially dried leaves that are piled up to ferment before being roasted.

In addition to ordinary teas, there are numerous varieties flavored with dried flower blossoms. Most popular are chrysanthemum, jasmine, lotus, hibiscus and rose. The dried flowers are generally left in the tea to expand beautifully and aromatically during infusion.

The Vietnamese word *ruou* for "wine" covers all alcoholic drinks made with any ingredient. One of the best-known national products is called *ruou de* or *choum*, a strong, colorless alcohol made from white glutinous rice (similar to the Japanese sake or the Chinese *kao liang* liquor.) A lesser-known charcoal-dark alcohol, called *ruou nep thang*, is made from a variety of black glutinous rice. Both spirits are very strong and may be served warm for toasting on special occasions.

Festive Foods

Festivals and holidays, always an integral part of Vietnam's culture, are celebrated with banquets that feature special foods. Tet, the Lunar New Year, is the most important of the holidays. On this occasion, homes around the country are adorned with peach blossoms, which represent luck and peace. Families gather to prepare and feast on traditional dishes, such as an abalone soup *(sup bao ngu)* or a special sharks' fin soup *(canh vay ca)*, fried spring rolls *(cha gio)*, glutinous rice cakes filled with meat and beans and boiled in banana leaves *(banh trung)* and candied fruits *(mut)*. After the festive meal, the family, dressed in traditional costumes, visits relatives to wish them joy, happiness and a long life. The children are given money wrapped in tiny red envelopes, and the adults exchange food. The celebration continues with more eating amidst the blasting of firecrackers and the playing of Vietnamese games of chance.

How to Order in Vietnamese Restaurants

According to State Department figures, America is home to more than 750,000 Vietnamese immigrants. Although there are Vietnamese restaurants throughout the country, this sophisticated cuisine still remains largely unknown to the general public.

In a restaurant it is often hard for one or two diners to sample more than a few dishes from a long and puzzling menu. Therefore, the best way to experience Vietnamese food is to gather a group of adventurous friends to go with you in order that a spectrum of tastes can be shared by all.

A typical meal for four persons should include one or two appetizers per person, a soup and three or four entrées. Try to experience the different methods of cooking; select one steamed dish, one simmered dish, one or two fried dishes, one roast and one rice or noodle dish.

In most restaurants you should be able to find the following classic Vietnamese dishes:

Hor d'oeuvres and appetizers (*mon an choi*):
Fried Spring Rolls (*Cha Gio*)
Barbecued Shrimp on Sugar Cane (*Chao Tom*)
Fresh Spring Rolls (sometimes describes as pork and shrimp rice rolls, *Goi Cuon*)
Steamed Rolled Ravioli (*Banh Cuon*)
Barbecued Pork Meatballs (*Nem Nuong*)
Grilled Beef with Lemon Grass (*Bo Xa Lui Nuong*)
Vietnamese Cold Plate (thinly sliced cold Vietnamese sausages)

Soups (*canh*):
Hanoi Soup (*Pho*)
Chicken and Cellophane Noodle Soup (*Mien Ga*)
Spicy and Sour Shrimp Soup (sometimes described as "Vietnamese Bouillabaisse," *Canh Chua Tom*)
Asparagus and Crabmeat Soup (*Mang Tay Nau Cua*)
Chicken and Corn Soup (*Sup Bap Ga*)

Entrées (*khai vi*):
Sweet-and-Sour Fish (*Ca Rang Chua Ngot*)
Pork or Fish Simmered in Caramel Sauce (*Thit/Ca Kho*)
Fried Chicken with Lemon Grass (*Ga Xao Sa Ot*)
Shrimp or Crab Fried in Salt and Pepper (*Tom Cua Rang Muoi*)
Roast Duck (*Vit Nuong*)
Rice and Chicken in a Clay Pot (*Com Ga*)
Crisp-Fried Egg Noodles with Meat and Vegetables (*Mi Xao Thap Cam*)
Vietnamese Fondues (*Bo Nhung Dam* or *Lau Thap Cam*)—if you order one, omit the soup and order fewer entrées.

Desserts (*trang mieng*):
In most restaurants dessert offerings are limited to canned fruits in syrup, such as litchi, longan, mango, rambutan, etc. At more sophisticated restaurants, you may try fried banana or pineapple flamed with rice wine (*chuoi/dua chien*) or the more traditional coconut-laced pudding desserts called *che*. Also traditional

Roast Chicken with Lemon Grass, Nuoc Cham, *Crisp-Fried Bean Curd in Tomato Sauce and Chicken and Mustard Greens Soup*

is a cold dessert-drink combination of ground mung bean, agar-agar and coconut milk often listed under Beverages as "Rainbow Drink." Of course, you may also opt for more westernized desserts, such as *Flan au Caramel*, fruit sorbets and ice creams.

Beverages (*rouc, nuoc*):

To accompany their meals, Vietnamese patrons usually drink tea, Asian beers (or Vietnam's own "33" or soft drinks, such as sweet soybean milk (*sua dau nanh*), iced French Coffee (*ca-phe sua da*), sugar cane juice (*nuoc mia*), soda (*nuoc ngot*) or a rich drink that combines club soda, milk and egg yolks (*soda sua hot ga*).

To conclude the meal, try French coffee (*ca-phe sau*). Note that the Vietnamese use condensed milk instead of fresh milk and sugar, and the coffee is served filtered into individual glasses (not cups as the French do at the table. If you prefer something more robust, order rice wine (*ruou de*).

Here is a variety of menus for different occasions. If Vietnamese cooking is new to you, you may want to begin by incorporating one dish into your standard menu. For example, try a Vietnamese salad with roast beef. When planning a menu, base your choice on the flavor combinations you find most appealing.

In general, ice-cold beer is a natural accompaniment to Vietnamese dishes. Try an Asian import or a light German brew. Vietnamese food also goes extremely well with wines. I usually pair light white wines and rosés with light or mild dishes. On the other hand, a full-bodied Burgundy or Gewürztraminer will give an interesting spark to spicier or richer dishes.

Fresh fruits are traditionally served to conclude ordinary meals while prepared desserts are reserved for special occasions. You may also choose fruit sorbets to end a Vietnamese meal gracefully.

I. Simple Menus

Menu 1:
Ground Pork Omelet (page 126)
Stir-Fried Long Beans with Shrimp (page 182)
Tomato and Egg Drop Soup (page 52)
Plain Rice

Menu 2:
Pork Simmered in Caramel Sauce (page 112)
Pickled Bean Sprouts (page 184)
Stir-Fried Water Spinach with Garlic (page 176)
Daikon and Pork Soup (page 56)
Plain Rice

Menu 3:
Crisp-Friend Bean Curd in Tomato Sauce (page 171)
Roast Chicken with Lemon Grass (page 97)
Chicken and Bamboo Mustard Cabbage Soup (page 56)
Plain Rice

${\cal A}$PPETIZERS

Boiled Shrimp and Pork Dumplings

BOILED SHRIMP AND PORK DUMPLINGS

BANH BOT LOC

These delicious dumplings come from the central region. Tapioca starch lends an interesting, chewy texture to these snacks.

■ ■ ■ ■ ■ ■ ■ ■ ■ ■ ■

4 *ounces ground pork*
4 *ounces raw medium shrimp, peeled, deveined and coarsely chopped*
2 *large garlic cloves, minced*
1½ *tablespoons* nuoc mam *(Vietnamese fish sauce)*
⅛ *teaspoon sugar*
   Freshly ground black pepper
2 *dried Chinese mushrooms*
1½ *teaspoons dried tree ear mushrooms*
2 *tablespoons vegetable oil*
2 *large shallots, chopped*
1 *teaspoon tomato paste*
¼ *cup chopped bamboo shoots, water chestnuts or jicama*
   Scallion oil (page 225), double the recipe
   Nuoc Cham *with Shredded Carrot and Daikon (page 212)*
1 *cup tapioca starch*
¼ *teaspoon salt*
32 *fresh coriander sprigs*

In a mixing bowl, combine the ground pork, shrimp, garlic, fish sauce, sugar and black pepper to taste. Mix well. Cover and refrigerate.

Soak the two types of mushrooms in hot water for 30 minutes. Squeeze the mushrooms dry; remove and discard the stems. Coarsely chop the mushroom caps.

Heat 1 tablespoon of the oil in a wok or skillet over high heat. Add the shallots and stir-fry for 30 seconds. Add the tomato paste and stir for 1 minute. Add the pork and shrimp mixture and stir-fry for 3 minutes. Add the mushrooms and bamboo shoots and cook until heated through. Transfer the filling to a dish to cool. (The recipe may be prepared to this point half a day in advance. Cover and refrigerate.)

Prepare the scallion oil. Transfer to a large bowl; set aside. Prepare the *Nuoc Cham* with Shredded Carrot and Daikon.

Prepare the dough: Combine the tapioca starch and salt in a mixing bowl. In a small saucepan, combine the remaining 1 tablespoon oil with ½ cup plus 2 tablespoons water. Bring to a rolling boil. Gradually pour the liquid over the tapioca starch. Working quickly, use chopsticks or a fork to stir the mixture until it forms a sticky mass. Cover the dough and let stand for 15 minutes, or until cool enough to handle. Lightly oil a work surface and knead the dough for 5 minutes, or until smooth.

Divide the dough into 2 equal parts. Work with half of the dough at a time; keep the other half covered with a damp cloth. Dust a work surface with flour. Knead each half of the dough for a few more minutes, until very smooth. Roll the dough with your hands to form a long rope about 1 inch in diameter. Cut each rope into 16 equal portions.

Cover the dough pieces with a damp cloth as you work. Working with 1 portion at a time, roll out each piece of dough into a 3¼-inch circle. Use a 3-inch cookie cutter to make a perfect round. To form each dumpling, place a heaping teaspoon of the filling on one half of the dough circle. Place 1 coriander sprig on top of the filling. Fold the dough over the filling and pinch the edges together to seal. Set the dumpling on an oiled tray and keep covered with a damp cloth. Continue in the same manner with the remaining dough portions, filling and coriander sprigs.

Bring a large pot of water to a boil. Place a large bowl of cold water and the bowl containing the scallion oil next to the stove. Working in batches of 6 to 8, add the dumplings to the boiling water and cook over moderate heat for 2 minutes. Do not crowd the pot. Use a wire mesh sieve or slotted spoon to remove the cooked dumplings. Drop them into the bowl of cold water and let soak for 1 minute, or until the dough turns translucent. Remove the dumplings from the water and drop them into the scallion oil. Soak until the dumplings are luke-warm, about 1 minute. Remove the dumplings to a platter. Cook the remaining dumplings in the same manner.

Serve with *Nuoc Cham* with Shredded Carrot and Daikon.

Yield: 32 dumplings

SHRIMP TOAST
BANH MI CHIEN VOI TOM

Nuoc Cham *(page 212)*
8 *ounces raw shrimp, peeled and deveined*
4 *garlic cloves*
6 *shallots, or 1 small onion*
½ *teaspoon grated fresh gingerroot*
½ *teaspoon salt*
1½ *teaspoons sugar*
1 *tablespoon potato starch or cornstarch*
 Freshly ground black pepper
1 *tablespoon* nuoc mam *(Vietnamese fish sauce)*
1 *narrow loaf of French bread, cut into ½-inch-thick slices*
1 *cup fine fresh bread crumbs (made in a food processor from bread crusts or trimmings)*
 Vegetable oil, for frying

Prepare the *Nuoc Cham*. Set aside.

In a food processor, combine the shrimp, garlic, shallots, ginger, salt, sugar, potato starch and pepper. Process until finely chopped (you want to retain some texture of the shrimp). With the motor running, pour the fish sauce through the feed tube and process until the mixture is well combined.

Spread about 1 tablespoon of the shrimp paste on each slice of bread, rounding off the top. Dip the shrimp-coated side in the bread crumbs, covering well. Refrigerate, covered, for up to 1 day.

In a wok or wide heavy pan, heat about 2 inches of oil to 360°F, or until bubbles form around a dry wooden chopstick when inserted in the oil. Working in batches, add the shrimp toasts, shrimp side down. Fry for about 1 minute, or until golden brown. Turn over, bread side down, and fry for 1 minute. Drain on paper towels and serve hot with *Nuoc Cham*.

Yield: About 20 shrimp toasts

Fresh Spring Rolls

Lettuce Rolls

FRESH SPRING ROLLS
GOI CUON

*T*his is nothing more than a Vietnamese salad with pork and shrimp rolled up in rice papers. The aromatic herbs in these traditional rolls give an incredibly refreshing taste. They may be served with either Peanut Sauce or *Nuoc Cham* with Shredded Carrot and Daikon.

■ ■ ■ ■ ■ ■ ■ ■ ■ ■ ■

Peanut Sauce (page 211), or Nuoc Cham *with Shredded Carrot and Daikon (page 212)*

*2 ounces thin rice vermicelli (*bun, *page 223), or ½ bundle Japanese alimentary paste noodles (*somen, *page 223)*

1 tablespoon roasted peanuts (page 220), ground

8 raw medium shrimp

12 ounces fresh bacon (pork belly) or boneless pork loin, in one piece

1 large carrot, shredded

1 teaspoon sugar

*8 rounds of rice paper (*banh trang*), each 8½ inches in diameter*

4 large red leaf or Boston lettuce leaves, thick stem ends removed and cut in half

1 cup fresh bean sprouts

½ cup mint leaves

16 sprigs Chinese chives, trimmed to 5-inch lengths (optional)

½ cup coriander leaves

Prepare the dipping sauce, noodles and roasted peanuts. Set aside.

Boil the shrimp for 3 minutes; refresh under cold water. Shell, devein and cut lengthwise in half. Set aside.

Cook the fresh bacon in boiling salted water for 20 minutes; refresh in cold water. Thinly slice into 1 by 2-inch pieces.

In a bowl, combine the shredded carrot with the sugar; let stand for 10 minutes to soften.

Have a basin of warm water ready to moisten the rice papers.

Work with only 2 sheets of rice paper at a time, keeping the remaining sheets covered with a barely damp cloth to prevent curling. Immerse each sheet individually into the warm water. Quickly remove and spread out flat on a dry towel, without letting the sheets touch one another. The rice paper will become pliable within seconds.

Lay one piece of lettuce over the bottom third of the rice paper. On the lettuce, place 1 tablespoon of noodles, 1 tablespoon of the shredded carrot, a few pieces of pork, bean sprouts and several mint leaves. Roll up the paper halfway into a cylinder. Fold both sides of the paper over the filling. Lay 2 shrimp halves, cut side down, along the crease. Tuck 2 chive sprigs under the shrimp at one end, leaving about 1 inch of the chives extending over the fold line. Place several coriander leaves next to the shrimp row. Keep rolling the paper into a cylinder to seal. Place the rolls on a plate covered with a damp towel so they will stay moist as you fill the remaining wrappers.

Pour the dipping sauce into small individual bowls and sprinkle with the ground nuts. Dip the rolls in the sauce as you eat.

NOTE These rolls can be prepared a few hours in advance, covered with a damp towel or plastic wrap and kept at room temperature until needed.

Yield: 8 rolls, or 4 servings

LETTUCE ROLLS
CUON DIEP

*T*his could be described as a rolled salad. The delicate rolls may be served with either *Nuoc Cham* or *Mam Tom*.

■ ■ ■ ■ ■ ■ ■ ■ ■ ■ ■

Nuoc Cham (*page 212*), *or* Mam Tom (*page 215*)
2 ounces thin rice vermicelli (bun, *page 223*), *or ½ bundle Japanese alimentary paste noodles* (somen, *page 223*)
4 egg pancakes (page 219), whole
4 ounces store-bought or homemade Vietnamese Pork Sausage (page 116), in one piece (optional)
8 raw medium shrimp
8 ounces fresh bacon (pork belly) or boneless pork loin, in one piece
8 young, thin scallions, trimmed
8 large red leaf or Boston lettuce leaves, thick stem ends removed
½ cup mint leaves
½ cup coriander leaves

Prepare the *Nuoc Cham* or *Mam Tom*. Prepare the egg pancakes. Thinly slice the pork sausage and then cut into 1½ by 2½-inch pieces. Boil the noodles; set aside.

Boil the shrimp for 5 minutes, then drain and rinse under cold water. Shell, devein and cut the shrimp lengthwise in half.

Boil the pork for 30 minutes, then drain and rinse with cold water. Thinly slice the fresh bacon into 1½ by 2½-inch pieces.

Roll each pancake into a cylinder; stack the rolled pancakes together and trim both ends. Cut the stack of pancakes crosswise into 4 equal pieces. You should have a total of sixteen 1½ by 2½-inch pieces of the egg pancakes.

Plunge the scallions into boiling water and remove immediately. Refresh the scallions in cold water; pat dry with paper towels.

On the narrow end of each piece of lettuce, place about 1 tablespoon of cooked noodles, 1 piece of shrimp, 2 slices of fresh bacon, 1 piece of egg pancake, 1 slice of pork sausage and a few mint and coriander leaves. Roll up everything into a neat cylinder shape, being careful not to tear the lettuce. Tie 1 piece of shrimp, 1 slice of pork, 1 piece of egg pancake and 1 slice of pork sausage around the rolled lettuce bundle with a scallion. Trim both ends of the lettuce roll with a knife or scissors to make it look neat and attractive. Repeat rolling with the remaining ingredients.

Serve with *Nuoc Cham* or *Mam Tom*.

NOTE These rolls can be prepared a few hours in advance, covered with plastic wrap and refrigerated until needed.

Yield: 8 rolls, or 4 servings

FRIED SHRIMP ROLLS
CHA GIO TOM

*T*his variation of the fried spring roll is equally delicious. A stuffing of beef, pork, crabmeat, vegetables and a whole shrimp is wrapped in a rice paper round, folded into a triangular shape and fried until crisp and golden brown.

■ ■ ■ ■ ■ ■ ■ ■ ■ ■ ■

Accompaniments
Nuoc Cham *with Shredded Carrot
    and Daikon (page 212)*
1 *bunch of mint*
1 *bunch of coriander*
Filling
1 *ounce cellophane (bean thread)
    noodles*
4 *ounces lean ground beef*
4 *ounces ground pork shoulder*
4 *ounces fresh or canned crabmeat,
    picked over and drained*
4 *shallots, minced*
4 *garlic cloves, minced*
½ *medium onion, minced*
1 *cup fresh bean sprouts*
2 *tablespoons* nuoc mam *(Vietnamese
    fish sauce)*
¼ *teaspoon freshly ground black pepper*
1 *egg*
Assembling and frying
½ *cup sugar*
24 *rounds of rice paper* (banh trang),
    each 8½ inches in diameter
24 *raw medium shrimp, peeled with tail
    section attached, deveined*
    Peanut oil, for frying

Prepare the *Nuoc Cham.* Wash and dry the mint and coriander leaves. Set aside.

Prepare the filling: Soak the noodles in warm water for 30 minutes. Drain. Cut into 1-inch lengths.

Combine the noodles with all of the remaining filling ingredients in a bowl. Mix with your hands to blend. Set aside.

Assemble the rolls: Fill a mixing bowl with 4 cups of warm water and dissolve the sugar in it. Rice paper is quite fragile. Work with only 2 sheets at a time, keeping the remaining sheets covered with a barely damp cloth to prevent curling.

Immerse 1 sheet of rice paper into the warm water. Remove and spread flat on a dry towel. Soak a second sheet of rice paper and spread it out without touching the other round. The rice papers will become pliable within seconds.

Fold up the bottom third of each round. Place ½ tablespoon of the filling in the center of the folded-over portion. Place 1 shrimp on the filling, leaving the tail section extended over the fold line. Top the shrimp with an additional ½ tablespoon of filling and press into a compact triangle, forming a point where the tail extends (it is important that the filling be flat so it can be wrapped entirely and tightly). Fold the sides over to enclose the filling. Fold in half from bottom to top to completely enclose the filling, then fold the remaining sides over to seal the compact triangle. The completed roll resembles a triangle with a handle. Fill the remaining wrappers in the same manner.

Fry the rolls: If possible, fry in 2 skillets. Pour 1 to 1½ inches of oil into each skillet and heat to 325°F. Add a few rolls to each skillet; don't let them touch or they will stick together. Cook over moderate heat for 10 to 12 minutes, turning often, until crisp and golden brown. Drain the rolls on paper towels. Keep warm in a low oven while frying the remaining rolls.

Serve the shrimp rolls as an appetizer with the *Nuoc Cham,* mint and coriander leaves.

NOTE These rolls may be cooked in advance then reheated in a 350°F oven for about 20 minutes, or until crispy.

Yield: 24 shrimp rolls

Fried Spring Rolls and Fried Shrimp Rolls

FRIED SPRING ROLLS
CHA GIO

Cha Gio, also called *nems,* can be considered the national dish of Vietnam. Since preparation is time consuming, it is generally produced at home only on special occasions, such as the Vietnamese New Year, weddings or banquets.

The rolls can be assembled one day in advance and then covered with plastic wrap and refrigerated. On the following day, the accompaniments can be prepared and the rolls fried. In fact, the rolls can even be fried weeks in advance and frozen. When needed, just thaw them and reheat in a 350°F oven.

■ ■ ■ ■ ■ ■ ■ ■ ■ ■

Accompaniments
8 ounces thin rice vermicelli (bun, page 223), or 2 bundles of Japanese alimentary paste noodles (somen, page 223)
Nuoc Cham with Shredded Carrot and Daikon (page 212)
Vegetable Platter (page 169)

Filling
6 dried Chinese mushrooms
1 tablespoon dried tree ear mushrooms
6 water chestnuts, or ½ small jicama, peeled and chopped
4 ounces fresh or canned lump crabmeat, picked over and drained
8 ounces raw shrimp, shelled, deveined and minced
12 ounces ground pork shoulder
1 medium onion, minced
4 shallots, minced
4 garlic cloves, minced
2 tablespoons nuoc cham (Vietnamese fish sauce)
1 teaspoon freshly ground black pepper
3 eggs

Assembling and frying
½ cup sugar
80 small rounds of rice paper (banh trang), each 6 ½ inches in diameter
Peanut oil, for frying

Boil the noodles. Prepare the *Nuoc Cham* and Vegetable Platter. Set aside.

Prepare the filling: Soak the two types of mushrooms in hot water until soft, about 30 minutes. Drain. Remove the stems from the mushrooms and squeeze to extract the liquid. Mince the mushrooms.

Combine the mushrooms with the remaining filling ingredients in a large bowl. Mix with your hands to blend. Set aside.

Assemble the rolls: Fill a mixing bowl with 4 cups of warm water and dissolve the sugar in it. The rice paper sheets are brittle and must be handled with care. (The water is used to soften the sheets for handling. Sweetening the water helps the rice paper turn a deep golden color when fried and also produces crispier rolls.)

Work with only 4 sheets of rice paper at a time, keeping the remaining sheets covered with a barely damp cloth to prevent curling. One at a time, immerse a sheet in the warm water. Quickly remove it and spread flat on a dry towel. Do not let the sheets touch each other. The rice paper will become pliable within seconds.

Fold up the bottom third of each round. Put 1 generous teaspoon of filling in the center of the folded-over portion. Press it into a compact rectangle. Fold one side of the paper over the mixture, then the other side. Roll from bottom to top to completely enclose the filling. Continue until all of the mixture is used.

Fry the rolls: If possible, fry in 2 skillets. Pour 1 to 1½ inches of oil into each skillet and heat to 325°F. Working in batches, add some of the rolls to each skillet, but do not crowd or let them touch, or they will stick together. Fry over moderate heat for 10 to 12 minutes, turning often, until golden and crisp. Remove the rolls with tongs and drain on paper towels. Keep warm in a low oven while frying the remaining rolls.

Traditionally, *Cha Gio* is served with the accompaniments suggested in this recipe.

To eat, each diner wraps a roll in a lettuce leaf along with a few strands of noodles and a variety of other ingredients from the Vegetable Platter before dipping it in the *Nuoc Cham*. If served as an hors d'oeuvre, allow 4 or 5 rolls per person; serve 8 to 10 as a main course.

NOTE Another popular way of serving this dish is to divide the noodles and elements of the Vegetable Platter evenly among individual bowls. Top with cut-up pieces of *Cha Gio,* ground roasted peanuts and *Nuoc Cham*.

As a quick and easy appetizer, *Cha Gio* can be served with just *Nuoc Cham*.

Yield: About 80 spring rolls

GRILLED FRESH YOUNG SQUID
MUC TUOI NUONG

*O*ne of my favorite ways of preparing squid consists of searing marinated squid quickly in a smoking hot skillet (cast iron sears extremely well when hot, but it has to be smoking hot before the squid is put in—be sure the ventilation fan is on), then brushing it with scallion oil to make a tasty appetizer.

The squid may also be cooked over a hot charcoal fire; just remember to baste the squid constantly with oil to avoid its drying out.

■ ■ ■ ■ ■ ■ ■ ■ ■ ■ ■

Scallion oil (page 225)
8 very young squid (about 1 pound total weight)
4 garlic cloves, chopped
1 tablespoon nuoc mam (Vietnamese fish sauce)
Freshly ground black pepper
Coriander leaves, for garnish

Prepare the scallion oil. Set aside.

Separate each squid head from the body section by gently pulling apart, being careful not to break the ink sac. Cut the tentacles from the head; discard the head and reserve the tentacles. Pull out the long, transparent sword-shaped "pen" from the body section and make a lengthwise cut along the body to open. Remove the insides and peel off the membrane from the body. Rinse the prepared squid and tentacles under cold running water. Pat dry.

In a bowl, combine the garlic, fish sauce and black pepper to taste. Rub the mixture over the squid and tentacles. Let marinate at room temperature for 30 minutes.

Heat a heavy cast-iron skillet or griddle until smoking. Brush the skillet generously with scallion oil. Spread the squid and tentacles in one layer without crowding and cook for about 20 seconds. Turn and cook for 20 seconds on the other side. Turn again and cook for 20 seconds longer.

Transfer the squid to a cutting board and cut into bite-size pieces. Arrange on a warm plate. Brush the squid with the remaining scallion oil and garnish with the coriander leaves. Serve hot.

Yield: 4 servings

FRIED SQUID
MUC CHIEN

*C*runchy outside, moist and chewy inside, this appetizer is a sure winner among squid lovers. Traditionally, *Muc Chien* is served with *Nuoc Cham,* but I find it equally exciting when served with ketchup, seasoned with a little soy sauce and a dash of Tabasco sauce. You may substitute smelts for the squid.

■ ■ ■ ■ ■ ■ ■ ■ ■ ■ ■

Nuoc Cham (*page 212*)
1 pound fresh squid
2 large garlic cloves, minced
2 teaspoons nuoc mam (*Vietnamese fish sauce*)
2 tablespoons chopped fresh dill
Freshly ground black pepper
Cornstarch, for coating
Vegetable oil, for deep-frying

Prepare the *Nuoc Cham.* Set aside.

Separate each squid head and body by gently pulling apart. Cut off and reserve the tentacles; discard the head. Pull out the "pen" and discard the entrails. Peel off the membrane from the body of the squid. Wash the squid under cold running water. Cut the body into rings.

In a bowl, combine the squid and tentacles with the garlic, fish sauce, dill and black pepper to taste; toss well. Let marinate at room temperature for 30 minutes. Dredge the squid rings and tentacles in cornstarch, shaking off any excess.

In a wok or wide heavy pan, heat 3 inches of oil to 365°F. Working in batches, drop in the squid pieces and deep-fry for 1 minute. Remove and drain on paper towels. Continue until all of the squid is fried.

Just before serving, heat the oil to 375°F. Add the squid and deep-fry for 30 seconds, or until golden brown. Remove and drain on paper towels.

Serve hot with the *Nuoc Cham.*

Yield: 4 servings

GRILLED BEEF STRIPS WITH BACON

BO DUN

*T*his dish is usually served as part of *Bo Bay Mon,* a festive meal that features seven different beef dishes.

It may be cooked over hot coals or under a broiler.

■ ■ ■ ■ ■ ■ ■ ■ ■ ■ ■

Nuoc Cham *(page 212)*
2 *tablespoons roasted peanuts (page 220), ground*
8 *garlic cloves, minced*
2 *teaspoons* nuoc mam *(Vietnamese fish sauce)*
¼ *teaspoon salt*
½ *teaspoon sugar*
2 *tablespoons peanut oil*
Freshly ground black pepper
8 *ounces rump roast of beef*
4 *ounces bacon, cut into 24 strips, each about 1½ inches long*
12 *bamboo skewers, soaked in water for 30 minutes*

Prepare the *Nuoc Cham* and roasted peanuts. Set aside.

Combine the garlic, fish sauce, salt, sugar, oil, black pepper to taste and the ground nuts in a bowl. Set the marinade aside.

Thinly slice the beef crosswise, against the grain, into 12 strips that are 1½ inches long and 4 to 5 inches wide. Mix the beef strips with the marinade; let stand for 30 minutes.

Sandwich each piece of meat between 2 pieces of bacon and thread on the skewers.

Grill the skewers over hot coals or under a broiler for 4 to 5 minutes, turning once. Serve immediately with *Nuoc Cham.*

Yield: 12 skewers

GRILLED BEEF PATTIES

CHA BO

$\mathcal{S}$imilar to a hamburger, this dish is one of seven beef dishes featured in *Bo Bay Mon* (Beef in Seven Ways), traditionally found in Vietnamese restaurants.

It may be cooked over charcoal or under a broiler.

■ ■ ■ ■ ■ ■ ■ ■ ■ ■

Nuoc Cham *(page 212)*
2 *tablespoons roasted peanuts (page 220), ground*
8 *ounces moderately lean ground beef*
2 *shallots, minced*
2 *teaspoons* nuoc mam *(Vietnamese fish sauce)*
2 *tablespoons coconut milk*
½ *teaspoon curry powder or ground cumin*
½ *teaspoon sugar*
¼ *teaspoon salt*
Freshly ground black pepper
8 *bamboo skewers, soaked in water for 30 minutes*

Prepare the *Nuoc Cham* and roasted peanuts.

Mix the ground peanuts with all of the remaining ingredients, except for the *Nuoc Cham*.

Divide the mixture into 16 portions. Shape each portion into a ball and then flatten lightly between the palms of your hands to form a 1½-inch patty.

Thread 2 patties on each skewer.

Grill the beef patties over hot coals or under a broiler for 5 to 6 minutes, turning once. Do not overcook; the beef should be rare in the middle.

Serve immediately with *Nuoc Cham*.

Yield: 4 servings

GRILLED STUFFED GRAPE LEAVES

BO NUONG LA GNO

*T*his recipe is an adaptation of a unique and famous Vietnamese dish called *Bo La Lot. La lot,* or *Piper lolot,* is an Asian aromatic. *La lot,* a large, shiny, heart-shaped leaf, bears a striking resemblance to a grape leaf and is believed to contain a narcotic. It is used as a wrapper for marinated beef. The grilling of these little rolls brings out the herb's unique, clean flavor. Its penetrating flavor suggests that of anise (with a hint of spiciness), incense or camphor.

Fortunately, the pleasures of eating *Bo La Lot* will not be diminished by substituting grape leaves for this rare herb.

These irresistible little bundles are traditionally grilled and served with *Mam Nem* (anchovy sauce) or *Nuoc Cham.*

■ ■ ■ ■ ■ ■ ■ ■ ■ ■ ■

Scallion oil (page 225)
Anchovy and Pineapple Sauce (Mam Nem, *page 216) or* Nuoc Cham *(page 212)*
2 *tablespoons roasted peanuts (page 220), ground*
24 *large grape leaves, packed in brine (available at specialty food stores)*
10 *ounces lean ground beef*
1 *tablespoon finely chopped fresh lemon grass, or 1 teaspoon grated lemon zest*
1 *medium onion, grated*
4 *garlic cloves, minced*
1 *teaspoon sugar*
1 *teaspoon* nuoc mam (*Vietnamese fish sauce)*
1 *teaspoon soy sauce*
1 *tablespoon vegetable oil*
 Freshly ground black pepper
6 *bamboo skewers, soaked in water for 30 minutes*

Prepare the scallion oil, *Mam Nem* and roasted peanuts. Set aside.

Wash the grape leaves thoroughly in cold water to remove the salt. Remove the stems, being careful not to tear the leaves. Drain.

In a bowl, mix the beef with the lemon grass, onion, garlic, sugar, fish sauce, soy sauce, oil and black pepper to taste. Marinate at room temperature for 30 minutes.

Place about 1 tablespoon of the mixture on the narrow end of each grape leaf. Fold the sides over, then roll up to enclose the filling, forming a neat package.

Thread 4 of the rolls on each skewer. Brush generously on both sides with the scallion oil.

Place the skewers over medium charcoals and grill for 5 to 6 minutes, brushing occasionally with the scallion oil and turning once.

If you don't have a grill, heat a griddle or large skillet over moderate heat. Brush generously with scallion oil. Omit the skewers and place the rolls on the hot pan. Cook for about 3 minutes on each side, brushing the rolls frequently, until nicely browned.

Transfer the rolls to a warm platter and brush with the remaining scallion oil. Garnish with ground roasted peanuts and serve with *Mam Nem* or *Nuoc Cham.*

Yield: 24 rolls

CURRIED TARO TURNOVERS
BANH KHOAI MON

*T*his Vietnamese version of the meat turnover has an unusual crust made of taro root, a vegetable that grows in abundance in Vietnam. Fried, the creamy pastry releases the fragrant aroma of its curried filling.

These delicious treats also make excellent picnic fare.

■ ■ ■ ■ ■ ■ ■ ■ ■

Nuoc Cham *with Shredded Carrot and Daikon (page 212)*
Filling
1 *stalk fresh lemon grass, or 1 tablespoon dried lemon grass*
8 *ounces ground pork*
2 *shallots, minced*
2 *cloves garlic, minced*
4 *teaspoons nuoc mam (Vietnamese fish sauce)*
1 *teaspoon cornstarch*
¼ *teaspoon sugar*
Freshly ground black pepper
3 *tablespoons vegetable oil*
1 *medium onion, chopped*
1 *tablespoon curry powder*
Dough
1 *pound taro root*
½ *cup cornstarch*
5 *tablespoons vegetable shortening*
1 *tablespoon sugar*
½ *teaspoon salt*
Assembling and frying
Cornstarch, for dusting
Vegetable oil, for deep-frying

Prepare the *Nuoc Cham*. Set aside.

Prepare the filling: If you are using fresh lemon grass, discard the outer leaves and upper half of the stalk; slice thin and finely chop. If you are using dried lemon grass, soak it in warm water for 1 hour, then drain and finely chop. Set aside.

In a bowl, combine the ground pork, shallots, garlic, fish sauce, cornstarch, sugar and black pepper. Marinate for 30 minutes.

Heat the oil in a skillet over moderate heat. Add the onion and lemon grass and stir-fry until the onion is lightly browned and the lemon grass is fragrant. Add the curry powder; stir for 30 seconds. Add the pork mixture. Fry, breaking up the lumps with a wooden spoon, until the mixture is cooked through, about 5 minutes. Remove and allow to cool.

Make the dough: Peel the taro root and cut crosswise into ¼-inch slices. Place the taro slices in a single layer on a steamer rack and steam until tender but not mushy, about 20 to 25 minutes. Remove the taro slices to a mixing bowl. Using a potato masher, food mill or electric mixer, mash the slices until no lumps remain. Allow the taro to cool thoroughly. Add the cornstarch, shortening, sugar and salt; mix the ingredients well until they form a soft dough. If the dough is too moist to handle, add a little more cornstarch.

Assemble the turnovers: Dust a countertop with cornstarch and knead the dough until it is smooth. Roll the dough into a

cylinder, then divide it into 12 portions. Work with one portion at a time, keeping the remaining portions covered with a cloth. Flatten the portion of dough with the palm of your hand into a 3-inch circle. Place 1 tablespoon of filling slightly below the center; lightly moisten the edges of the dough with water. Fold the dough over the filling and seal securely, either by pressing the edges together with a fork or by pinching and folding the edges to seal. Make the remaining 11 turnovers in the same manner.

NOTE These pastries can be prepared half a day in advance, then covered and refrigerated until needed.

Fry the turnovers: Pour 3 inches of oil into a wok or deep-fryer and heat to 350°F. Deep-fry 3 or 4 turnovers at a time, until they rise to the surface and are lightly brown, about 2 minutes. Remove the fried turnovers to a heatproof pan lined with a double thickness of paper towels, and keep warm in a 200° F oven while frying the remaining turnovers. Increase the oil temperature to 375°F and deep-fry the turnovers, in batches, a second time, until they turn crisp and golden brown, about 2 minutes. Drain on paper towels.

Serve immediately with *Nuoc Cham* with Shredded Carrot and Daikon.

Yield: 12 turnovers

SALADS

Warm Beef Salad

WARM BEEF SALAD
BO LUC LAC

This recipe has adapted the French technique of sautéing beef as well as the use of olive oil. It would be right at home on a French menu.

■ ■ ■ ■ ■ ■ ■ ■ ■ ■ ■

Dressing

1 *medium red onion, peeled and cut into paper-thin strips*
2 *garlic cloves, finely minced*
½ *teaspoon sugar*
½ *teaspoon salt*
¼ *cup distilled white vinegar*
¼ *cup plus 2 tablespoons olive oil*
  Freshly ground black pepper

Beef

1 *pound beef sirloin or other tender cut (eye of round, filet of beef)*
10 *garlic cloves, minced*
1 *tablespoon* nuoc mam *(Vietnamese fish sauce)*
1 *tablespoon soy sauce*
1 *teaspoon sugar*
  Freshly ground black pepper
1 *head chicory (frisée)*
½ *head of soft lettuce, such as Boston, red leaf or oak leaf*
1 *small bunch of watercress*
2 *tablespoons vegetable oil*

Make the dressing: Combine the onion, garlic, sugar, salt, vinegar, olive oil and black pepper to taste in a large salad bowl; mix well. Set aside.

Prepare the beef: Cut the beef against the grain into thin 1 by 2-inch strips. In a bowl, combine the beef, half of the minced garlic (reserve remaining half for frying), fish sauce, soy sauce, sugar and ground black pepper to taste. Let stand for 30 minutes.

Clean the lettuces and watercress. Drain and pat dry with paper towels. Add the greens to the dressing, but do not toss.

Preheat a large skillet over high heat and add the vegetable oil. Fry the remaining minced garlic until fragrant and golden. Add the beef and sauté quickly, shaking the pan, over high heat to sear, about 1 minute (the beef should be medium-rare). Pour the seared meat over the greens and toss gently. Divide the warm salad among 4 individual plates.

Sprinkle with freshly ground black pepper and serve with French bread, if desired.

NOTE You can create your own salad combinations according to availability of lettuces, or you can substitute chicken, liver, seafood or even fish for the beef.

Yield: 4 servings

SHREDDED CABBAGE AND CHICKEN SALAD

GA XE PHAI

*I*n Vietnam, *Ga Xe Phai* is as popular as cole slaw is in the U.S. Like most Vietnamese salads, this one uses very little oil and may be served with shrimp chips.

In my family, this dish is almost always served along with Chicken and Cellophane Noodle Soup. My mother would remove the cooked hen from the broth, along with the gizzards and liver, shred everything and then add the pieces to the salad and the soup.

■ ■ ■ ■ ■ ■ ■ ■ ■ ■ ■

2 chile peppers, seeded and minced
3 garlic cloves, minced
2 tablespoons sugar
1 tablespoon rice vinegar
3 tablespoons fresh lime juice
3 tablespoons nuoc mam *(Vietnamese fish sauce)*
3 tablespoons vegetable oil
1 medium onion, thinly sliced
    Freshly ground black pepper
2 cups shredded cooked chicken
4 cups finely shredded white cabbage
1 cup shredded carrot
½ cup shredded fresh mint
    Coriander sprigs, for garnish

In a bowl, combine the chiles, garlic, sugar, vinegar, lime juice, fish sauce, oil, onion and black pepper in a bowl. Let the dressing stand for 30 minutes.

In a large mixing bowl, combine the shredded chicken, cabbage, carrot and mint. Sprinkle the dressing over all and toss well.

Transfer the salad to a serving platter and garnish with the coriander sprigs. Sprinkle with additional black pepper and serve with shrimp chips, if desired.

Yield: 4 to 6 full servings

GREEN PAPAYA SALAD
GOI DU DU

*I*n Vietnam, this salad is eaten as a snack rather than a full dish. To be authentic, use unripe papaya, which is available in Southeast Asian markets or Caribbean grocery stores. Green mango makes an excellent substitute. This salad is usually accompanied by glutinous rice.

■ ■ ■ ■ ■ ■ ■ ■ ■ ■ ■

Grilled Dried Beef (page 106; see Note)
2 garlic cloves, minced
½ teaspoon salt
2 teaspoons sugar
¼ cup distilled white vinegar
1 tablespoon chile sauce (sriracha or sambal oeleck) or Tabasco sauce
1 green papaya (about 1½ pounds), peeled, seeded and finely shredded
1 medium carrot, finely shredded
1 cup finely shredded coriander leaves

Prepare the Grilled Dried Beef. Cut the beef pieces into thin strips with a scissors. Set aside.

Combine the garlic, salt, sugar, vinegar and chile sauce in a bowl. Stir to blend. Set the dressing aside.

In a large salad bowl, combine shredded papaya, carrot, grilled beef strips and coriander. Pour on the dressing and toss well.

Transfer the salad to a serving platter.

NOTE "Beef jerky," available at Chinese and Vietnamese markets, is the best substitute for Grilled Dried Beef.

Yield: 4 to 6 servings

Papaya Salad, Steamed Glutinous Rice and Grilled Dried Beef

SALAD OF VEGETABLE, MEAT AND GRAPEFRUIT

NOM TRAI BUOI

*P*lace bite-size portions of this salad on top of shrimp chips so they can be easily picked up and eaten with the hands, or impress your guests by serving this irresistible salad in hollowed grapefruit shells at a sit-down dinner party.

In Vietnam, Pomelo, a thick-skinned grapefruit the size of a honeydew melon, is used. Pink grapefruit, which lends a beautiful color to this dish, may be substituted for Pomelo.

■ ■ ■ ■ ■ ■ ■ ■ ■ ■ ■

About 40 shrimp chips (page 221)
2 tablespoons roasted peanuts (page 220), ground
2 tablespoons toasted sesame seeds (page 225), ground
2 egg pancakes (page 219), cut into thin strips
2 ounces store-bought or homemade Vietnamese Pork Sausage (page 116)
2 garlic cloves, minced
2 fresh red chile peppers, seeded and minced
1 tablespoon sugar
1 tablespoon fresh lime juice
1 tablespoon rice vinegar
3 tablespoons nuoc mam (Vietnamese fish sauce)
1 ounce dried shrimp
4 ounces pork belly or shoulder
4 ounces raw shrimp in the shell
2 ounces cooked chicken meat
½ teaspoon salt
2 medium cucumbers, unpeeled, halved lengthwise, seeded and thinly sliced
1 large carrot, shredded
2 cups fresh bean sprouts
1 large grapefruit, peeled, sectioned and cut crosswise into 1-inch pieces
Coriander leaves, for garnish

Prepare the shrimp chips, roasted peanuts, toasted sesame seeds and egg pancakes. Cut the pork sausage into thin strips. Set aside.

Combine the garlic, chiles, sugar, lime juice, vinegar and fish sauce in a bowl. Stir to blend. Set the dressing aside.

Soak the dried shrimp in hot water for 30 minutes. Drain. Pound or process the dried shrimp in a food processor until very fine. Set aside.

Cover the pork with water in a small saucepan and bring to a boil over high heat. Reduce the heat to moderate and boil the pork for 25 to 30 minutes, or until the juices run clear when the meat is pierced with a knife. Refresh the pork in cold water. Drain. Shred into thin strips and set aside.

Cook the raw shrimp in boiling water until just pink, about 2 minutes. Refresh the shrimp in cold water. Drain. Peel, devein and cut the shrimp lengthwise in half. Shred the shrimp. Set aside.

Cut the cooked chicken into thin strips. Set aside.

Sprinkle the salt over the cucumbers and shredded carrot and let stand for 15 minutes. Rinse under cold running water and squeeze dry with your hands (it is very important that the vegetables be completely dry to ensure their crunchiness).

Dip the bean sprouts in salted boiling water for 30 seconds. Refresh under cold water. Drain.

In a large salad bowl, combine the egg pancake strips, dried shrimp, pork, shredded shrimp, chicken, pork sausage, cucumbers, carrot, bean sprouts, grapefruit and sesame seeds. Mix well with your hands. Pour the dressing over the salad and mix thoroughly.

Transfer the salad to a serving platter and sprinkle on the ground peanuts. Garnish with coriander. Serve with shrimp chips.

NOTE A variation on this salad uses dried, shredded jellyfish instead of the grapefruit. It is called *Nom Sua.*

Yield: about 6 full servings, or 40 hors d'oeuvres

ROAST BEEF SALAD
LAP

A typical Vietnamese salad is never plain; it is always composed of numerous ingredients so the final dish is tasty and colorful with contrasting textures. Traditionally, these salads are not served as such by themselves, but rather as the first course at a dinner party. However, they may also be served as a light main course for lunch or for dinner.

This recipe is my mother's adaptation of a very popular Laotian dish called *Laub*, a mixture of finely chopped raw beef seasoned with lime juice and several varieties of herbs. The meat is grilled just long enough to sear and seal the juices inside, then sliced paper-thin. When dressed, the rare meat will be "cooked" a little further by the acidity of the lime juice. Glutinous rice goes well with this light beef salad.

■ ■ ■ ■ ■ ■ ■ ■ ■ ■ ■ ■

2 *tablespoons roasted rice powder (page 220)*
2 *stalks fresh lemon grass, or 2 tablespoons dried lemon grass*
1 *red chile pepper, seeded*
3 *garlic cloves, peeled*
2 *tablespoons* nuoc mam *(Vietnamese fish sauce)*
Juice of 3 limes
1 *large red onion, sliced very thin*
1 *pound beef filet or lean boneless beef (sirloin or eye of round)*
¼ *cup finely shredded fresh basil*
1 *small head of Boston lettuce, separated into whole leaves*
Freshly ground black pepper
Red chile peppers, for garnish
Coriander leaves, for garnish

Prepare the roasted rice powder. Set aside.

If you are using fresh lemon grass, remove and discard the outer leaves and upper half of the stalk. Cut the stalk into thin slices and coarsely chop. If you are using dried lemon grass, soak in warm water for 1 hour. Drain and coarsely chop.

Pound the lemon grass, chile and garlic to a fine paste in a mortar. Combine the paste with the fish sauce, lime juice and red onion in a large salad bowl. Stir to blend the dressing.

If grilling, cook the beef, covered, over hot coals for 8 to 10 minutes on each side. Do not overcook; the beef should be rare in the middle. If you don't have a grill, heat a greased cast-iron skillet or griddle over high heat and sear the beef for 8 to 10 minutes on each side.

Let the roast stand for 10 minutes; the meat will continue to cook. The juices that accumulate in the center will spread throughout the piece of meat, which will make carving easier.

Trim and discard all fat from the roast. Slice the meat across the grain into thin 1½ by 2½-inch strips. Add the sliced beef and basil to the dressing. Toss well and let stand for a few minutes to allow the flavors to blend.

To serve, line a large platter with lettuce leaves. Mound the beef on top and sprinkle the roasted rice powder and black pepper over the beef. Garnish with the chiles and coriander leaves.

Yield: 2 to 4 servings

SOUPS

Asparagus and Crabmeat Soup

ASPARAGUS AND CRABMEAT SOUP
MANG TAY NAU CUA

This soup was probably created by some homesick Frenchman. White asparagus (a French import, packed in jars or cans, is used for this recipe). Traditionally, crumbled, salted duck egg yolk is added to season the soup.

If white asparagus is unavailable, use frozen or fresh asparagus (in this case, add the fresh asparagus to the broth from the very beginning and cook until tender before adding the remaining ingredients).

■ ■ ■ ■ ■ ■ ■ ■ ■ ■ ■

4 cups chicken broth
1 tablespoon plus 2 teaspoons nuoc mam (Vietnamese fish sauce)
½ teaspoon sugar
¼ teaspoon salt
1 tablespoon vegetable oil
6 shallots, chopped
2 garlic cloves, chopped
8 ounces fresh or canned lump crabmeat, picked over and drained
Freshly ground black pepper
2 tablespoons cornstarch or arrowroot, mixed with 2 tablespoons cold water
1 egg, lightly beaten
1 jar (15 ounces) white asparagus spears, cut into 1-inch sections with canning liquid reserved
1 tablespoon shredded coriander
1 scallion, thinly sliced

Combine the broth, 1 tablespoon of the fish sauce, the sugar and salt in a 3-quart soup pot. Bring to a boil. Reduce the heat and simmer.

Meanwhile, heat the oil in a skillet. Add the shallots and garlic and stir-fry until aromatic. Add the crabmeat, the remaining 2 teaspoons fish sauce and black pepper to taste. Stir-fry over high heat for 1 minute. Set aside.

Bring the soup to a boil. Add the cornstarch mixture and stir gently until the soup thickens and is clear. While the soup is actively boiling, add the egg and stir gently. Continue to stir for about 1 minute. Add the crabmeat mixture and asparagus with its canning liquid; cook gently until heated through.

Transfer the soup to a heated tureen. Sprinkle on the coriander, scallion and freshly ground black pepper.

Yield: 4 to 6 servings

CREAMED CORN AND CHICKEN SOUP

SUP BAP GA

A combination of puréed and whole-kernel corn gives interesting flavor and texture to this delicious soup. Although fresh corn is plentiful in Vietnam, canned corn, one of the many convenience foods introduced by the French, is used in this recipe. Although pork stock is preferred here, chicken broth can be substituted.

■ ■ ■ ■ ■ ■ ■ ■ ■ ■ ■

4 cups pork stock or chicken broth
1 pound chicken thighs, skin and fat removed
2 cans (each 17 ounces) creamed sweet corn
2 tablespoons vegetable oil
4 garlic cloves, minced
4 shallots, thinly sliced
4 scallions, thinly sliced
1 tablespoon nuoc mam (Vietnamese fish sauce)
1 can (8 ounces) whole corn kernels, drained
¼ teaspoon salt
4 teaspoons cornstarch or arrowroot, mixed with 1 tablespoon cold water
1 egg, lightly beaten
2 tablespoons shredded coriander leaves
Freshly ground black pepper

Place the stock and chicken thighs in a 3-quart soup pot and bring to a rolling boil. Reduce the heat and skim the surface to remove the foam. Continue skimming until the foam ceases to rise. Simmer for 30 minutes, or until the chicken is tender. Remove the chicken; refresh under cold running water. Pull the chicken meat apart into small pieces with your fingers; set aside. Discard the bones.

Place the creamed corn in a blender and process to a fine purée. Strain the mixture through a fine sieve, pressing to extract as much of the solids as possible, into a bowl. Discard the pulp and reserve the purée.

Heat the oil in a large skillet. Add the garlic, shallots and scallions and sauté until aromatic. Add the shredded chicken and fish sauce; stir-fry for 1 minute. Set aside.

Stir the corn purée, corn kernels and salt into the stock. Bring the soup to a boil. Add the cornstarch mixture to the soup and stir gently until thickened. While the soup is actively boiling, add the egg and stir gently. Continue to stir for 1 minute. Add the chicken mixture to the soup and cook gently until heated through.

Transfer the soup to a heated tureen. Sprinkle on the coriander and freshly ground black pepper.

Yield: 4 to 6 servings

Clockwise from top: Bean Curd and Chinese Chive Buds Soup, Daikon and Pork Soup, Tomato and Egg Drop Soup and Spicy and Sour Shrimp Soup

SPICY AND SOUR SHRIMP SOUP
CANH CHUA TOM

*T*his southern soup, with a nation-wide appeal, is one of the most delicious dishes imaginable. What makes it so special is the subtle combination of sweet-and-sour ingredients.

To be really authentic, this soup should include two special ingredients: One is an aromatic souring herb called *la kinh gioi,* or *ngo om,* sometimes called "rice-paddy herb." The other is the spongy stem from an aquatic plant called *rau rap mong.* These two edibles can be found occasionally at Southeast Asian markets. If they cannot be obtained, however, this recipe will still taste delightful. If a spicier soup is desired, pass fresh chile peppers at the table.

■ ■ ■ ■ ■ ■ ■ ■ ■ ■ ■

2 ounces lump tamarind, or 2
    tablespoons tamarind concentrate
½ cup boiling water
8 ounces raw shrimp, shelled and
    deveined
2 garlic cloves, chopped
¼ cup plus 1 teaspoon nuoc mam
    (Vietnamese fish sauce)
    Freshly ground black pepper
2 tablespoons vegetable oil
2 shallots, thinly sliced
3 stalks fresh lemon grass, white bulb
    crushed and cut into 2-inch sections
1 large ripe tomato, cored, seeded and
    cut into wedges
2 tablespoons sugar
¼ fresh ripe pineapple, cored, cut into
    ¼-inch slices and then cut crosswise
    into small chunks
½ cup fresh or canned bamboo shoots,
    drained and thinly sliced
1 teaspoon salt
2 fresh red chile peppers, minced
½ cup fresh bean sprouts
1 scallion, thinly sliced
2 tablespoons shredded mint

Soak the lump tamarind in the boiling water for 15 minutes, or until the tamarind is soft. Force the tamarind through a fine sieve into a small bowl. If tamarind concentrate is used, dilute it with only ¼ cup of warm water.

Cut each shrimp lengthwise in half. In a bowl, combine the shrimp, garlic, 1 teaspoon of the fish sauce and pepper to taste. Let stand for 30 minutes.

Heat the oil in a 3-quart saucepan. Add the shallots and lemon grass and sauté briefly, without browning. Add the tomato and sugar and cook over moderate heat until slightly soft. Add the pineapple and bamboo shoots and cook, stirring, for about 2 minutes. Add 5 cups of water and bring to a boil over high heat. Stir in the tamarind liquid, salt and the remaining ¼ cup fish sauce. Reduce the heat to moderate and simmer the broth for 5 minutes.

Stir in the shrimp, chiles and bean sprouts and cook for 30 seconds more. Add the scallion and mint. Remove from the heat. Remove and discard the lemon grass.

Ladle the soup into a heated tureen and serve at once.

NOTE Do not overcook the shrimp or they will toughen. Catfish, red snapper or any other firm white-fleshed fish can replace the shrimp.

Yield: 4 to 6 servings

TOMATO AND EGG DROP SOUP
CANH TRUNG CA TRUA

This soup originated in southern Vietnam. It is probably derived from Chinese egg drop soup but given a new twist when combined with tomatoes, which grow abundantly in the south.

While preparing this soup one day, I experimented by including other ingredients I had on hand. The addition of lime leaves and galangal introduced a new, fresh taste and stimulated all of the flavors in the soup.

■ ■ ■ ■ ■ ■ ■ ■ ■ ■ ■

4 *lime leaves, frozen or dried (optional)*
4 *galangal slices, frozen or dried (optional)*
2 *tablespoons vegetable oil*
4 *shallots, thinly sliced*
5 *large ripe tomatoes, cored, seeded and cut into wedges*
1 *teaspoon sugar*
5 *cups chicken broth*
¼ *teaspoon salt*
1 *tablespoon* nuoc mam *(Vietnamese fish sauce)*
5 *eggs, lightly beaten*
1 *scallion, finely sliced*
1 *tablespoon shredded coriander*
  Freshly ground black pepper

If using dried lime leaves and galangal, soak them in hot water for 30 minutes. Drain.

Heat the oil in a 3-quart saucepan over moderate heat. Add the shallots and sauté until fragrant. Add the tomatoes and sugar and cook for 5 minutes, or until the tomatoes are very soft. Add the chicken broth and bring to a boil over high heat. Stir in the lime leaves, galangal, salt and fish sauce. Reduce the heat, cover the pan and let the broth simmer for 30 minutes.

Remove and discard the lime leaves and galangal. Bring the soup back to a boil. While the soup is actively boiling, pour in the eggs in a thin slow stream and stir gently for 30 seconds. Add the scallion and coriander.

Transfer the soup to a heated tureen. Sprinkle with freshly ground black pepper and serve hot.

Yield: 4 servings

WATER SPINACH AND BEEF SOUP
CANH RAU MUONG THIT BO

*T*he most outstanding attribute of water spinach is the contrast in texture between the crunchy stem and limp leaves when cooked. It is mainly available at Chinese markets where it is called *ong choi,* and *rau muong* at Vietnamese markets. If it is unavailable, substitute regular spinach.

■ ■ ■ ■ ■ ■ ■ ■ ■ ■

Beef and marinade
6 ounces lean beef (sirloin, filet or chuck)
2 garlic cloves, chopped
1 shallot, thinly sliced
¼ teaspoon sugar
2 teaspoons nuoc mam *(Vietnamese fish sauce)*
Freshly ground black pepper
Soup
1 small bunch of water spinach, or 4 ounces fresh spinach
3 tablespoons nuoc mam *(Vietnamese fish sauce)*
1 tablespoon fresh lemon juice
Freshly ground black pepper
1 fresh red chile pepper, finely sliced (optional)

Prepare the beef and marinade: Thinly slice the beef against the grain into strips that are 1 inch wide by 2 inches long. Mix the beef with the garlic, shallot, sugar, fish sauce and black pepper to taste in a bowl. Marinate for 30 minutes.

Meanwhile, prepare the soup: If using water spinach, wash it first. Smash the stems with the back of a heavy cleaver. Cut into 2-inch sections. If using fresh spinach, do not remove the stems; clean with several changes of water to remove any sand; drain.

In a 3-quart saucepan, bring 5 cups of water to a boil. Add the spinach and bring back to a boil. Season the broth with the fish sauce. Add the beef and turn off the heat. Separate the beef slices with chopsticks or a fork and stir to heat through. Stir in the lemon juice.

Ladle the soup into a heated tureen and sprinkle with freshly ground black pepper. Serve with the hot chile pepper on the side, if desired.

Yield: 4 to 6 servings

RICE AND BEEF SOUP
CHAO THIT BO

My mother never failed to feed us a large bowl of this delicious soup whenever we were sick or had a bad cold. Lemon grass and ginger are believed to cure the common cold.

■ ■ ■ ■ ■ ■ ■ ■ ■ ■ ■ ■

Beef and marinade

8 ounces ground lean beef (eye or bottom round)
1 small onion, minced
1 tablespoon nuoc mam (Vietnamese fish sauce)
Freshly ground black pepper

Soup

2 tablespoons roasted peanuts (page 220), ground
½ ounce cellophane (bean thread) noodles
2 tablespoons vegetable oil
1 teaspoon grated fresh gingerroot
⅓ cup raw long-grain rice
3 tablespoons nuoc mam (Vietnamese fish sauce)
1 tablespoon sugar
1½ teaspoons salt
2 large garlic cloves, minced
1 tablespoon fresh minced lemon grass
1 tablespoon shredded coriander
2 scallions, thinly sliced
Freshly ground black pepper

Prepare the beef and marinade: In a soup tureen, combine the beef, onion, fish sauce and black pepper to taste. Mix well, cover and refrigerate.

Prepare the soup: Prepare the roasted peanuts. Set aside. Soak the cellophane noodles in warm water for 20 minutes. Drain and cut into 2-inch lengths. Set aside.

In a 4-quart saucepan, heat 1 tablespoon of the oil. Add the ginger and rice and stir until the rice puffs up and becomes milky white, about 1 minute. Add 7 cups of water and bring to a boil. Reduce the heat to low and simmer, partially covered, for about 20 minutes, or until the rice is very tender. Stir in the fish sauce, sugar and salt.

Heat the remaining 1 tablespoon oil in a small skillet. Add the garlic and lemon grass and sauté over low heat until fragrant and golden, about 1 minute. Stir the mixture into the soup; add the cellophane noodles.

Bring the soup to a boil. Pour the hot soup over the meat mixture in the soup tureen. Use chopsticks or a fork to break the lump of meat into small pieces. The boiling broth will cook the beef instantly.

Sprinkle on the ground peanuts, coriander, scallions and black pepper before serving.

Yield: 4 to 6 servings

BEAN CURD AND CHINESE CHIVE BUDS SOUP
CANH DAU PHU HE

*T*he creamy bean curd contrasts nicely with the "onion" flavor of the chive buds in this seasoned broth. This soup is a homey meal-in-a-bowl all by itself, or, if you like, serve it with rice and simmered meat to lend a refreshing note to a simple meal.

If Chinese chive buds are unobtainable, substitute young, tender scallions.

■ ■ ■ ■ ■ ■ ■ ■ ■ ■ ■

Pork and marinade
6 ounces lean pork shoulder, thinly sliced
1 teaspoon nuoc mam (*Vietnamese fish sauce*)
Freshly ground black pepper
Soup
5 cups chicken broth
¼ teaspoon salt
¼ teaspoon sugar
1 tablespoon nuoc mam (*Vietnamese fish sauce*)
1 small bunch of Chinese chive buds (*about ¼ pound*), tough ends trimmed, cut into 2-inch lengths
6 ounces soft bean curd (*tofu*), cut into 1-inch cubes

In a bowl, combine the pork, fish sauce and black pepper to taste. Let stand for 30 minutes.

Prepare the soup: Combine the pork and chicken broth in a 3-quart soup pot and bring to a boil. Reduce the heat and skim the surface to remove the foam. Continue skimming until the foam ceases to rise. Simmer until broth is well flavored and the pork is cooked, about 10 minutes.

Stir in the salt, sugar and fish sauce; simmer for 5 minutes longer. Add the Chinese chives and bean curd. Wait for the liquid to come to a boil and then remove from the heat. The vegetables should be bright green.

Ladle into heated soup bowls and serve at once.

Yield: 4 to 6 servings

CHICKEN AND BAMBOO MUSTARD CABBAGE SOUP

CANH CAI GA

This soup is exceptionally light and delicious. Traditionally, mustard cabbage is used but broccoli rabe, broccoli or turnip greens may be substituted.

■ ■ ■ ■ ■ ■ ■ ■ ■ ■ ■ ■

8 ounces chicken wings
5 cups chicken broth
2 teaspoons grated fresh gingerroot
¼ teaspoon salt
¼ teaspoon sugar
4 teaspoons nuoc mam (Vietnamese fish sauce)
8 ounces mustard cabbage, trimmed and cut into 2-inch pieces, including stalks
Freshly ground black pepper

Place the chicken wings and broth in a 3-quart saucepan. Bring to a rolling boil and reduce the heat. Skim the surface to remove the foam. Continue skimming until the foam ceases to rise. Add the ginger, salt, sugar and fish sauce. Simmer gently for 30 minutes.

Remove the wings with a slotted spoon. Set aside until cool enough to handle. Pull off the meat and return it to the saucepan. Discard the bones.

Bring the soup to a fast boil. Add the mustard cabbage. Cook for 1 minute, or until the leaves are just wilted.

Transfer the soup to a heated tureen and sprinkle with freshly ground black pepper.

Yield: 4 servings

DAIKON AND PORK SOUP

CANH CU CAI

If you serve this soup alongside a spicy entrée, it will lend a refreshing note to the whole meal.

■ ■ ■ ■ ■ ■ ■ ■ ■ ■ ■ ■

6 ounces pork shoulder, thinly sliced
1 teaspoon plus 1 tablespoon nuoc mam (Vietnamese fish sauce)
Freshly ground black pepper
5 cups chicken broth
¼ teaspoon salt
¼ teaspoon sugar
2 cups thinly sliced peeled daikon
2 scallions, thinly sliced

In a bowl, combine the pork, 1 teaspoon of the fish sauce and black pepper to taste. Let marinate for 30 minutes.

In a 3-quart soup pot, combine the pork and chicken broth. Bring to a rolling boil. Reduce the heat and skim the surface to remove the foam. Continue skimming until the foam ceases to rise. Simmer until the broth is well flavored and the pork cooked, about 10 minutes.

Stir in the salt, sugar and the remaining 1 tablespoon fish sauce; simmer for 5 minutes longer. Add the daikon, cover and simmer until tender, about 15 minutes. Remove from the heat.

Transfer the soup to a heated tureen. Garnish with the scallions and sprinkle with freshly ground black pepper.

Yield: 4 to 6 servings

BEEF AND PINEAPPLE SOUP
CANH THIT BO NAU DUA

*T*he use of fruits in cooking is typical of the cuisine of southern Vietnam. Pineapples are so abundant that they are interchangeably used as a fruit and a vegetable. They are usually combined with beef, poultry or seafood. When quite ripe, pineapples develop a high percentage of sugar and malic acids that produce a very pleasant aroma.

Do not use canned pineapple in this recipe; it does not approach fresh pineapple in fragrance and delicacy of flavor.

■ ■ ■ ■ ■ ■ ■ ■ ■ ■ ■

Beef and marinade
8 ounces not-too-lean beef chuck or
    bottom round
2 teaspoons nuoc mam (*Vietnamese
    fish sauce*)
¼ teaspoon sugar
2 garlic cloves, chopped
2 shallots, finely sliced
    Freshly ground black pepper
Soup
3 tablespoons vegetable oil
½ medium onion, cut into thin slivers
1 large ripe tomato, cored, seeded and
    cut into wedges
½ fresh ripe pineapple, cored, cut into
    ¼-inch-thick slices and then
    crosswise into small pieces
1 tablespoon sugar
1½ teaspoons salt
3 tablespoons nuoc mam (*Vietnamese
    fish sauce*)
1 scallion, thinly sliced
1 tablespoon shredded coriander
    Freshly ground black pepper

Prepare the beef: Slice the beef against the grain into thin strips, about ⅛ inch thick by 2 inches long. Combine the beef, fish sauce, sugar, garlic, shallots and black pepper to taste in a small bowl. Let marinate for 30 minutes.

Prepare the soup: Heat 1 tablespoon of the oil in a 3-quart soup pot over high heat. Add the beef and stir-fry briefly over high heat, about 1 minute; the beef should still be pink. Transfer the beef to a bowl.

Heat the remaining 2 tablespoons of oil in the same soup pot. Add the onion and sauté until lightly browned. Add the tomato, pineapple and sugar and stir-fry over moderate heat for about 2 minutes. Add 5 cups of water, the salt and fish sauce. Bring to a boil. Reduce heat to moderate and simmer the broth for about 5 minutes.

Stir the cooked beef into the soup. Remove from the heat. Add the scallion and coriander and stir to combine.

Transfer the soup to a heated tureen. Sprinkle with freshly ground black pepper and serve hot.

Yield: 4 to 6 servings

$\mathcal{F}$ISH AND $\mathcal{S}$EAFOOD

Stuffed Squid

STUFFED SQUID

MUC NHOI

*This dish may be served as part of a meal or as an appetizer, with *Nuoc Cham*.*

■ ■ ■ ■ ■ ■ ■ ■ ■ ■ ■

Nuoc Cham *(page 212)*
6 *large dried Chinese mushrooms*
1 *ounce cellophane (bean thread) noodles*
8 *young squid (about 1 pound total weight; see Note)*
12 *ounces ground pork*
3 *shallots, chopped*
3 *large garlic cloves, chopped*
1 *tablespoon* nuoc mam *(Vietnamese fish sauce)*
¼ *teaspoon salt*
¼ *teaspoon sugar*
  Freshly ground black pepper
¼ *cup vegetable oil*

Prepare the *Nuoc Cham*. Set aside.

Soak the mushrooms in hot water and the cellophane noodles in warm water for 30 minutes. Drain. Remove and discard the mushroom stems. Coarsely chop the mushroom caps and noodles.

Clean each squid by gently pulling the head with its tentacles from the body section, being careful not to break the ink sac. Discard the head and reserve the tentacles.

Pull out the long, transparent, sword-shaped "pen" from the body section. Remove the insides and rinse the mantle thoroughly under cold running water. Peel off the membrane from the outside of the mantle. Pat the squid dry, inside and out; set aside. Mince the tentacles.

In a large bowl, combine the minced tentacles, mushrooms, noodles, pork, shallots, garlic, fish sauce, salt, sugar and black pepper to taste. Mix well with your hands.

Stuff the mixture into the squid mantles, packing firmly so as to leave no air pockets, and stuffing the squid two-thirds full. Sew the openings shut with a coarse needle and heavy thread.

Heat the oil in a large skillet over moderate heat. When the oil is hot, add the stuffed squid and cook for about 5 minutes, turning several times to coat with the oil. Using a fork, pierce each squid body all over to release the water. Be careful, as the water can cause the oil to splatter. Continue cooking the squid for 10 minutes more, turning occasionally, until nicely browned on all sides.

If using larger squid, cook 5 minutes longer.

Remove the threads. Slice each squid into ¼-inch rounds. Serve with rice and *Nuoc Cham*.

NOTE If young squid are not available, substitute 4 large squid (about 1 pound total weight). For variation, boil 6 live blue crabs. Pick out the meat and add to the filling. Stuff into the crab shells and fry until the filling turns golden brown.

Yield: 4 servings

DEEP-FRIED FLOUNDER

CA RAN

Every part of the fish is used in this dish; after the fillets are removed, the bones are fried to a golden crisp and used as a natural and spectacular serving boat for the fried fish nuggets. These bones are so crisp and tasty they can be eaten like potato chips.

Flounder is used here but any small, flat, white-fleshed fish, such as sole, turbot or halibut, can also be prepared this way. Plan to serve 8 ounces per person.

■ ■ ■ ■ ■ ■ ■ ■ ■ ■ ■

4 *flounders, about 8 ounces each*
  Vegetable oil, for deep-frying
  All-purpose flour, for dredging
  Nuoc Cham *with Shredded Carrot and*
    Daikon (page 212)
4 *scallions, cut into 2-inch pieces*
4 *4-inch red chiles*
  Coriander sprigs, for garnish

Fillet the fish, leaving the skin attached to each fillet (or have the fish dealer do this for you); reserve the skeleton, with head and tail attached. Cut each fillet into 1½-inch squares.

Early in the day, prepare the fish boats: Pour 3 inches of oil in a wok or deep fryer and heat to 330°F. Dredge the reserved skeletons with flour, shaking off any excess. Dip the head in the hot oil, holding the tail with tongs above the oil, forming a curve. Hold until the curve is set and the bones have become brown and crisp, about 10 minutes. Reverse the position of the bones (now the tail is curved up in the oil and you are holding the head above the oil) and finish deep-frying. Remove and drain on paper towels. Repeat with the remaining 3 skeletons. Place the boats on a baking sheet; set aside. Strain and reserve the oil for frying the fish fillets.

Prepare the *Nuoc Cham*. Set aside.

Make scallion flowers: Use a sharp paring knife to cut each scallion halfway up, lengthwise, into 6 or 8 sections. Make chile flowers: Use scissors to make long, uniform cuts from the top of each chile pepper halfway in toward the stem end. Place the carved scallions and chile peppers in cold water. Cover and refrigerate until the "petals" open, about 1 hour.

Reheat the fish boats in a 300°F oven while you fry the fish.

Pour the reserved oil into a wok or deep fryer and heat to 375°F. This temperature must be maintained for the entire frying process. Dredge the fish pieces with flour. Gently drop them, one at a time, into the hot oil. Deep-fry a few pieces at a time until they turn golden brown and crispy, about 1½ minutes. Remove the fish pieces as they are cooked to drain on paper towels. Keep them warm in the oven while frying the remaining fish pieces. If the fish is not crispy enough, deep-fry briefly a second time.

Distribute the fish pieces among the fish boats. Garnish with the coriander sprigs and scallion and chile flowers. To serve, dip the fried fish in *Nuoc Cham*. Break the fish boats into small pieces and eat like potato chips.

Yield: 4 servings

SHRIMP AND SWEET POTATO CAKES

BANH TOM

Also called *Banh Cong,* these delicious shrimp cakes are always served wrapped in crisp lettuce leaves with fresh herbs and dipped in *Nuoc Cham.*

If you are fortunate enough to find fresh prawns, you can leave the 16 shrimp unshelled to place on top of the batter. You may also substitute Idaho potatoes for sweet potatoes.

■ ■ ■ ■ ■ ■ ■ ■ ■ ■ ■ ■

Nuoc Cham *with Shredded Carrot*
    and Daikon (page 212)
Vegetable Platter (page 169)
24 *raw medium shrimp (about*
    1½ pounds)
  1 *tablespoon* nuoc mam *(Vietnamese*
    fish sauce)
  2 *large garlic cloves, minced*
    Freshly ground black pepper
  2 *cups cake flour*
  2 *tablespoons sugar*
  1 *tablespoon salt*
  1 *teaspoon baking powder*
¾ *teaspoon turmeric*
  1 *large sweet potato (about 8 ounces)*
  2 *scallions, finely sliced*
    Vegetable oil, for deep-frying

Prepare the *Nuoc Cham* and Vegetable Platter. Set aside.

Shell and devein the shrimp, leaving the tails attached on 16 of the shrimp. Combine the whole shrimp, the fish sauce, garlic and black pepper to taste in a bowl. Mix well and refrigerate. Cut the shrimp without tails into fine pieces. Using the back of a cleaver, mash the shrimp but do not reduce to a paste. You want to retain some of the texture of the shrimp. Set aside.

In a large mixing bowl, sift together the flour, sugar, salt, baking powder, turmeric and black pepper. Make a well in the center and pour in 1¼ cups of cold water, stirring constantly with a whisk. Whisk until very smooth; the batter should have the consistency of thick cream.

Pare the sweet potato. Slice it paper-thin and then shred into very thin strands. Add the shredded potato, scallions and mashed shrimp to the batter; mix well.

In a heavy 12-inch skillet, heat 1 inch of oil until very hot but not smoking.

Meanwhile, make the cakes: Spoon about 2 heaping tablespoons of the potato mixture into a saucer and lightly press a whole shrimp into the center. Holding the saucer close to the surface of the oil, gently push the cake into the oil with a spoon. Fry the cakes, 3 or 4 at a time, for about 2 minutes, spooning the hot oil over each cake. Regulate the heat so that cakes cook evenly without burning. Carefully turn the cakes, shrimp side down, and cook for another 2 minutes. When the cakes are crisp and golden brown, drain on paper towels. Keep warm in a low oven while you fry the remaining cakes.

Arrange the shrimp cakes, shrimp side up, on a heated platter. To serve, diners place a piece of the shrimp cake on a leaf of lettuce, then add selected ingredients from the Vegetable Platter along with some shredded carrot and daikon from the sauce. The bundle is rolled up, dipped in *Nuoc Cham* and eaten out of hand.

NOTE These fritters can be prepared in advance and reheated in a 350°F oven before serving.

Yield: 16 cakes

STEAMED WHOLE FISH
CA HAP

*M*ost Vietnamese are very fond of fish, and this is one classic way of cooking it. Although steamed fish is usually family-style fare, it is also a beloved party dish.

Traditionally, carp is used in this dish, but sea bass, red snapper or sea trout make good substitutes. Freshwater carp and fresh bacon (pork belly) can be purchased at many of the fish dealers and butcher shops in Chinatown.

■ ■ ■ ■ ■ ■ ■ ■ ■ ■ ■

4 *dried Chinese mushrooms*
1 *tablespoon dried tree ear mushrooms*
½ *ounce cellophane (bean thread) noodles*
1 *tablespoon* nuoc mam *(Vietnamese fish sauce)*
2 *teaspoons soy sauce*
½ *teaspoon salt*
2 *teaspoons sugar*
2 *garlic cloves, minced*
1 *teaspoon Oriental sesame oil*
1 *whole white-fleshed fish (2½ to 3 pounds), cleaned, with head and tail left on*
1 *tablespoon peanut oil*
1 *small onion, thinly sliced*
1 *tablespoon shredded fresh gingerroot*
4 *ounces fresh bacon (pork belly), thinly shredded*
1 *celery rib, thinly sliced*
1 *tomato, cut into 8 wedges*
3 *scallions, cut into 2-inch sections, finely shredded*
2 *fresh red chile peppers, finely shredded*
  Freshly ground black pepper
  Coriander sprigs, for garnish

Soak the Chinese and tree ear mushrooms in hot water and the cellophane noodles in warm water for 30 minutes. Drain. Remove and discard the stems from the Chinese mushrooms. Squeeze the mushroom caps dry; cut into thin strips. Cut the noodles into 2-inch lengths.

In a small bowl, combine the fish sauce, soy sauce, salt, sugar, garlic, sesame oil and 1 tablespoon of water. Set the sauce aside.

Wash the fish; pat dry with paper towels. Lightly score the fish on each side, from the gills to the tail, at 1-inch intervals. Brush the fish, inside and out, with the sauce mixture. Place the fish on a heatproof plate that will fit in a large steamer. (If the fish is too long for the plate, cut it in half for steaming. For serving, restore it to its original shape.)

Heat the peanut oil in a skillet over high heat. Add the onion and ginger and stir-fry briefly. Add the fresh bacon and fry for 1 minute, or until lightly browned. Add the celery, tomato wedges and mushrooms and stir to combine. Pour the mixture over the fish.

Set up a large steamer and bring the water to a boil. Put the plate with the fish on the steaming rack, cover and steam over high heat for 10 minutes.

Uncover the steamer and baste the fish with the juices collected in the plate. Scatter the noodles, shredded scallions and chiles over the fish. Baste again, cover and steam for 10 minutes.

Sprinkle the fish with black pepper and garnish with the coriander sprigs. Serve the fish at once, directly from the plate.

Yield: 4 servings

BATTER-FRIED SHRIMP
TOM CHIEN BOT

*T*he flavor of these light and crispy fritters is further enhanced by zesty Sweet-and-Sour Dipping Sauce.

Scallops, oysters, clams and pieces of lobster can be substituted for the shrimp.

■ ■ ■ ■ ■ ■ ■ ■ ■ ■ ■

Sweet-and-Sour Dipping Sauce (page 214)
1 *pound raw medium shrimp*
1 *tablespoon* nuoc mam *(Vietnamese fish sauce)*
2 *large garlic cloves, minced*
  Freshly ground black pepper
1 *cup all-purpose flour, sifted*
2 *tablespoons baking powder*
1 *teaspoon sugar*
½ *teaspoon salt*
¼ *teaspoon turmeric*
  Vegetable oil, for deep-frying
  Cornstarch, for dredging

Prepare the Sweet-and-Sour Dipping Sauce. Set aside.

Shell and devein the shrimp, leaving the tail section attached. Combine the shrimp, fish sauce, garlic and black pepper to taste in a bowl. Mix well; set aside to marinate for 30 minutes.

Combine the flour, baking powder, sugar, salt, turmeric and ¼ teaspoon of black pepper in a bowl. Make a well in the center. Stir in 1¼ cups of cold water until smooth. Let rest for 1 hour.

Heat 2 inches of oil in a wok or deep fryer to 365°F, or until a drop of batter sizzles and rises to the surface. Dredge the shrimp in cornstarch, shaking off any excess. One by one, dip the shrimp in the batter, holding each one by the tail, and coat well. Carefully add the shrimp to the hot oil, a few at a time. Fry, turning once, for 2 to 3 minutes, or until golden brown and crisp. Drain on paper towels. Continue coating and frying until all of the shrimp are cooked.

Serve hot, with Sweet-and-Sour Sauce as part of a meal or as an appetizer.

NOTE The same batter may be used for vegetables, such as cauliflower, sweet potato, zucchini or mushrooms. Substitute *Nuoc Cham* for the Sweet-and-Sour Sauce.

Yield: 4 to 6 servings

Fried Crab with Salt and Pepper

Boneless Stuffed Whole Fish

FRIED CRAB WITH SALT AND PEPPER
CUA RANG MUOI

This dish is to the Vietnamese what a Crab Boil is to Americans. Throughout Vietnam, it is traditionally served along with other seafood specialties at outdoor get-togethers.

Traditionally, live, freshwater crabs are used for this recipe. Here in America, I find the blue crabs best suited, as they are small in size and the shells are not too hard.

In order to enjoy this treat to the fullest, be sure to have on hand plenty of cold beer or iced tea, lots of napkins and, of course, lots of company.

■ ■ ■ ■ ■ ■ ■ ■ ■ ■

1 dozen small live blue crabs
3 tablespoons peanut oil
4 garlic cloves, chopped
1 teaspoon salt
½ teaspoon freshly ground black pepper

Drop the live crabs into a large quantity of boiling water in a soup pot. Immediately remove the pot from the heat and let stand for 1 minute. Drain and refresh the crabs in cold water.

Detach the claws and open each shell. With a toothpick, scrape all the roe from the shell and body into a bowl; cover and refrigerate. Crack the claws with a mallet or the flat side of a heavy cleaver. Set aside.

Remove and discard the gills. Clean the shell of each crab with a vegetable brush under cold running water.

Lay a crab on a cutting board and place a heavy cleaver, blade edge down, across the center of the crab body. Using a mallet, firmly strike the top of the cleaver to split the crab in half. Cut each half crosswise into 2 pieces.

Heat the oil in a wok or Dutch oven over high heat. When the oil is smoking, add the garlic and stir-fry until fragrant. Add the crabs and claws and stir-fry for 2 minutes. Cover the pan and continue to cook over high heat for 10 minutes, tossing frequently.

Uncover the pan and sprinkle on the salt and pepper. Toss well. Add the crab roe and stir-fry for 1 minute to combine.

Transfer the crabs to a large heated serving platter and serve at once. If desired, dip the picked crabmeat in a mixture of salt, freshly cracked black pepper and freshly squeezed lemon juice.

NOTE You may substitute fresh, unshelled jumbo shrimp for the crabs, or soft-shell crabs for the blue crabs (in this case, they should be coated with flour first, then fried only briefly.

Yield: 2 to 4 servings

BONELESS STUFFED WHOLE FISH
CA RUT XUONG DON THIT

Stuffed whole fish is a prized dish frequently offered at Vietnamese banquets. The fish head itself is considered a delicacy; it is commonly believed that eating a fish head will bring much luck—probably the reason that fish is often served whole at the table.

Buy a fresh, whole 3-pound fish (red snapper, sea bass or carp) with the head and tail left on.

The fish may be grilled over a charcoal fire; just remember to baste frequently with oil to avoid its drying out.

■ ■ ■ ■ ■ ■ ■ ■ ■ ■

Nuoc Cham (*page 212*)
Pickled Carrots (page 184)
½ *tablespoon dried tree ear mushrooms*
½ *ounce cellophane (bean thread)*
   noodles
 4 *shallots, minced*
 4 *garlic cloves, minced*
¼ *teaspoon salt*
¼ *teaspoon sugar*
 1 *tablespoon* nuoc mam (*Vietnamese*
   fish sauce)
   Freshly ground black pepper
 1 *2½-to-3-pound red snapper, boned*
   and cleaned, with head and tail
   left on
 4 *ounces ground pork*
 2 *ounces fresh lump crabmeat, picked*
   over well
½ *medium onion, minced*
 1 *egg, lightly beaten*
   Vegetable oil
   Lemon and lime wedges
   Coriander sprigs

Prepare the *Nuoc Cham* and Pickled Carrots. Set aside.

Preheat the oven to 400°F.

Soak the tree ears in hot water and the cellophane noodles in warm water for 30 minutes. Drain. Mince the tree ears. Cut the cellophane noodles into 1-inch lengths.

In a medium bowl, mix together the shallots, garlic, salt, sugar, fish sauce and black pepper to taste. Rub half of the seasoning inside the fish. Combine the remaining half with the pork, crabmeat, onion, egg and the noodles and mushrooms. Mix well. Fill the fish cavity with the stuffing. Close the opening with string.

Line a baking pan with a double thickness of aluminum foil, leaving excess foil at both ends so the fish can be removed by lifting the foil. Generously oil the foil. Place the fish on it and brush oil on the fish.

Bake, uncovered, until the fish flakes easily when tested with a fork, and the pork is cooked through, 30 to 35 minutes.

Transfer the fish to a large platter. Arrange the pickled carrots, lemon and lime wedges and coriander sprigs around the fish. Pass the *Nuoc Cham* separately.

Yield: 4 to 6 servings

CURRIED FROGS' LEGS

ECH NAU CA-RI

This delicious lemon grass and co-conut-laced curry comes from southern Vietnam. If you prefer a very hot curry, simply use more chile peppers.

■ ■ ■ ■ ■ ■ ■ ■ ■ ■ ■

4 pairs of jumbo frogs' legs (about 1 pound), trimmed
1 stalk fresh lemon grass, or 1 tablespoon dried lemon grass
2 fresh red chile peppers, seeded and sliced
2 shallots, sliced
2 garlic cloves, crushed
1½ teaspoons sugar
1 teaspoon curry paste (page 231)
2 teaspoons curry powder
¼ teaspoon salt
2 tablespoons nuoc mam (Vietnamese fish sauce)
2 ounces cellophane (bean thread) noodles
2 tablespoons vegetable oil
1 small onion, chopped
1 cup chicken broth or water
½ cup coconut milk or heavy cream
1 teaspoon cornstarch
Freshly ground black pepper
Coriander sprigs, for garnish

Cut the frogs' legs into bite-size pieces. Rinse with cold water to remove any chipped bones. Pat dry and refrigerate.

If you are using fresh lemon grass, discard the outer leaves and upper half of the stalk. Cut into thin slices and finely chop. If you are using dried lemon grass, soak it in warm water for 1 hour. Drain and finely chop.

In a blender, combine the lemon grass with the chiles, shallots, garlic, sugar, curry paste, curry powder, salt and 1 tablespoon of the fish sauce. Process to a very fine paste. Rub the paste over the frogs' legs. Cover and refrigerate for 30 minutes.

Meanwhile, soak the cellophane noodles in warm water for 30 minutes. Drain. Cut into 2-inch sections.

Heat the oil in a saucepan over moderate heat. Add the onion and sauté until translucent. Add the frogs' legs and brown well on all sides, about 3 minutes. Add the chicken broth and bring to a boil. Reduce the heat, cover and simmer for 15 minutes.

Uncover the pan and add the coconut milk, the cornstarch diluted in 1 tablespoon of cold water and the remaining 1 tablespoon fish sauce. Cook, stirring, until the sauce thickens, about 15 minutes.

Add the cellophane noodles and bring the mixture to a boil. Remove from the heat.

Sprinkle with black pepper and garnish with coriander sprigs.

Serve immediately with rice, French bread or over rice noodles.

NOTE Instead of discarding the upper half of the lemon grass, crush it and cook it with the frogs' legs for extra flavor. Remove the stalk before serving.

Yield: 4 servings

SWEET-AND-SOUR FISH
CA RANG CHUA NGOT

*U*nlike the classic Cantonese sweet-and-sour dish, this recipe is more subtle, pairing crisp-fried fish, fresh pineapple and light sweet-and-sour sauce. Often served on special occasions, this dish is also of symbolic significance: the whole fish stands for totality, and the red color of the sauce for good luck.

■ ■ ■ ■ ■ ■ ■ ■ ■ ■ ■

1 *sea bass or red snapper (2½ to 3 pounds), cleaned, with head and tail left on*
1½ *teaspoons salt*
   Freshly ground black pepper
10 *dried tiger lily buds*
4 *dried Chinese mushrooms*
¼ *cup unsweetened pineapple juice*
¼ *cup distilled white vinegar*
½ *teaspoon salt*
2 *tablespoons plus 1 teaspoon sugar*
1 *tablespoon ketchup*
2 *tablespoons* nuoc mam *(Vietnamese fish sauce)*
3 *tablespoons light soy sauce*
4½ *teaspoons cornstarch*
1 *tablespoon grated fresh gingerroot*
2 *tablespoons vegetable oil*
6 *garlic cloves, minced*
1 *small onion, cut into thin slivers*
1 *cup fresh pineapple chunks, or 1 can (8¼ ounces) pineapple chunks in their own juice, drained*
1 *medium carrot, halved lengthwise and cut on a diagonal into ⅛-inch slices*
1 *large celery rib, cut on a diagonal into ⅛-inch slices*
3 *scallions, cut into 2-inch sections*
1 *small tomato, cut into 8 wedges*
¼ *cup pickled shallots (page 233), shredded*
1 *red chile pepper, thinly sliced*
   Vegetable oil, for frying
   All-purpose flour, for coating
   Coriander leaves, for garnish

Wash the fish under cold running water and pat completely dry with paper towels. Lightly score the fish on each side at 1-inch intervals, starting from behind the head. Rub it inside and out with the salt and black pepper. Set aside.

Soak the tiger lily buds and dried mushrooms in hot water for 30 minutes. Drain, reserving ¼ cup of the soaking liquid. Cut away and discard the hard ends of the lily buds and tie a knot in the center of each. Cut away and discard the mushroom stems; slice the caps crosswise into ¼-inch strips.

In a small bowl, combine the reserved soaking liquid, pineapple juice, vinegar, salt, sugar, ketchup, fish sauce, soy sauce, cornstarch and ginger. Mix the sauce until the sugar and cornstarch dissolve.

In a heavy saucepan, heat the 2 tablespoons of oil over moderate heat until a light haze forms above it. Stirring for about 30 seconds after each addition, drop in the garlic, onion slivers, pineapple, carrots, mushrooms, lily buds, celery, scallions and the tomato wedges.

Add the sauce and bring to a boil, stirring constantly, over moderate heat. Still stirring, cook briskly for 2 to 3 minutes, or until the sauce thickens. Add the pickled shallots and chile slices to the sauce. Remove from the heat.

Heat 2 inches of oil in a heavy skillet large enough to hold the fish. (If the fish is too long for the skillet, cut it in half crosswise.) Restore it to its original length after frying. Dredge the fish in flour, shaking off any excess. The oil should be hot but not smoking. Fry the fish in the hot oil for 8 to 10 minutes on each side, or until the fish is firm and delicately browned. Spoon the hot oil over the fish while frying. Turn it carefully with two long-handled spatulas. Remove and drain on paper towels.

Transfer the fish to a large, heated platter. Reheat the sauce, stirring gently, for 1 to 2 minutes. Pour the sauce over the fish, spreading the vegetables attractively on top. Garnish with coriander leaves. Serve at once with rice.

Yield: 4 to 6 servings

DILLED SQUID CAKES
CHA MUC

*T*raditionally, these flavorful squid cakes call for pounded squid but the food processor does as good a job as a mortar and pestle.

Freeze the tentacles for use in other dishes, such as Grilled Fresh Young Squid, Stir-Fried Squid with Pickled Mustard Greens or Fried Squid.

I usually prepare a double batch of this recipe, shaping half into patties as described below and the other half into meatball-size portions that are steamed and frozen. When a quick appetizer is needed, I thaw them and reheat by frying, baking, steaming or barbecuing.

■ ■ ■ ■ ■ ■ ■ ■ ■ ■

Nuoc Cham *(page 212)*
1 *pound fresh squid*
3 *shallots, sliced*
6 *garlic cloves, crushed*
1 *ounce rock sugar (page 234), crushed, or 1 tablespoon granulated sugar*
4 *ounces pork fat, cut into small chunks*
2 *teaspoons* nuoc mam *(Vietnamese fish sauce)*
1 *egg, lightly beaten*
2 *tablespoons chopped fresh dill*
⅛ *teaspoon freshly ground black pepper*
½ *cup vegetable oil*

Prepare the *Nuoc Cham.* Set aside.

Clean each squid by gently pulling the head with its tentacles from the body section, being careful not to break the ink sac. Discard the head and reserve the tentacles for other use.

Pull out the long, transparent sword-shaped "pen" from the body section. Make a lengthwise cut along the body to open it. Remove the insides; peel off the outer membrane from the body. Rinse the prepared squid under cold running water. Pat dry with paper towels (it is very important that the squid be completely free of moisture). Cut the body into 2-inch pieces.

Place the squid, shallots, garlic and sugar in the work bowl of a food processor. Process to a very smooth and sticky paste (it should spring back to the touch), stopping as necessary to scrape down the sides of the bowl. Transfer the paste to a bowl.

Place the pork fat in the processor and coarsely chop (do not reduce to a paste). Add the squid paste, fish sauce, egg, dill and black pepper to the processor. Pulse briefly, only enough to blend all of the ingredients.

Pour ¼ cup of the vegetable oil into a small bowl. Dip your fingers in the oil and then mold about 2 tablespoons of the squid paste into a small round cake, about 2½ inches in diameter. Continue until all of the squid paste is used.

Heat the remaining ¼ cup vegetable oil in a large skillet over moderate heat. Fry 3 or 4 cakes at a time for 2 to 3 minutes on each side, or until puffy and golden brown.

Remove the cakes to a serving platter lined with a double thickness of paper towels. Keep warm in a low oven. Continue cooking the remaining cakes.

Cut each cake into bite-size pieces. Serve with plain rice and *Nuoc Cham.*

NOTE Scallops, shrimp, cuttlefish or any white, firm-fleshed fish are excellent substitutes for squid in this recipe.

Yield: 4 to 6 servings

Barbecued Shrimp Paste on Sugar Cane, Extra-Thin Rice Vermicelli and Peanut Sauce

Deep-Fried Flounder and Nuoc Cham *with Shredded Carrot and Daikon*

BARBECUED SHRIMP PASTE ON SUGAR CANE

CHAO TOM

*A*lthough this dish can be baked in an oven, I strongly suggest you grill it over charcoal, for the result is far superior.

The dish may be prepared over 2 consecutive days. On day one, prepare the dipping sauce and condiments. The Vegetable Platter and shrimp paste can be assembled the following day.

Fresh sugar cane may be obtained at Caribbean markets; canned sugar cane is available at Asian grocery stores.

■ ■ ■ ■ ■ ■ ■ ■ ■ ■ ■

1 *tablespoon roasted rice powder (page 220)*
  Scallion oil (page 225)
  Crisp-fried shallots (page 226)
1 *tablespoon roasted peanuts (page 220), ground*
1 *pound raw shrimp in the shell*
1 *tablespoon salt*
6 *garlic cloves, crushed*
6 *shallots, crushed*
2 *ounces rock sugar (page 234), crushed to a powder, or 1 tablespoon granulated sugar*
4 *ounces pork fat*
4 *teaspoons nuoc mam (Vietnamese fish sauce)*
  Freshly ground black pepper
  Peanut Sauce (page 211)
  Vegetable Platter (page 169)
8 *ounces 6½-inch rice paper rounds (banh trang)*
  12-inch piece fresh sugar cane, or 1 can (12 ounces) sugar cane packed in light syrup, drained
12 *8½-inch bamboo skewers, soaked in water for 30 minutes*
  Vegetable oil, for shaping shrimp paste
8 *ounces extra-thin rice vermicelli (banh hoi, page 222)*

Prepare the roasted rice powder, scallion oil, crisp-fried shallots and roasted peanuts. Set aside.

Shell and devein the shrimp. Sprinkle the salt over the shrimp and let stand for 20 minutes. Rinse the shrimp thoroughly with cold water. Drain and squeeze between your hands to remove excess water. Dry thoroughly with paper towels. Coarsely chop the shrimp.

Boil the pork fat for 10 minutes. Drain and finely dice.

In a food processor, combine the shrimp, garlic, shallots and sugar. Process until the shrimp paste pulls away from the sides of the container, stopping as necessary to scrape down the sides. The paste should be very fine and sticky.

Add the pork fat, roasted rice powder, fish sauce and black pepper to taste to the processor. Pulse briefly, only enough to blend all of the ingredients. Cover and refrigerate.

Meanwhile, prepare the Peanut Sauce and Vegetable Platter. Cover the rice papers with a damp towel and a sheet of plastic wrap; keep at room temperature until needed.

Peel the fresh sugar cane; cut crosswise into 4-inch sections. Split each section lengthwise into quarters. (If using canned sugar cane, split each section lengthwise in half only, then thread 2 pieces lengthwise onto a skewer.)

Pour about ¼ cup of oil into a small bowl. Oil your fingers. Pick up and mold about 2 tablespoons of the shrimp paste around and halfway down a piece of fresh sugar cane. Leave about 1½ inches of the sugar cane exposed to serve as a handle. (If using canned sugar cane, there is no need to leave a handle. The skewers will serve as handles.) Press firmly so that the paste adheres to the cane. Proceed until you have used all the shrimp paste.

Prepare a charcoal grill or preheat the oven to broil.

Meanwhile, steam the noodles, then garnish with the scallion oil, crisp-fried shallots and ground roasted peanuts. Keep warm. Pour the peanut sauce into individual bowls and place the Vegetable Platter and rice papers on the table.

Grill the shrimp paste on the sugar cane over medium coals, turning frequently, for about 8 minutes. Or broil, on a baking sheet lined with foil, under the broiler, about 6 inches from the heat, for 3 minutes on each side, or until browned. Transfer to a warm platter.

To serve, each diner dips a rice paper round in a bowl of warm water to make it pliable, then places the paper on a dinner plate. Different ingredients from the Vegetable Platter, some noodles and a piece of the shrimp paste, which has been removed from the sugar cane, are added. The rice paper is then rolled up to form a neat package. The roll is dipped in the Peanut Sauce and eaten out of hand.

The remaining sugar cane may be chewed.

NOTE If both types of sugar cane are unavailable, use skewers. Shape the shrimp paste into meatballs and thread 3 or 4 on each skewer.

Yield: 4 to 6 servings

FRIED FISH STEAKS IN TOMATO SAUCE
CA CHIEN SOT CA CHUA

This common dish is delicious and very easy to prepare. Usually tuna steaks are used for this recipe, but any firm-fleshed fish may be substituted.

■ ■ ■ ■ ■ ■ ■ ■ ■ ■ ■

Nuoc Cham *(page 212)*
4 *tuna, tilefish or halibut steaks, each cut 1 inch thick*
3 *tablespoons* nuoc mam *(Vietnamese fish sauce)*
Freshly ground black pepper
All-purpose flour, for dredging
¼ *cup vegetable oil*
4 *shallots, thinly sliced*
4 *garlic cloves, thinly sliced*
4 *large ripe tomatoes (about 1½ pounds), cored, seeded and diced*
1 *teaspoon sugar*
2 *scallions, sliced*
2 *tablespoons shredded coriander*

Prepare the *Nuoc Cham.* Set aside.

In a bowl, coat the fish steaks with 1 tablespoon of the fish sauce and sprinkle with ½ teaspoon black pepper. Let marinate for 30 minutes.

Dredge the fish steaks with flour, shaking off any excess.

Heat the oil in a wok or large skillet over moderate heat. Add the fish steaks and cook for 4 minutes on one side. Turn and cook for 4 minutes longer. Drain the fish steaks on a platter lined with a double layer of paper towels. Keep warm in a low oven while making the tomato sauce.

Pour off the oil from the wok, leaving about 2 tablespoons in the pan. Add the shallots and garlic to the wok and stir-fry over moderate heat until fragrant. Add the tomatoes and cook for 1 minute. Add the remaining 2 tablespoons fish sauce, the sugar and ¼ cup of water. Simmer, stirring occasionally, for 5 minutes. Add the scallions and coriander and stir to combine.

Return the fish steaks to the wok and turn to coat evenly with the sauce. Cook until the fish is just heated through. Transfer the fish to a hot platter and spoon the sauce over the fish. Sprinkle with freshly ground black pepper.

Serve with rice and the *Nuoc Cham.*

Yield: 4 servings

STIR-FRIED SQUID
WITH PICKLED MUSTARD GREENS
MUC XAO CAI CHUA

*I*n this dish the sourness and crispiness of the pickled greens contrast sharply with the chewiness of the squid and the clear taste of the celery leaves. Combined with the seasonings, all these ingredients create a spectrum of flavors and textures.

Pickled Chinese mustard greens come vacuum-packed in brine and can be purchased at most Vietnamese or Chinese grocery stores. A recipe is provided on page 189.

■ ■ ■ ■ ■ ■ ■ ■ ■ ■ ■

Nuoc Cham (*page 212*)
1 *pound pickled mustard greens*
1 *pound large fresh squid*
4 *garlic cloves, chopped*
2 *tablespoons* nuoc mam (*Vietnamese fish sauce*)
¼ *teaspoon sugar*
Freshly ground black pepper
1 *large onion*
4 *celery ribs, with leaves*
2 *large tomatoes*
4 *scallions*
4 *tablespoons peanut oil*
3 *tablespoons chopped fresh dill*
Coriander leaves, for garnish

Prepare the *Nuoc Cham*. Set aside.

Soak the pickled greens for at least 2 hours, or overnight, changing the water several times to remove the salt.

Clean each squid by gently pulling the head with its tentacles from the body section, being careful not to break the ink sac. Discard the head and reserve the tentacles.

Pull out the long, transparent sword-shaped "pen" from the body section and make a lengthwise cut along the mantle to open it. Remove the insides. Peel off the membrane from the outside of the mantle. Rinse the prepared squid and tentacles under cold running water. Pat dry with paper towels.

Cut the squid mantles lengthwise into 2-inch strips. Diagonally score the inside surface of each strip, cutting only two-thirds of the way through. Repeat the same diagonal cuts in the opposite direction to form diamond-shape designs. Cut the strips into 2-inch pieces.

In a bowl, mix the squid with half of the chopped garlic, 1 tablespoon of the fish sauce, the sugar and black pepper to taste. Cover and refrigerate for 30 minutes.

Meanwhile, drain the pickled greens and squeeze dry. Cut crosswise into 1-inch pieces. Cut the onion into slivers. Cut the celery on the diagonal into 1½-inch-long slices. Core each tomato and cut each into 8 wedges. Cut the scallions into 2-inch pieces.

Arrange all of the vegetables and squid on a large platter to facilitate the final cooking.

Place a large skillet over high heat. Add 2 tablespoons of the oil. When hot, add the squid and stir-fry until the pieces curl, about 30 seconds; remove. Reheat the skillet. Add the remaining 2 tablespoons oil. Stir-fry the onion and the remaining garlic until fragrant. Add the tomatoes and cook for 1 minute. Add the greens and celery and stir-fry for 2 minutes. Season the mixture with the remaining 1 tablespoon fish sauce. Add the squid, scallions and dill and mix well.

Transfer to a warm platter. Sprinkle with black pepper and garnish with the coriander. Serve with rice and *Nuoc Cham*.

NOTE Cuttlefish may be substituted for the squid.

Yield: 4 servings

Stir-Fried Squid with Pickled Mustard Greens and Stir-Fried Pickled Bamboo Shoots with Fresh Bacon

FROGS' LEGS SIMMERED WITH LEMON GRASS AND CHILE PEPPER

ECH KHO XA OT

*T*his is a delicious and unusual way to prepare these delicate frogs' legs. Serve them with rice, Pickled Bean Sprouts or Pickled Mustard Greens and soup for a complete dinner. Frogs' legs are available fresh or frozen at well-stocked fish markets.

■ ■ ■ ■ ■ ■ ■ ■ ■ ■

Caramel Sauce (page 217)
4 pairs of jumbo frogs' legs (about 1 pound), trimmed
1 stalk fresh lemon grass, or 1 tablespoon dried lemon grass
1 red chile pepper, seeded and chopped
2 teaspoons vegetable oil
Freshly ground black pepper (optional)

Prepare the Caramel Sauce. Set aside.

Cut the frogs' legs into bite-size pieces and rinse with cold water to remove any chipped bones. Pat dry and refrigerate.

If you are using fresh lemon grass, discard the outer leaves and upper half of the stalk. Cut into thin slices and finely chop. If you are using dried lemon grass, soak it in warm water for 1 hour. Drain and finely chop.

In a saucepan, combine the cooled Caramel Sauce, lemon grass, chile, oil and frogs' legs. Bring the mixture to a boil. Cover the pan and simmer over low heat, stirring occasionally, for 20 to 30 minutes, or until the meat is tender. Sprinkle with black pepper, if desired.

NOTE For variation, marinate whole frogs' legs in the Caramel Sauce, then grill over hot coals. Just remember to baste the legs with oil to prevent their drying out.

Yield: 4 servings

FISH SIMMERED IN CARAMEL SAUCE

CA KHO TO

*C*a Kho To is another popular national dish of Vietnam. To be authentic, simmer the fish in an earthenware crock and present it at the table where diners serve themselves directly from it. Offer alongside Spicy and Sour Shrimp Soup and Pickled Bean Sprouts or simply slices of cucumbers for a refreshing note to a spicy meal.

■ ■ ■ ■ ■ ■ ■ ■ ■ ■

Pickled Bean Sprouts (page 184)
Caramel Sauce (page 217)
1 teaspoon chile paste (tuong ot tuoi)*, or 2 fresh red chiles, seeded and minced*
4 catfish, halibut or tilefish steaks, each cut 1 inch thick
Freshly ground black pepper

Prepare the Pickled Bean Sprouts and Caramel Sauce. Stir the chile paste into the cooled caramel sauce and set aside.

Add the fish to the Caramel Sauce in a clay pot or heavy-bottomed saucepan and bring to a boil. Reduce the heat to low, cover the pot and simmer for about 45 minutes, turning the fish occasionally.

Sprinkle with black pepper, if desired, and serve with rice and Pickled Bean Sprouts.

Yield: 4 servings

FRIED WHOLE FISH WITH LEMON GRASS

CA CHIEN XA

*T*he scent of fried lemon grass is so aromatic, refreshing and comforting that I will forever associate it with my mother's kitchen. If possible, use whole catfish to prepare this recipe. Rock cod, tilefish, red snapper, striped bass, shelled fresh prawns or any firm, white-fleshed fish may be substituted.

The fish may also be grilled over a hot charcoal fire instead of deep-fried (it is then called *Ca Nuong*). Just remember to baste the fish constantly with oil to avoid its drying out.

■ ■ ■ ■ ■ ■ ■ ■ ■ ■ ■ ■

3 *stalks fresh lemon grass, or 2 table-*
   spoons dried lemon grass
4 *garlic cloves, crushed*
4 *shallots, sliced*
3 *fresh red chile peppers, seeded and*
   sliced
2 *tablespoons sugar*
2 *tablespoons* nuoc mam (*Vietnamese*
   fish sauce)
   Freshly ground black pepper
1 *whole white-fleshed fish (2½ to 3*
   pounds), cleaned, with head and tail
   left on
   Anchovy and Pineapple Sauce (Mam
   Nem, *page 216*)
8 *ounces thin rice vermicelli* (bun, *page*
   223), *or 2 bundles Japanese*
   alimentary paste noodles (somen,
   page 223)
   Vegetable Platter (*page 169*)
8 *ounces 6½-inch rice paper rounds*
   (banh trang)
   Vegetable oil, for deep-frying
   All-purpose flour, for dredging

If you are using fresh lemon grass, discard the outer leaves and upper half of the stalk. Cut into thin slices and coarsely chop. If you are using dried lemon grass, soak it in warm water for 1 hour. Drain and coarsely chop.

In a mortar, pound the lemon grass, garlic, shallots, chiles and sugar into a paste. Stir in the fish sauce and black pepper to taste. Set aside.

Wash the fish and pat dry with paper towels. Score the fish lightly at 1-inch intervals on each side, starting from behind the head. Rub the lemon grass mixture on the inside and outside of the fish. Set aside to marinate for 1 hour.

Meanwhile, prepare the Anchovy and Pineapple Sauce, noodles and Vegetable Platter. Set aside. Cover the rice papers with a damp cloth and a sheet of plastic wrap. Keep at room temperature until needed.

In a heavy skillet large enough to hold the fish, heat 2 inches of oil until hot but not smoking. Meanwhile, dredge the fish with flour, shaking to remove the excess flour. (If the fish is too long for the skillet, cut it in half crosswise. Restore to its original length after frying.

Add the fish by sliding it headfirst into the hot oil. Fry the fish for 8 to 10 minutes on each side, or until it is firm and delicately browned. Spoon the hot oil over the fish while frying. Turn it carefully with 2 long-handled spatulas. Remove and drain on paper towels.

Divide the dipping sauce among 4 to 6 individual bowls. Carve the fish into individual portions, without cutting through the spine. Discard the head and spine.

To serve, each diner dips a rice paper round in a bowl of warm water to make it pliable. Selected ingredients from the Vegetable Platter, some noodles and a piece of fried fish are added. The rice paper is then rolled up to form a neat package. The roll is dipped in the sauce and eaten out of hand.

NOTE You may also try this fish with *Nuoc Cham* and plain rice as part of a simple meal.

Yield: 4 to 6 servings

POULTRY

Chicken with Pineapple and Cashews

CHICKEN WITH PINEAPPLE AND CASHEWS

GA XAO DUA, HANH

*S*elect a ripe, firm pineapple for this dish. If the pineapple is not fully ripe, seal it in a brown bag with banana peels or a ripe apple, and keep in a cold oven for a day or two. Both give off a gas that hastens the ripening of the pineapple.

For a spectacular presentation, serve this festive dish individually in halved, hollowed pineapple shells.

■ ■ ■ ■ ■ ■ ■ ■ ■ ■

Nuoc Cham (*page 212*)
1 cup whole cashews
3 tablespoons oyster sauce
4 tablespoons nuoc mam (*Vietnamese fish sauce*)
4 teaspoons sugar
3 tablespoons vegetable oil
4 garlic cloves, minced
½ teaspoon chile paste, or 2 fresh red chile peppers, chopped
6 chicken thighs (1 ½ pounds) boned, skinned and cut crosswise into 1 ¼ x 1-inch strips
1 medium onion, cut into 1-inch cubes
1 red bell pepper, cut into 1-inch squares
1 fresh pineapple, peeled, cored and cut into 1-inch cubes
1 can (15 ounces) straw mushrooms, drained
4 scallions, cut into 2-inch lengths
Freshly ground black pepper
Coriander sprigs, for garnish

Prepare the *Nuoc Cham*. Set aside.

Place the cashews in a dry skillet set over moderate heat. Stir constantly for about 5 minutes, or until the nuts are nicely browned. Set aside.

Combine the oyster sauce, 2 tablespoons of the fish sauce, 2 teaspoons of the sugar and 2 tablespoons of water in a small bowl. Stir to blend. Set the sauce aside.

Heat 2 tablespoons of the oil in a wok or large skillet over high heat. Add the garlic and chile paste and fry until fragrant, about 15 seconds. Add the chicken strips and sauté until browned, about 3 minutes. Stir in the sauce and continue to cook until slightly thickened. Remove the chicken to a plate.

Add the remaining 1 tablespoon oil to the wok. Add the onion and fry for 1 minute. Add the bell pepper, pineapple, the remaining 2 tablespoons fish sauce and the remaining 2 teaspoons sugar. Sauté over high heat until the pineapple is nicely glazed, about 2 minutes. Return the chicken to the wok, along with the straw mushrooms. Toss thoroughly. Add the scallions and cashews and stir to blend well.

Transfer the mixture to a heated platter or divide among hollowed pineapple shells. Sprinkle with the black pepper and garnish with coriander sprigs. Serve with rice; pass the *Nuoc Cham* separately.

Yield: 4 to 6 servings

CHICKEN CURRY, VIETNAMESE STYLE

CA-RI GA

*T*his is a stew-like dish with chicken and vegetables cooked in varying combinations of ground herbs and spices, known as curry paste. Vietnamese curries are not as incendiary as most curries of other Southeast Asian countries. If you prefer a very hot curry, simply use more chile peppers.

Like most stews, this curry improves in flavor with mellowing and also freezes well. For best results, defrost slowly in the refrigerator before reheating. Since freezing can tame the spice aroma and herb bouquet, be sure to taste and adjust the seasoning before serving. More water may be necessary to thin the condensed sauce.

■ ■ ■ ■ ■ ■ ■ ■ ■ ■

3 stalks fresh lemon grass, or 3
  tablespoons dried lemon grass
4 shallots
6 large garlic cloves, crushed
2 fresh red chile peppers, seeded
1 teaspoon sugar
2 tablespoons curry paste (page 231)
3 tablespoons curry powder
¼ cup nuoc mam (Vietnamese fish sauce)
  Freshly ground black pepper
1 chicken (4 pounds), cut into serving
  pieces
  Vegetable oil, for frying
2 large Idaho potatoes, pared and cut
  into 1½-inch pieces
2 bay leaves
2 large onions, each cut into eighths
2 large ripe tomatoes, cored, seeded and
  each cut into 8 wedges
2 cups chicken broth or water
1 tablespoon salt
2 large carrots, cut into 1½-inch pieces
2 tablespoons cornstarch
3 cups coconut milk (page 227) or heavy
  cream

If you are using fresh lemon grass, discard the outer leaves and upper half of the stalks. Cut into thin slices and finely chop. If you are using dried lemon grass, soak in warm water for 1 hour. Drain and finely chop.

In a blender or food processor, combine the lemon grass with the shallots, garlic, chiles, sugar, curry paste, curry powder, fish sauce and black pepper to taste. Process to a very fine paste.

Arrange the chicken pieces in a large shallow dish and spread the paste over both sides of the chicken. Cover and refrigerate for 1 hour.

Heat ½ inch of vegetable oil in a Dutch oven over moderately high heat. Add the potatoes and brown on all sides, about 5 minutes. Remove with a slotted spoon and drain on a platter lined with a double thickness of paper towels.

Remove all but 3 tablespoons of the oil from the Dutch oven. When the oil is hot, scrape the paste off the chicken pieces and reserve it and add the chicken to the Dutch oven without crowding. Brown on all sides. Transfer the chicken to the platter.

Pour off all but 3 tablespoons of the chicken fat from the Dutch oven. Add the paste and bay leaves and stir for 2 minutes. Add the onions and cook, stirring frequently, until lightly browned, about 3 minutes. Add the tomatoes and stir for 2 minutes. Add the chicken broth, salt and chicken leg pieces and bring the mixture to a boil. Reduce the heat, cover and simmer for 30 minutes.

Add the chicken breast pieces and carrots and simmer, stirring occasionally, for 30 minutes longer, or until the chicken pieces are very tender.

Meanwhile, dissolve the cornstarch in the coconut milk. When the cooking time is up, stir in the coconut milk-cornstarch mixture. Continue simmering, uncovered, stirring to prevent sticking, until the sauce thickens, about 15 minutes.

Transfer the curry to a heated bowl and serve with rice or French bread.

Yield: 4 to 6 servings

ROAST QUAIL
CHIM QUAY

*T*raditionally, small, tender squab is used for this dish, but I prefer the more delicate quail. Once cooked, the bird becomes so crispy that you can eat it bones and all. The so-called roast quail is actually a marinated bird that is steamed and then deep-fried. This technique yields quail that are extremely crispy on the outside, with moist flesh inside. You may apply this same cooking technique to Cornish game hens (split lengthwise), duck legs or chicken legs.

In Vietnam, game birds, such as squab, pigeon or quail, are prized foods and reserved for family celebrations and banquets only. The roast bird is usually served dipped in a salt-and-pepper mixture or in *Nuoc Cham*. Serve cold beer alongside.

■ ■ ■ ■ ■ ■ ■ ■ ■ ■ ■

2 ounces rock sugar (page 234), or 2
  tablespoons granulated sugar
1 ounce fresh gingerroot, grated
4 shallots, minced
4 garlic cloves, minced
¼ cup light soy sauce
2 tablespoons rice wine or dry Sherry
  (optional)
1 teaspoon five-spice powder
½ teaspoon freshly ground black pepper
8 quail, or 4 small squab
  Vegetable oil, for deep-frying
  Watercress, for garnish

In a mortar, pound or crush the rock sugar, ginger, shallots and garlic to a fine paste. In a small nonreactive saucepan, mix the paste with the soy sauce, rice wine, five-spice powder, black pepper and ½ cup of water. Stir to combine. Bring the liquid to a boil and stir until the sugar dissolves. Allow to cool slightly. Add the quail and turn to coat evenly. Marinate, turning occasionally, for at least 2 hours or overnight.

Drain the quail. Pour 1 inch of water into a wok or wide pot. Place a steamer rack or bamboo steamer over the water. Arrange the quail in a single layer on the rack. Cover and steam for 15 minutes. Remove and allow to cool thoroughly.

Pat the quail dry with paper towels. Cut in half lengthwise, using poultry shears.

Heat 3 inches of oil in a clean wok or deep fryer to 365°F (or until bubbles form around a dry wooden chopstick when inserted in the oil). This temperature must be maintained for the entire frying process. Add the quail, a few pieces at a time, and fry, turning once, until golden brown, about 2 minutes (longer if using squab or pigeon). Drain on paper towels and serve immediately on a serving platter lined with watercress.

NOTE If using squab or pigeon, hack each half into smaller pieces so diners can pick them up with their fingers and eat out of hand.

Yield: 4 servings

ROAST DUCK, BARBECUED STYLE

VIT QUAY

*T*he Chinese influence is evident in this close adaptation of the famous Peking duck. Roast duck, also called lacquered duck, is an important part of formal Vietnamese dinners and banquets. Instead of separating the crisp skin from the meat, the duck is carved then served wrapped in lettuce leaves, along with steamed rice vermicelli and *Nuoc Cham.*

Roast duck may be served plain with rice, French bread, steamed bread, noodles, glutinous rice, or added to rice or noodle soups.

■ ■ ■ ■ ■ ■ ■ ■ ■ ■ ■

1 *roasting duck (about 5 pounds)*
¼ *cup scallion oil (page 225)*
1 *tablespoon roasted peanuts (page 220),*
   ground
   Crisp-fried shallots (page 226)
   Nuoc Cham (page 212)
   Vegetable Platter (page 169)
1 *scallion, cut into 2-inch lengths*
4 *slices fresh gingerroot*
2 *coriander sprigs*
   Basting sauce
2 *large garlic cloves, minced*
1 *tablespoon grated fresh gingerroot*
¼ *teaspoon crushed black peppercorns*
½ *teaspoon crushed coriander seeds*
1 *teaspoon five-spice powder*
⅛ *teaspoon salt*
½ *teaspoon ground cinnamon*
2 *star anise, or ½ teaspoon aniseed*
2 *tablespoons light soy sauce*
2 *tablespoons honey*
1 *tablespoon light corn syrup*
¼ *cup chicken broth*
2 *teaspoons tomato paste*
   Accompaniments
8 *ounces extra-thin rice vermicelli (banh*
   hoi, page 222)

Three days in advance, remove the neck and giblets from the duck. Discard any excess fat. Cut off the duck wing tips and reserve with neck and giblets for stock or soup. Wash the duck; dry thoroughly with paper towels. Place the duck, breast side up, directly on a refrigerator rack (allow enough space for air to circulate freely). Place a pan on the shelf below to catch drippings. Refrigerate for 3 days, turning the duck once each day.

Early in the day, prepare the scallion oil, roasted peanuts, crisp-fried shallots, *Nuoc Cham* and Vegetable Platter. Set aside.

Preheat the oven to 450°F. Adjust the oven racks to the lowest and second-lowest positions.

Stuff the duck cavity with the scallion, ginger and coriander.

Combine all of the basting sauce ingredients in a small nonreactive saucepan. Simmer gently for 10 minutes, until the honey melts and all of the spices are well infused. Strain the sauce through a fine sieve into a bowl.

Put a large roasting pan half-filled with hot water on the lowest oven rack to catch the drippings and provide moisture during roasting. Prick the skin on the back and sides of the duck with the tip of a knife or fork (do not pierce the breast). Place the duck, breast side up, directly on the oven rack above the pan. Roast for 30 minutes.

Turn the duck over and roast for 15 minutes longer.

Reduce the oven temperature to 300°F. Prick the duck skin again and continue roasting for 45 minutes longer, turning and basting the duck with sauce every 10 minutes. The duck skin should be shiny, a dark caramel color and very crispy.

Transfer the duck to a cutting board and let stand for 10 minutes.

While the duck is resting, dip the rice vermicelli cakes in hot water. Steam for 5 minutes (while steaming, keep sprinkling more water over the noodles if they are still too dry).

Transfer the noodles to a serving platter and sprinkle with the scallion oil, crisp-fried shallots and ground roasted peanuts.

Carve the duck: Place the duck breast side up and cut in half lengthwise. Cut off the wings and legs. Cut off the backbone on each half of the bird; cut the backbone into bite-size pieces and reassemble on the serving platter. Cut each wing and leg into 2 or 3 pieces and arrange on each side of the backbone. Chop the remaining bird into bite-size pieces. Reassemble each half to its original shape.

To serve, diners roll a piece of roast duck in a lettuce leaf along with a little coriander, mint, selected vegetables and some noodles, and then dip the whole package in *Nuoc Cham* and eat out of hand.

Yield: 3 or 4 servings

STIR-FRIED CHICKEN GIBLETS WITH GINGER

LONG GA XAO GUNG

Nuoc Cham (*page 212*)
3 tablespoons vegetable oil
1 large onion, cut into thin slivers
1 pound of chicken livers, cut into bite-
    size pieces
6 garlic cloves, minced
1½ tablespoons thinly shredded fresh
    gingerroot
1 pound mixed chicken gizzards and
    hearts, trimmed and thinly sliced
1 tablespoon sugar
2½ tablespoons nuoc mam (*Vietnamese
    fish sauce*)
4 scallions, cut into 2-inch lengths
    Freshly ground black pepper
    Coriander sprigs

Prepare the *Nuoc Cham.* Set aside.

In a large nonstick skillet, heat half of the oil over moderately high heat. When the oil is hot, add the onion and cook until fragrant, about 1 minute. Add the chicken livers and stir-fry for 3 minutes. Remove to a plate. Add the remaining 1½ tablespoons of oil to the pan. Fry the garlic and ginger until aromatic. Add the gizzards, hearts and sugar and cook for 2 minutes longer. Return the livers to the pan along with the fish sauce and ¼ cup of water. Stir-fry for 2 minutes, or until the sauce reduces slightly. Add the scallions and stir-fry for 30 seconds. Transfer to a heated platter.

Sprinkle with black pepper and garnish with coriander sprigs.

Serve with rice and *Nuoc Cham.*

Yield: 4 to 6 servings

CHICKEN WINGS
IN CARAMEL SAUCE AND GINGER
CANH GA KHO GUNG

If you are in a hurry, try this quick and simple dish for a delicious meal. Traditionally, a whole chicken is cut up and used for this recipe. Since I love eating with my fingers, I think using the wings alone makes the dish more fun to eat.

Pickled Mustard Greens may be substituted for the Pickled Bean Sprouts as an accompaniment to this dish. Round off the meal with a soup such as Bean Curd and Chive Buds.

■ ■ ■ ■ ■ ■ ■ ■ ■ ■

Pickled Bean Sprouts (page 184)
Caramel Sauce (page 217)
2 pounds chicken wings
1 tablespoon finely shredded fresh
  gingerroot
Freshly ground black pepper

Prepare the Pickled Bean Sprouts and Caramel Sauce. Set aside.

Cut each chicken wing into 3 pieces: the main wing joint, the second joint and the wing tip. Reserve the wing tips for soups or stocks.

In a 3-quart saucepan, add the chicken wing pieces and shredded ginger to the cooled Caramel Sauce. Stir to combine. Set over high heat and bring the mixture to a rapid boil. Cover the pan, reduce the heat to low and simmer, stirring occasionally, for 30 to 40 minutes, or until the chicken is very tender. Skim off any excess fat.

Transfer the chicken wings and sauce to a serving dish. Sprinkle with black pepper, if desired.

To serve, spoon some of the sauce over rice and serve with Pickled Bean Sprouts.

NOTE Instead of simmering, you can grill the marinated chicken wings over medium charcoals, basting regularly with the marinade.

Yield: 4 to 6 servings

FRIED BONELESS CHICKEN WITH HONEY AND GINGER

GA XAO GUNG, MAT ONG

This toothsome and aromatic dish is fast and easy to put together. You can also try it with duck, pork or fresh prawns, shelled or unshelled. Serve with rice, a vegetable dish and a soup for a very satisfying meal.

■ ■ ■ ■ ■ ■ ■ ■ ■ ■ ■

2 tablespoons vegetable oil
1 large onion, cut into wedges
1 pound boned chicken thighs, cut into 2-inch pieces
6 large garlic cloves, thinly sliced
1 tablespoon thinly shredded gingerroot
2 tablespoons honey
2 tablespoons nuoc mam (Vietnamese fish sauce)
2 tablespoons soy sauce
½ teaspoon five-spice powder
Freshly ground black pepper
Coriander sprigs, for garnish

Heat the oil in a wok or skillet over high heat. Add the onion and stir-fry until lightly browned. Add the chicken and stir-fry until browned, about 3 minutes. Add the garlic and ginger and stir-fry until fragrant. Stir in the honey, fish sauce, soy sauce and five-spice powder. Toss to combine the ingredients and cook until the chicken pieces are nicely glazed with the sauce, about 3 minutes. Remove to a hot platter.

Sprinkle with black pepper and garnish with coriander sprigs. Serve with rice.

Yield: 4 servings

STUFFED BONELESS CHICKEN LEGS

DUI GA GNOI THIT

■ ■ ■ ■ ■ ■ ■ ■ ■ ■ ■

Nuoc Cham *(page 212)*
5 chicken legs with thighs attached
1 tablespoon dried tree ear mushrooms
2 ounces cellophane (bean thread) noodles
2 stalks fresh lemon grass, or 2 tablespoons dried lemon grass
2 red chile peppers, seeded
4 shallots, sliced
4 garlic cloves, crushed
1 teaspoon sugar
2 tablespoons nuoc mam (Vietnamese fish sauce)
¼ teaspoon salt
¼ teaspoon freshly ground black pepper
8 ounces lean ground pork
2 tablespoons vegetable oil

Prepare the *Nuoc Cham*. Set aside.

Bone chicken legs: Rotate a sharp paring knife around the end of the drumstick, cutting the tendons from the bone. Using paper towels, grasp the leg firmly with both hands and bend the joints backward to break the drumstick bone from the thigh. With the blade of the knife, cut the tendons and scrape the meat down the drumstick bone, turning back the skin as you progress. Withdraw and discard the bone.

Bone the thigh: Place the chicken leg flat on a cutting board, inner side up, to expose the thighbone. Using a sharp paring knife, make a slit along each side of the thighbone. With the blade of the knife, scrape the meat away from the bone, being careful not to damage the skin. To withdraw the thighbone, cut around and under the cartilage, being careful not to cut through the skin. Discard the bone.

You should have a boned chicken leg with only the thigh part butterflied. Repeat with the other legs.

Discard the skin from 1 chicken leg. Cut the meat into thin strips; coarsely chop. Set aside.

Soak the mushrooms in hot water and the cellophane noodles in warm water to cover for 30 minutes. Drain; coarsely chop.

If you are using fresh lemon grass, discard the outer leaves and upper half of the stalk. Cut into thin slices and finely chop. If you are using dried lemon grass, soak in warm water for 1 hour. Drain and finely chop.

In a bowl, grind or pound the lemon grass, chiles, shallots, garlic and sugar to a fine paste. Add the fish sauce, salt and pepper. Stir to blend.

Preheat the oven to 350°F.

In a food processor, combine the ground pork, chopped chicken meat, mushrooms, cellophane noodles and the lemon grass mixture. Blend for about 15 seconds to mix the force-meat with the spices.

Stuff the chicken legs with the mixture, using your fingers to force the stuffing into the drumstick parts. Do not over-stuff the thigh; pack the mixture neatly so that you are able to fold the butterflied thigh meat over.

Place the legs, stuffed side neatly tucked down, in a roasting pan lined with foil. Brush the legs with some of the oil. Bake for 45 minutes, basting frequently with the oil.

Heat the broiler. Place the chicken legs under the broiler, about 6 inches from the heat. Broil for 5 minutes, until nicely browned and crisp all over.

Cool slightly before slicing into ¼-inch rounds. Serve with rice, *Nuoc Cham* and a pickled vegetable as part of a family meal.

NOTE For a superb appetizer, use the same stuffing with boned chicken wings. Instead of baking, coat the wings with cornstarch and deep-fry for about 12 minutes.

Yield: 4 servings

BOILED DUCK WITH GINGER RICE SOUP

CHAO VIT

*T*his versatile dish stands somewhere between a rice soup and a main dish. The boiled duck is eaten with a ginger sauce and fresh mint; the broth is transformed into a delicious soup (more like a consommé) with the addition of rice and mushrooms and served on the side. If you have leftovers, add the shredded meat to the rice soup to make a wholesome meal the next day.

The amount of ginger used in this recipe is guaranteed to cure the most stubborn cold. Pickled ginger is sold in 4-ounce containers at Asian markets.

■ ■ ■ ■ ■ ■ ■ ■ ■ ■ ■

Ginger Dipping Sauce (page 213)
1 duck (5 pounds), including the giblets and liver
1 ounce gingerroot, crushed
4 dried Chinese mushrooms
4 shallots, thinly sliced
½ cup raw long-grain rice
¼ cup nuoc mam *(Vietnamese fish sauce)*
½ teaspoon salt
1 bunch of watercress
1 bunch of mint leaves
Pickled ginger
2 tablespoons finely shredded gingerroot
2 tablespoons shredded coriander leaves
2 scallions, thinly sliced
Freshly ground black pepper

Prepare the Ginger Dipping Sauce. Set aside.

Place the duck, giblets, liver and crushed ginger in a large kettle. Add water to cover (about 3 quarts). Bring the water to a boil and cook, skimming the froth as it rises to the surface, about 15 minutes. Reduce the heat to low and simmer, uncovered, skimming frequently, for 15 minutes. Remove the giblets and liver; refresh with cold water and slice into thin pieces. Set aside. Continue to simmer the duck and broth for 30 minutes more.

Meanwhile, soak the mushrooms in hot water for 30 minutes. Drain, Remove and discard the stems; cut the mushroom caps into thin strips. Set aside.

When the duck is cooked, remove it to a large platter; wrap with foil and set aside.

Skim the fat from the broth, reserving 2 tablespoons of fat for the rice. Boil over high heat to reduce the liquid to about 2 quarts.

Place the reserved duck fat in a skillet over moderate heat. Add the shallots and cook until translucent, about 1 minute. Add the rice and stir until it turns white, about 3 minutes. Add the rice and shallots to the broth, along with the mushrooms, fish sauce and salt. Cover and simmer for about 20 minutes, or until the rice is tender.

Meanwhile, skin the duck and halve it lengthwise with a cleaver. Remove the legs and hack them into bite-size pieces. Remove and discard the backbone and cut each half crosswise into bite-size pieces.

Arrange a bed of watercress on a platter and place the cut-up duck on it. Surround the platter with fresh mint and pickled ginger.

Divide the soup among heated soup bowls and garnish each bowl with slices of the giblets and the liver, some of the shredded ginger, coriander and scallions. Sprinkle with black pepper.

To serve, diners dip duck pieces in the Ginger Dipping Sauce, then eat with the accompanying watercress, fresh mint and pickled ginger. Serve the soup on the side.

Yield: 4 to 6 servings

VIETNAMESE FRIED CHICKEN
GA CHIEN

*H*ere's a way to transform a simple fried chicken into an exotic delight.

■ ■ ■ ■ ■ ■ ■ ■ ■ ■ ■

Nuoc Cham *(page 212)*
6 *garlic cloves, crushed*
4 *shallots, thinly sliced*
2 *teaspoons sugar*
2 *tablespoons* nuoc mam *(Vietnamese fish sauce)*
2 *tablespoons light soy sauce*
Freshly ground black pepper
4 *chicken legs with thighs attached (about 2 pounds)*
All-purpose flour, for dredging
Vegetable oil, for deep-frying

Prepare the *Nuoc Cham.* Set aside.

In a mortar or blender, pound or grind the garlic, shallots and sugar to a fine paste. Add the fish sauce, soy sauce and black pepper to taste. Stir to blend.

Rub the paste on the chicken legs. Marinate for at least 1 hour in a shallow pan.

Halve the chicken legs at the joint and dredge them with flour; shake to remove any excess flour.

Heat 3 inches of oil in a wok or deep fryer to 375°F. This temperature must be maintained for the entire frying process. Deep-fry the chicken pieces, a few at a time, turning once, until golden and tender, about 10 minutes. Remove and drain on paper towels; keep warm. Continue frying the remaining chicken pieces. The skin of the chicken should be crispy and the meat very tender and highly aromatic. If a crispier skin is desired, deep-fry briefly a second time.

Hack the chicken pieces into bite-size morsels and reassemble on a serving platter. Serve hot or at room temperature, with rice and *Nuoc Cham.*

NOTE The marinated chicken legs are also delicious grilled over charcoal.

Yield: 4 servings

ROAST CHICKEN WITH LEMON GRASS
GA NUONG XA

*R*oast chicken doesn't have to be boring. Gild it with spices—lemon grass, chile peppers, garlic and shallots—and you have an exotic meal. The rich, golden brown, flavorful skin is achieved by basting the chicken with vegetable oil. Duck may replace the chicken; in this case, no basting is necessary.

■ ■ ■ ■ ■ ■ ■ ■ ■ ■ ■

Nuoc Cham *(page 212)*
3 stalks fresh lemon grass, or 3 tablespoons sliced dried lemon grass
6 garlic cloves, crushed
4 shallots, sliced
2 red chile peppers, seeded
1 tablespoon sugar
½ teaspoon salt
1 tablespoon nuoc mam *(Vietnamese fish sauce)*
1 roasting chicken (about 4 pounds)
2 tablespoons vegetable oil

Prepare the *Nuoc Cham.* Set aside.

If you are using fresh lemon grass, discard the outer leaves and upper half of the stalk. Cut into thin slices and finely chop. If you are using dried lemon grass, soak in warm water for 1 hour. Drain and finely chop.

In a mortar or blender, pound or grind the lemon grass, garlic, shallots, chiles and sugar to a paste. Add the salt and the fish sauce and stir to blend.

Rinse the chicken well; pat dry. Carefully loosen the skin on the breast and legs of the chicken by pushing your fingers between the skin and meat to form a pocket. Rub half of the lemon grass paste all over the meat under the skin. Rub the remaining lemon grass paste all over the chicken skin and the cavity. Tuck the wings under the chicken; tie the legs together with twine. Let stand for 30 minutes.

Preheat the oven to 425°F.

Place the chicken on a rack in a roasting pan. Roast for 15 minutes. Reduce the oven temperature to 375°F and continue roasting for 1¼ hours, basting the chicken as it roasts with the oil and the pan juices. The chicken is done when it registers 180° to 185°F on an instant-reading meat thermometer, or when a leg moves freely in its joint. Let the chicken stand for 10 minutes.

To carve the chicken: Place the chicken breast side up and cut in half lengthwise. Cut off the wings and legs. Cut off the backbone on each half of the bird, and then cut the backbone into bite-size pieces and reassemble on a serving platter. Cut each wing and leg into 2 or 3 pieces and arrange on each side of the backbone. Chop the remaining bird into bite-size pieces. Reassemble each half to its original shape.

Serve with rice and *Nuoc Cham.*

Yield: 4 servings

$\mathcal{B}$ E E F

Beef Stew

BEEF STEW

THIT BO KHO

*S*tew lovers will find this concoction most comforting. Like most stews, this dish is delicious made in advance and reheated before serving.

■ ■ ■ ■ ■ ■ ■ ■ ■ ■ ■

2 *stalks fresh lemon grass, or 2 table-*
  spoons dried lemon grass
2 *pounds stewing beef or beef chuck, cut*
  into 2-inch cubes
2 *fresh red chile peppers, seeded and*
  minced
2 *teaspoons sugar*
2 *tablespoons grated fresh gingerroot*
2 *teaspoons ground cinnamon*
2 *teaspoons curry powder*
3 *tablespoons* nuoc mam *(Vietnamese*
  fish sauce)
  Freshly ground black pepper
2 *teaspoons salt*
3 *tablespoons vegetable oil*
1 *large onion, minced*
6 *cloves garlic, minced*
¼ *cup tomato paste*
4 *star anise*
2 *medium carrots, cut into 1-inch chunks*
2 *medium potatoes, peeled and cut into*
  1-inch chunks
1 *small daikon, or 2 medium turnips,*
  peeled and cut into 1-inch chunks

If you are using fresh lemon grass, discard the outer leaves and upper half of the stalk. Slice paper-thin; chop very fine. If you are using dried lemon grass, soak in warm water for 1 hour. Drain and finely chop.

In a bowl, combine the beef with the lemon grass, chiles, sugar, ginger, cinnamon, curry powder, fish sauce and black pepper to taste. Sprinkle in 1 teaspoon of the salt; mix well. Let stand for 30 minutes.

Heat 2 tablespoons of the oil in a large, heavy saucepan or pot over high heat. Add the beef and marinade and stir quickly to sear, about 2 minutes. Remove the meat to a bowl.

Add the remaining 1 tablespoon oil to the saucepan. When the oil is hot, add the onion and garlic and stir-fry until fragrant, about 1 minute. Add the tomato paste and stir for 2 minutes. Add the beef, star anise, the remaining 1 teaspoon salt and 4 cups of water. Bring the mixture to a boil. Reduce the heat to low, cover the pan and simmer until the beef is tender, about 1½ hours.

Add the carrots and simmer for 10 minutes. Add the potatoes and continue simmering for 10 minutes longer. Add the daikon and cook for another 10 minutes.

Serve hot over rice, noodles or bread.

Yield: 4 to 6 servings

STEAMED BEEF PÂTÉ

CHA DUM

This dish is part of *Bo Bay Mon,* a traditional meal that features 7 different beef dishes.

In Vietnam, this specialty is wrapped in banana leaves, steamed and served with grilled coconut-rice paper *(banh da nuoc dua nuong)*. Here, I simply serve them with shrimp chips; banana leaves can be omitted.

■ ■ ■ ■ ■ ■ ■ ■ ■ ■ ■

Scallion oil (page 225)
Nuoc Cham (page 212)
1 *tablespoon roasted peanuts (page 220), ground*
20 *shrimp chips (page 221)*
1 *tablespoon small dried tree ear mushrooms*
½ *ounce cellophane (bean thread) noodles*
8 *ounces lean ground beef (eye or bottom round)*
1 *small onion, minced*
2 *garlic cloves, minced*
1 *tablespoon* nuoc mam *(Vietnamese fish sauce)*
½ *teaspoon sugar*
Freshly ground black pepper
2 *eggs*
Coriander sprigs, for garnish

Prepare the scallion oil, *Nuoc Cham,* roasted peanuts and shrimp chips. Set aside.

Soak the mushrooms in hot water and the cellophane noodles in warm water for 30 minutes. Drain. Remove the stems from the mushrooms. Coarsely chop the mushrooms and noodles.

In a large bowl, combine the beef, mushrooms, noodles, onion, garlic, fish sauce, sugar and black pepper to taste. Stir to blend. Make a well in the center, break the eggs into it and beat the meat into the eggs.

Pack the pâté mixture, pressing firmly, into an oiled, small heatproof bowl (2-cup capacity). Pour 1 inch of water into a wok or deep pot. Place a steamer rack or bamboo steamer over the water. Set the bowl on the rack. Cover and steam over high heat for 20 to 25 minutes. Remove and set aside to cool slightly.

Loosen the steamed pâté by running the pointed end of a small knife around the edge. Invert it onto a serving platter. Sprinkle with scallion oil and ground peanuts. Garnish with the coriander.

Serve with shrimp chips, or rice, and *Nuoc Cham.*

Yield: 4 to 6 servings

GRILLED BEEF WITH LEMON GRASS
BO XA LUI NUONG

In this recipe, lemony and spicy slices of lean beef are grilled over charcoal. The meat can be cooked on a barbecue grill (the traditional way), under a broiler or even in a skillet. (Cast iron sears extremely well when hot, but it has to be smoking hot when the meat is put on. Be sure the ventilation fan is on.) Whether you barbecue or broil, cook the meat about 6 inches from the heat source.

■ ■ ■ ■ ■ ■ ■ ■ ■ ■ ■

Nuoc Cham *with Shredded Carrot and Daikon (page 212)*
Vegetable Platter (page 169)
8 *ounces thin rice vermicelli (*bun, *page 223), or 2 bundles Japanese alimentary paste noodles (*somen, *page 223)*
2 *stalks fresh lemon grass, or 2 tablespoons dried lemon grass*
4 *shallots, sliced*
4 *garlic cloves, crushed*
1 *tablespoon sugar*
2 *fresh red chile peppers, seeded*
2 *tablespoons* nuoc mam *(Vietnamese fish sauce)*
1 *tablespoon Oriental sesame oil*
1 *tablespoon peanut oil*
2 *tablespoons sesame seed*
1 *pound rump roast or sirloin*
24 *8-inch bamboo skewers soaked in water for 30 minutes*

Prepare the *Nuoc Cham*, Vegetable Platter and noodles. Set aside.

If you are using fresh lemon grass, discard the outer leaves and upper half of the stalk. Slice paper-thin and chop very fine. If you are using dried lemon grass, soak in warm water for 1 hour. Drain and chop very fine.

Combine the lemon grass, shallots, garlic, sugar and chiles in a mortar and pound to a fine paste. Transfer the paste to a large bowl. Stir in the fish sauce, sesame oil, peanut oil and sesame seed; stir to blend.

Cut the beef crosswise, against the grain, into very thin strips, 1½ inches by 4 to 5 inches long. Add the beef strips to the paste and fold gently with your hands, to coat both sides of the meat with the seasonings. Set aside to marinate for 30 minutes.

Weave a skewer through each strip of meat.

Place the skewers over hot charcoals and grill for about 1 minute, or until the beef can be lifted from the grill without sticking. Turn the skewers and cook for 1 minute longer. Transfer to a heated serving platter. (If using a skillet, brush a cast-iron skillet or a griddle with 1 tablespoon of oil. Heat until quite hot. Without crowding, spread the unthreaded beef slices on the surface and brown briefly, about 20 seconds. Turn and cook for 20 seconds on the second side.)

To serve, each diner fills a lettuce leaf with some coriander, mint, bean sprouts, cucumber, a few strands of cooked noodles and some of the barbecued beef. The leaf is then wrapped into a neat roll and dipped in small individual bowls of *Nuoc Cham* and eaten out of hand.

NOTE For an excellent appetizer, wrap *Bo Xa Lui Nuong* in fresh store-bought or homemade rice noodle sheets. Serve with *Nuoc Cham* or Peanut Sauce. You may substitute chicken breast for beef.

Yield: 4 servings

VIETNAMESE ROAST BEEF
BE THUI

*P*robably of Mongolian origin, this northern specialty dish is very popular throughout Vietnam. Originally, whole sides of young calves were roasted over the pits, very much like the Mongolians used to prepare it. For the most authentic flavors, grill the piece of beef over charcoals, if possible.

■ ■ ■ ■ ■ ■ ■ ■ ■ ■ ■

Soybean and Ginger Sauce (page 215)
Vegetable Platter (page 169)
8 ounces thin rice vermicelli (bun, page 223), or 2 bundles Japanese alimentary paste noodles (somen, page 223)
5 tablespoons roasted rice powder (page 220)
4 garlic cloves, crushed
¼ teaspoon salt
1 tablespoon vegetable oil
Freshly ground black pepper
1 pound beef filet or eye of round
2 scallions, cut into 2-inch sections and finely shredded

Prepare the Soybean and Ginger Sauce, Vegetable Platter, noodles and roasted rice powder. Set aside.

In a mortar, pound the garlic and salt to a fine paste. Stir in the oil and black pepper to taste. Rub the meat with the garlic-oil mixture.

If grilling, cook the beef, covered, over hot charcoals, for 8 to 10 minutes on each side. Do not overcook; the beef should be rare in the middle. If you don't have a grill, oil a cast-iron skillet or griddle and set over high heat. Sear the beef for 8 to 10 minutes on each side.

If baking, place the meat in a baking pan lined with aluminum foil. Bake in a preheated 450°F oven for 18 to 20 minutes.

Let the roast rest for 10 minutes; the meat will continue to cook during this period.

Slice the beef across the grain into thin 2-inch-square pieces. Arrange the slices in overlapping layers on a large platter; sprinkle on the roasted rice powder. Distribute the shredded scallions over the beef. Sprinkle with additional black pepper, if desired.

To serve, each diner rolls a few slices of roast beef in a lettuce leaf along with a little coriander, mint, selected vegetables and a few strands of noodles. The whole package is dipped in the ginger sauce and eaten out of hand.

Yield: 4 servings

BEEF WITH SHRIMP SAUCE AND LEMON GRASS

BO RANG MAM TOM XA OT

After tasting this dish, you will be convinced that beef and shrimp sauce are made for each other.

■ ■ ■ ■ ■ ■ ■ ■ ■ ■ ■

4 *stalks fresh lemon grass, or 4*
   tablespoons dried lemon grass
4 *shallots, thinly sliced*
4 *garlic cloves, minced*
2 *red chile peppers, seeded and minced*
3 *tablespoons sugar*
2 *tablespoons vegetable oil*
2 *pounds lean ground beef*
2½ *tablespoons shrimp sauce (page 134)*
   Freshly ground black pepper
1 *cucumber, peeled, halved and sliced*
   ¼ inch thick
   Coriander sprigs, for garnish

If you are using fresh lemon grass, discard the outer leaves and upper half of the stalk. Slice thin and finely chop. If you are using dried lemon grass, soak in warm water for 1 hour. Drain and finely chop.

In a mortar or blender, pound or grind the lemon grass, shallots, garlic, chiles and 1 teaspoon of the sugar to a fine paste.

Heat the oil in a wok or large skillet over moderately high heat. Add the paste and stir-fry until fragrant, about 1 minute. Add the ground beef and stir to break up the lumps. Cook until browned, about 5 minutes. Add the remaining 2 tablespoons plus 2 teaspoons sugar. Reduce the heat to low and keep stirring for 5 minutes, or until the beef is lightly caramelized. Add the shrimp sauce and stir for 3 minutes longer.

Transfer to a serving platter. Sprinkle with black pepper. Serve over rice with the cucumber slices and garnish with coriander.

Yield: 4 servings

GRILLED DRIED BEEF

THIT BO KHO

*T*his Vietnamese-style "beef jerky" is delicious served with drinks. The Vietnamese enjoy eating it as a snack with glutinous rice. It is also an ingredient in Green Papaya Salad.

■ ■ ■ ■ ■ ■ ■ ■ ■ ■ ■

1 *pound lean bottom round or sirloin, in one piece, about 6 inches in diameter*

2 *stalks fresh lemon grass, or 2 tablespoons dried lemon grass*

2 *small red chile peppers, seeded*

2½ *tablespoons sugar or honey*

1 *tablespoon* nuoc mam *(Vietnamese fish sauce)*

3 *tablespoons light soy sauce*

Cut the beef across the grain into very thin 3 by 3-inch slices.

If you are using fresh lemon grass, discard the outer leaves and upper half of the stalk. Cut into thin slices and finely chop. If you are using dried lemon grass, soak in warm water for 1 hour. Drain and finely chop.

Combine the chiles and sugar in a mortar and pound to a fine paste. Add the chopped lemon grass, fish sauce and soy sauce and stir to blend. (If using a blender, combine all of these and blend to a very fine paste.) Spread the paste over the beef pieces to coat both sides. Let marinate for 30 minutes.

Spread out each slice of marinated beef on a large, flat wire rack or baking sheet. Let stand in the sun until both sides are completely dried, about 12 hours. (You can also place a rack on a jelly roll pan and let the beef dry in the refrigerator for 2 days.)

Grill the beef over a medium charcoal fire or transfer the rack from the refrigerator to the middle of a preheated 400°F oven and bake until brown and crisp, about 10 minutes.

Serve with glutinous rice.

NOTE After cooking, the meat may be kept for up to 1 week in a covered jar at room temperature.

Yield: 4 servings

BEEF FONDUE WITH VINEGAR

BO NHUNG GIAM

In Vietnam, to celebrate special occasions families often serve a seven-course dinner, *Bo Bay Mon,* or "Beef in Seven Ways." All the courses are made of beef and are served in small portions.

This meal always begins with Beef Fondue and ends with Beef Rice Soup. In between, the other five dishes are Warm Beef Salad, Skewered Beef with Bacon, Grilled Stuffed Grape Leaves, Grilled Beef Patties and Steamed Beef Pâté.

In order to cut the beef into paper-thin slices, freeze the piece of meat for 60 minutes, or until partly frozen, before slicing it.

Accompaniments for serving
Anchovy and Pineapple Sauce (page 216)
1 cup roasted peanuts (page 220), coarsely ground
Vegetable Platter (page 169)
2 bundles Japanese alimentary paste noodles (somen, page 223)
8 ounces 6½-inch rice paper rounds (banh trang)

Beef Platter
1½ pounds sirloin of beef or eye of round, trimmed of fat and sliced paper-thin across the grain
2 scallions, minced
2 small onions, sliced and separated into rings
3 tablespoons vegetable oil
Freshly ground black pepper

Broth
2 tablespoons vegetable oil
4 garlic cloves, minced
2 tablespoons chopped fresh lemon grass
6 thin slices fresh gingerroot
2 cups distilled white vinegar
¼ cup sugar
1½ tablespoons salt
2 scallions, chopped

Prepare the accompaniments: Make the dipping sauce, peanuts, Vegetable Platter and noodles, then refrigerate. Cover the rice papers with a damp cloth and then with plastic wrap and keep at room temperature until needed.

Prepare the beef platter: Arrange the beef slices in overlapping layers on 1 large or 2 medium platters. Garnish with the chopped scallions and onion rings. Sprinkle the oil and black pepper over all. Cover with plastic wrap and refrigerate.

Prepare the broth: In a heavy nonreactive saucepan, heat the oil. Add the garlic, lemon grass and ginger and stir-fry until fragrant. Add the vinegar, sugar, salt and 2 cups of water. Bring to a boil.

Transfer the broth to a tabletop fondue pot. Add the chopped scallions and maintain at a simmer.

Pour the dipping sauce into individual bowls and place all of the prepared platters alongside the fondue pot on the table.

To eat, dip a rice paper round in a bowl of warm water to make it pliable; place the paper on a dinner plate. Add different ingredients from the Vegetable Platter, some noodles and a teaspoon of the ground peanuts. Using chopsticks, dip a few slices of beef and onion rings in the simmering broth for about 1 minute, or until the beef loses its pinkness on the outside but is still rare inside. Remove the meat and add to the vegetable mound. Roll the rice paper up to form a neat package, then dip it in the anchovy sauce and eat out of hand.

Yield: 4 to 6 servings

BEEF BALLS

THIT BO VIEN

These crunchy little beef balls are very popular among the Vietnamese. They are served mainly as appetizers or added to noodle soups. Chile sauce (*tuong ot*) is the usual accompaniment, but any hot red pepper sauce can be served alongside.

■ ■ ■ ■ ■ ■ ■ ■ ■ ■

¼ cup plus 1 tablespoon nuoc mam
     (*Vietnamese fish sauce*)
1 tablespoon plus 1 teaspoon potato
     starch
1 teaspoon baking powder
1 teaspoon sugar
¼ teaspoon freshly ground black pepper
2 pounds trimmed boneless beef hind
     shank
4 garlic cloves, crushed
1 teaspoon Oriental sesame oil
     Vegetable oil, for shaping meatballs

In a shallow dish, mix the fish sauce, potato starch, baking powder, sugar and black pepper.

Slice the meat into ⅛-inch-thick pieces. Add to the marinade and mix well. Cover and refrigerate for at least 4 hours, or overnight.

Before proceeding, transfer the meat to the freezer for 30 minutes.

Work with half of the beef at a time; do not overload the work bowl. In a food processor, combine half of the beef with half of the garlic and sesame oil. Process to a completely smooth but stiff paste, about 3 minutes. Stop occasionally to scrape down the sides of the work bowl. The completed paste should spring back to the touch. Transfer the paste to a bowl. Process the remaining beef, garlic and sesame oil the same way.

Rub some vegetable oil on one hand. Grab a handful of the meat paste and close your hand into a fist, squeezing out a small portion of the mixture, about 1 teaspoon, between your thumb and index finger. Keep rolling and resqueezing that same portion between your thumb and index finger until you obtain a smooth rounded ball. Scoop out the meatball with an oiled spoon. Repeat until all of the paste is used.

Pour 1 inch of water into a wok or wide pot. Place a steamer rack or bamboo steamer over the water. Arrange the meatballs without crowding in a single layer on the rack. Cover and steam for 5 minutes.

Serve as an appetizer with chile sauce. These beef balls can also be added to a well-seasoned beef broth, sprinkled with chopped scallions and black pepper and served as a soup (noodles may be added).

NOTE These meatballs may be frozen. Thaw them thoroughly, then steam or simmer in boiling water until just heated through.

Yield: about 60 meatballs

STIR-FRIED BEEF WITH LEMON GRASS

THIT BO XAO XA OT

*L*emon grass and beef are often paired because they complement each other perfectly. Whenever I serve this spicy and aromatic dish to my guests, it becomes an instant hit.

■ ■ ■ ■ ■ ■ ■ ■ ■ ■

2 *stalks fresh lemon grass, or 2 table-*
 spoons dried lemon grass
1 *pound lean beef filet or eye of round*
2 *fresh red chile peppers, seeded and*
 minced
6 *garlic cloves, minced*
3 *tablespoons* nuoc mam *(Vietnamese*
 fish sauce)
1 *teaspoon arrowroot or cornstarch*
 Freshly ground black pepper
6 *tablespoons vegetable oil*
2 *medium onions, cut into slivers*
1 *tablespoon sugar*
¼ *cup roasted peanuts (page 220),*
 coarsely ground
 Coriander sprigs, for garnish

If you are using fresh lemon grass, discard the outer leaves and upper half of the stalk. Slice paper-thin and chop very fine. If you are using dried lemon grass, soak in warm water for 1 hour. Drain and chop very fine.

Cut the beef across the grain into very thin 2 by 3-inch slices. Pound the meat lightly with the flat side of a cleaver.

In a bowl, combine the beef with the lemon grass, chiles, half of the garlic, 2 tablespoons of the fish sauce, the arrowroot, black pepper to taste and 2 tablespoons of the oil. Mix well. Set aside for 30 minutes.

Heat a large skillet over moderately high heat and add 2 tablespoons of the oil. When the oil is hot, add the onions and the remaining garlic; stir-fry for about 3 minutes, or until golden brown. Remove the onions with a slotted spoon to a plate. Add the remaining 2 tablespoons oil. When the oil is hot, add the beef, the remaining 1 tablespoon fish sauce and the sugar. Sauté over high heat for 1 or 2 minutes, or until the beef is just cooked. Transfer the mixture to a heated platter.

Arrange the sautéed onions around the meat mixture; sprinkle the peanuts and black pepper over all. Garnish with coriander.

NOTE For a delicious sandwich, stuff a crusty French bread with the stir-fried beef. You may substitute chicken or shrimp for beef.

Yield: 4 servings

$\mathscr{P}$ORK

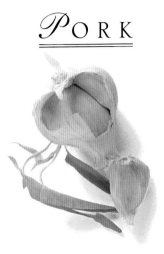

Pork Simmered in Caramel Sauce, Stir-Fried Water Spinach and Pickled Bean Sprouts

PORK SIMMERED IN CARAMEL SAUCE

THIT KHO

*T*he true simmered pork in caramel sauce is cooked in an old-fashioned clay pot, the kind used in the countryside for long simmering. This dish originated with peasants of northern Vietnam, whose midday meal in the fields included a simmered dish (meat, fish or poultry) with day-old rice and maybe a pickled vegetable.

Many Vietnamese prefer using pork belly (also called fresh bacon, available at Asian butcher shops) for this specific dish, but if calorie counting is an issue, try this recipe with shrimp, which is also authentic, and you will come up with *Tom Rim* (simmering shrimp).

■ ■ ■ ■ ■ ■ ■ ■ ■ ■

Pickled Bean Sprouts (page 184)
Caramel Sauce (page 217)
1 pound fresh ham or fresh bacon (pork belly)

Prepare the Pickled Bean Sprouts and Caramel Sauce. Set aside.

Cut the ham into thin 1 x 2-inch pieces. Add the meat to the cooled Caramel Sauce in a heavy-bottomed saucepan. Mix well and bring to a boil. Reduce the heat to low, cover the pan and simmer for 45 minutes, stirring occasionally.

Sprinkle with black pepper, if desired, and serve with rice and the Pickled Bean Sprouts.

NOTE For the Vietnamese version of "surf and turf," use half pork and half shrimp in the shell, instead of all pork.

Yield: 4 servings

CHARCOAL BROILED PORK
WITH RICE VERMICELLI

BUN CHA

*T*his delicious northern Vietnamese specialty is always barbecued over a charcoal fire. Smoke from the grilling adds a distinctive taste to the dish.

This versatile dish may be served in one of two ways: When served as a one-dish meal, it is turned into a noodle dish. Cold noodles are topped with shredded lettuce, vegetables, herbs (ingredients normally included in the traditional Vegetable Platter) and grilled meat. *Nuoc Cham* and ground roasted peanuts are passed at the table so each diner can season his or her own bowl as desired.

The second style of serving, described below, is usually reserved for celebrating special occasions, when more than one dish is offered.

■ ■ ■ ■ ■ ■ ■ ■ ■ ■ ■ ■

Nuoc Cham *with Shredded Carrot and Daikon (page 212)*
Vegetable Platter (page 169)
8 ounces thin rice vermicelli (bun, *page 223), or 2 bundles Japanese alimentary paste noodles (somen, page 223)*
Caramel Sauce (page 217)
1 pound fresh bacon (pork belly) with skin attached
1 pound ground beef (chuck)
8 garlic cloves, minced
24 bamboo skewers, soaked in water for 30 minutes

Prepare the *Nuoc Cham*, Vegetable Platter, noodles and Caramel Sauce. Set aside.

Remove and discard any bones in the pork belly. Cut the pork against the grain into ¼-inch slices, about 2 inches long.

Put the sliced pork belly and ground beef into two separate bowls. Add the garlic and half of the Caramel Sauce to the beef; add the remaining Caramel Sauce to the pork. Blend each mixture separately with your hands until well combined. Let stand for 30 minutes.

Prepare a charcoal grill or preheat the broiler. Shape the ground beef into 24 meatballs. Slightly press each ball into a 1½-inch patty.

Skewer the beef patties and pork slices separately (4 pieces to a skewer), so they will lie flat on the grill or under the broiler.

Place the pork skewers on the grill, or on a baking sheet lined with aluminum foil under the broiler, about 6 inches from the heat. Cook for 10 to 15 minutes, or until nicely browned and crispy. Turn the skewers. Add the skewers of beef and cook for 5 minutes. Turn the beef skewers and cook for 5 minutes, or until browned.

Arrange the meat skewers attractively on a serving platter.

To serve, each diner rolls a few pieces of meat in a lettuce leaf along with coriander, mint, vegetables from the Vegetable Platter and some noodles. The whole package is then dipped in individual dishes of *Nuoc Cham*.

Yield: 4 servings

GROUND PORK IN TOMATO SAUCE
HEO SOT CA CHUA

*H*ere's the Vietnamese interpretation of the universal spaghetti meat sauce. Because of the ingredients used, the texture and flavors differ sharply from its Italian counterpart. In keeping with its true Vietnamese character, this meat sauce should be served with rice, raw lettuce and the omnipresent *Nuoc Cham.*

■ ■ ■ ■ ■ ■ ■ ■ ■ ■ ■

1 *small head of soft leaf lettuce, finely*
   shredded
4 *scallions, cut into 2-inch lengths and*
   finely shredded
½ *cup shredded mint leaves*
1 *cup whole coriander leaves*
   Nuoc Cham *(page 212)*
2 *tablespoons vegetable oil*
1 *pound ground pork*
1 *tablespoon sugar*
3 *tablespoons* nuoc mam *(Vietnamese*
   fish sauce)
6 *garlic cloves, chopped*
1 *large onion, slivered*
3 *large ripe tomatoes, cored, seeded and*
   diced
1 *cup chicken broth or water*
2 *tablespoons tomato paste*
   Freshly ground black pepper

Combine the shredded lettuce, scallions, mint and coriander in a large bowl. Cover and refrigerate.

Prepare the *Nuoc Cham.* Set aside.

Heat 1 tablespoon of the oil in a wok or skillet over high heat. Add the ground pork and fry, breaking up the lumps, for 8 minutes. Add the sugar and 1 tablespoon of the fish sauce and cook for 2 minutes. Remove the meat to a bowl and set aside.

Heat the remaining 1 tablespoon oil in the wok. Add the garlic and onion and fry until fragrant. Add the tomatoes and cook for 5 minutes over moderate heat.

Return the pork to the wok, along with the broth, tomato paste and the remaining 2 tablespoons fish sauce. Simmer, stirring occasionally, for 15 minutes. Transfer the mixture to a serving bowl and sprinkle with the black pepper.

To serve, each diner puts some meat sauce and shredded lettuce over rice and then drizzles everything with *Nuoc Cham* before eating.

Yield: 4 servings

VIETNAMESE PORK SAUSAGE
CHA LUA / GIO

*T*he texture of this sausage matches perfectly its name *cha lua,* meaning, "silky sausage." Always served cold, it usually accompanies rice or glutinous rice as part of a meal or is stuffed in French bread for a sandwich. For best results, make this sausage 1 day in advance and refrigerate. It will improve in flavor. Refrigerate left-over sausage for up to 1 week, or freeze.

Use banana leaves if you can get them; they will give the sausage a wonderful fragrance. Although this recipe requires pork only, you may replace it with skinned chicken breast, or use half pork and half chicken. Shredded pork skin is added for extra texture but can be omitted. *Cha lua* or *gio* also can be purchased in Vietnamese groceries.

■ ■ ■ ■ ■ ■ ■ ■ ■ ■ ■

¼ *cup* nuoc mam *(Vietnamese fish sauce)*
2 *teaspoons potato starch*
1 *teaspoon sugar*
1 *teaspoon baking powder*
 Freshly ground white pepper
1 *pound lean boneless fresh ham*
2 *ounces fresh or dried pork skin (page 233) (optional)*
2 *ounces pork fat, cut into small cubes*
 For wrapping
2 *squares (12 inches) plastic wrap*
1 *square (12 inches) aluminum foil*
1 *banana leaf (12-inch square), brushed on one side with 1 tablespoon oil (optional)*

Combine the fish sauce, starch, sugar, baking powder, white pepper to taste and 3 tablespoons of water in a large bowl. Mix well. Set the marinade aside.

Remove all the fat from the fresh ham and cut into ¼-inch-thick slices. Place the meat in the marinade and toss well to coat. Cover the bowl and refrigerate for at least 4 hours, or overnight.

If using fresh pork skin, remove all of the fat attached to it with a very sharp knife (trim as close to the skin as possible). Cut the skin into very thin strips. Cook the shredded pork skin in boiling salted water for 1 minute. Drain and set aside. If using dried pork skin, soak in warm water for 30 minutes; drain. Cook in boiling salted water for 30 seconds. Drain and set aside.

Before processing the meat, transfer the bowl to the freezer and partially freeze the meat, about 30 minutes.

Place the meat in a food processor and process to a very fine paste. Stop every now and then to scrape down the sides of the bowl. The paste is ready when the meat turns pinkish, is sticky and springs back to the touch. Transfer the meat paste to another bowl.

Process the pork fat to a fine paste. Add the meat paste to the processed fat and pulse briefly, only enough to blend (if you overwork the paste at this point, it will turn into mush).

Transfer the paste to a bowl. If desired, fold the shredded pork skin into the paste.

Stack the wrapping sheets as follows: Lay 1 sheet of the plastic wrap flat on the counter. Place the aluminum foil on top. Cover the foil with the banana leaf, oiled side up. (If banana leaf is unavailable, the foil will do.)

Place the meat paste in the center of the banana leaf. Moisten your hands with water and shape the mixture into an 8 by 3-inch sausage shape. Bring the 2 large sides together as if wrapping a gift. Keep folding the gathered edges until they touch the sausage. Fold in the sides of the package to seal.

Place the package, folded side down, in the remaining sheet of plastic. Wrap the package. Cross-tie the package with string.

Place the package in a pot of cold water and bring to a boil over high heat. Reduce the heat to moderately low and cook, uncovered, for 1 hour, or until the internal temperature of the sausage reaches 140°F. For even cooking, place a heavy heat-proof weight on top of the package to keep it immersed in water. Add more water if necessary during cooking. When the cooking time is up, remove the sausage from the water and set aside to cool completely.

To serve the sausage as part of a meal, cut it into finger-size sticks and eat with rice and *Nuoc Cham;* or use as specified in other recipes.

Yield: One 8 by 3-inch sausage

BARBECUED SPARERIBS
SUON NUONG

*T*his is one of my favorite dishes. If you don't have a sturdy cleaver, ask the butcher to cut the ribs for you.

■ ■ ■ ■ ■ ■ ■ ■ ■ ■

1/3 *cup Caramel Sauce (page 217)*
2 *stalks fresh lemon grass, or 2*
    tablespoons sliced dried lemon grass
4 *shallots*
4 *garlic cloves*
2 *small fresh chile peppers, seeded*
2 *pounds lean spareribs, cut into*
    individual ribs

Prepare the Caramel Sauce. Set aside.

If you are using fresh lemon grass, discard the outer leaves and upper half of the stalk. Cut into thin slices and finely chop. If you are using dried lemon grass, soak in warm water for 1 hour. Drain and finely chop.

Combine the lemon grass, shallots, garlic and chiles in a mortar and pound to a paste (or blend in a spice grinder). Stir the paste into the cooled Caramel Sauce.

Place the ribs in a large dish. Pour the sauce over the ribs and turn to coat evenly. Let marinate in the refrigerator for at least 1 hour, or until ready to barbecue.

Drain the ribs, reserving the marinade for basting.

Place the ribs on a hot grill over medium coals and cook for 45 to 50 minutes, depending on the thickness. Turn the ribs frequently and brush with the marinade.

The spareribs may be baked in a foil-lined roasting pan in a preheated 350°F oven. Turn and baste the ribs frequently for 30 to 35 minutes. Place the ribs under a broiler and broil for 5 more minutes on each side, or until nicely glazed.

Serve as an appetizer or part of a family meal, with rice and Pickled Bean Sprouts or Pickled Mustard Greens.

Yield: 4 servings

Glazed Spareribs

Nha Trang Skewered Meatballs and Peanut Sauce

GLAZED SPARERIBS
SUON RANG

*T*his toothsome dish is most delicious served with Pickled Bean Sprouts. In Vietnam, tiny freshwater shrimp called *con tep* are usually cooked in the same manner, but without the bell peppers.

■ ■ ■ ■ ■ ■ ■ ■ ■ ■ ■

1 tablespoon vegetable oil
3 pounds lean spareribs, cut into 2-inch
　　pieces
2 tablespoons sugar
2 tablespoons nuoc mam (*Vietnamese
　　fish sauce*)
1 tablespoon soy sauce
2 medium onions, each cut into eighths
　　and separated
8 garlic cloves, crushed
2 small red bell peppers, each cut into
　　eighths
1 bunch of scallions, cut into 2-inch
　　sections
　　Freshly ground black pepper
　　Coriander sprigs, for garnish

Heat the oil in a wok or large skillet. Add the ribs and cook on both sides until browned, about 25 minutes.

Add the sugar and stir for 10 minutes.

Pour off all but 1 tablespoon of fat from the wok. Add the fish sauce and soy sauce and stir for 5 minutes. Add the onions, garlic, bell peppers and scallions. Stir-fry for 3 minutes longer, or until the onions are lightly browned and the peppers are slightly soft. Remove to a serving platter.

Sprinkle with black pepper and garnish with coriander sprigs. Serve with rice.

Yield: 4 to 6 servings

NHA TRANG SKEWERED MEATBALLS
NEM NUONG

*A*lthough this dish is a specialty of the central region, it is enjoyed throughout the country. As in most classical Vietnamese dishes, this one requires pounding the pork to achieve that certain crunchiness very much appreciated by food aficionados. I break with tradition here by using a food processor, since I prefer the convenience, and the result is more than satisfying. If you are fortunate enough to find Chinese chives, include them in the Vegetable Platter for authenticity.

■ ■ ■ ■ ■ ■ ■ ■ ■ ■ ■

Peanut Sauce (page 211)
Vegetable Platter (page 169)
3 *tablespoons roasted rice powder (page 220)*
8 *ounces thin rice vermicelli (bun, page 223), or 2 bundles Japanese alimentary paste noodles (somen, page 223)*
8 *ounces 6½-inch rice paper rounds (banh trang)*
1½ *pounds fresh ham, trimmed of excess fat*
4 *shallots, sliced*
8 *garlic cloves, sliced*
2 *tablespoons* nuoc mam *(Vietnamese fish sauce)*
2 *teaspoons ground rock sugar (page 234) or granulated sugar*
Freshly ground black pepper
4 *ounces pork fat*
Vegetable oil
12 *bamboo skewers, soaked in water for 30 minutes*

Prepare the Peanut Sauce, Vegetable Platter and roasted rice powder. Boil the noodles (can be prepared half day in advance and refrigerated). Cover the rice papers with a damp cloth and then with plastic wrap, and keep at room temperature until needed.

Thinly slice the fresh ham. Place in a shallow dish and add the shallots, garlic, fish sauce, sugar and pepper. Mix well. Cover the dish and marinate for at least 30 minutes.

Before processing the meat, transfer the dish to the freezer for about 30 minutes.

Place the partially frozen mixture in a food processor (avoid overloading the work bowl) and process to a completely smooth but stiff paste. The paste should be sticky and spring back to the touch. Stop every now and then to scrape down the sides of the bowl. Scrape the mixture into a bowl.

Add the pork fat to the processor and blend to a fine paste. Add the meat paste to the processed fat, along with the roasted rice powder and pulse briefly, only enough to blend (if you overwork the paste, it will turn into mush).

Pour a little oil into a bowl. Rub one hand with the oil. Grab a handful of the meat mixture and close your hand into a fist, squeezing out a small ball between your thumb and index finger; keep squeezing out the same ball until you have a round and smooth ball. Scoop out the ball with an oiled spoon. Continue until all of the paste is used.

Thread the meatballs onto bamboo skewers. Grill the skewered meatballs over a low charcoal fire, or under a broiler about 6 inches from the heat, for about 30 minutes, or until golden brown. Turn the meatballs occasionally so that all sides cook evenly. Pour the dipping sauce into individual bowls and serve in the following manner:

Dip a rice paper round in a bowl of warm water to soften and make it pliable. Place the paper on a dinner plate. Add different ingredients from the Vegetable Platter along with some noodles and a few meatballs. Roll up everything to form a neat package. Dip the roll in the Peanut Sauce and eat out of hand.

Yield: 4 to 6 servings

SWEET-AND-SOUR PORK
HEO XAO CHUA NGOT

Pork

1½ pounds pork shoulder, cut into 1-inch
    cubes
3 garlic cloves, chopped
1 teaspoon grated fresh gingerroot
2 tablespoons nuoc mam (Vietnamese
    fish sauce)
    Freshly ground black pepper
    Vegetable oil, for deep-frying
    Cornstarch, for coating

Sauce

¼ cup unsweetened pineapple juice
2 tablespoons nuoc mam (Vietnamese
    fish sauce)
3 tablespoons light soy sauce
¼ cup distilled white vinegar
1 tablespoon ketchup
2 tablespoons sugar
½ teaspoon salt
2 teaspoons cornstarch
1 tablespoon grated fresh gingerroot

Assembly

2 tablespoons vegetable oil
3 garlic cloves, minced
1 medium onion, cut in 1-inch chunks
    and separated
1 small carrot, cut on the diagonal into
    ¼-inch slices
1 small green bell pepper, cut into
    1-inch chunks
1 small red bell pepper, cut into
    1-inch chunks
2 large tomatoes, each cut into
    8 wedges
¼ fresh pineapple, cut into 1-inch
    chunks, or 1 can (8¼ ounces)
    pineapple chunks in their own juice,
    drained
2 scallions, cut into 2-inch sections
    Freshly ground black pepper
    Coriander sprigs, for garnish

Prepare the pork: In a bowl, combine the pork with the garlic, ginger, fish sauce and black pepper. Let stand for 30 minutes.

Heat 2 inches of oil in a wok or deep fryer to 360°F. The temperature should be maintained during the entire frying process. Coat the pork with cornstarch. Add one-fourth of the pork pieces to the oil and fry for 4 minutes. Remove with a slotted spoon and drain on paper towels. Continue cooking the remaining 3 batches.

Increase the oil temperature to 375°F. Deep-fry the pork in batches for a second time, until golden brown and very crisp, about 4 minutes. Remove and drain thoroughly on paper towels. Keep warm in a 200°F oven while you cook the vegetables. (The pork can be fried ahead of time and refrigerated.)

Prepare the sauce: Combine the ingredients for the sauce in a small bowl. Stir well. Set aside.

Finish the dish: Heat 2 tablespoons of fresh oil in a wok or skillet until very hot. Add the garlic and onion and stir-fry until lightly browned. Add the carrots and bell peppers and stir-fry for a few minutes, or until crisp-tender. Add the tomatoes, pineapple and scallions and cook for 1 minute longer. Remove the mixture to a platter.

Stir the sauce and add to the hot wok. Add the twice-fried pork to the sauce. Stir gently until pork is heated through and the sauce is slightly thickened. Stir in the vegetables and toss gently to coat with the sauce. Transfer the mixture to a hot platter.

Sprinkle with black pepper and garnish with coriander sprigs. Serve at once with rice.

NOTE You may replace the pork with spareribs that have been cut into 1-inch pieces.

Yield: 4 to 6 servings

STEAMED MEAT LOAF

MAM HAP

*T*his excellent dish—one of the first ones my nanny taught me how to cook—is best appreciated on a cold winter day, served with a steaming hot bowl of rice and sliced fresh cucumbers.

■ ■ ■ ■ ■ ■ ■ ■ ■ ■ ■

Nuoc Cham *(page 212)*
1 *ounce cellophane (bean thread) noodles*
4 *dried Chinese mushrooms*
1 *pound ground pork*
3 *garlic cloves, chopped*
3 *shallots, chopped*
1 *tablespoon nuoc mam (Vietnamese fish sauce)*
4 *eggs*
1 *can (2 ounces) anchovy fillets in olive oil, minced*
2 *fresh red chile peppers, seeded and minced*
Freshly ground black pepper

Prepare the *Nuoc Cham*. Set aside.

Soak the noodles in warm water and the mushrooms in hot water to cover for 30 minutes. Drain. Coarsely chop the noodles. Remove and discard the mushroom stems; cut the mushroom caps into thin strips.

In a large mixing bowl, combine the pork, garlic, shallots, and fish sauce. Make a well in the center of the mixture and break 3 of the eggs into the well. Beat the eggs into the pork with your hand, using a rapid circular motion.

Add the mushrooms, noodles, anchovies, chiles and black pepper. Stir to blend.

Pack the mixture in a 6½-inch round heatproof dish, 2½ inches deep, and smooth the surface. Lightly beat the remaining egg. Brush the egg on top of the meat loaf.

Pour 1 inch of water into a wok or wide pot. Place a steamer rack or bamboo steamer over the water. Place the heatproof dish on the rack. Cover and steam over high heat for about 45 minutes, or until the juices run clear when pierced with a chopstick. Be sure to have boiling water ready to replenish the steamer as needed.

Serve the meat loaf with rice and *Nuoc Cham*.

Yield: 4 to 6 servings

RICE SAUSAGE
GIO NEP

This very unusual sausage is delicious as well as economical. If you have leftovers, do not refrigerate; keep the sausage at room temperature for up to 2 days. Serve it as is. This sausage is excellent plain or dipped in *Nuoc Cham*.

■ ■ ■ ■ ■ ■ ■ ■ ■ ■ ■ ■

2 cups raw glutinous rice
  Nuoc Cham (page 212)
2 tablespoons dried shrimp
2 tablespoons preserved vegetables (page 233)
8 feet hog casing
1 pound chicken thighs, boned, skinned and coarsely ground
3 tablespoons nuoc mam (Vietnamese fish sauce)
10 garlic cloves, minced
½ cup chicken broth or water
1 teaspoon sugar
½ teaspoon freshly ground black pepper
¼ teaspoon cayenne pepper
½ teaspoon salt
1 teaspoon Oriental sesame oil
¼ cup plus 2 tablespoons vegetable oil
10 shallots, minced

Soak the glutinous rice overnight in water to cover, or for at least 8 hours. Drain.

Prepare the *Nuoc Cham*. Set aside.

Soak the dried shrimp and preserved vegetables in 1½ cups of hot water for 30 minutes. Drain, reserving 1 cup of the soaking liquid. Set aside. Coarsely chop the shrimp and vegetable mixture. Set aside.

Soak the sausage casing in warm vinegared water until soft, about 1 hour. Run cold water through the casing to check for any holes; cut off at the spot where there is a hole. Drain. Make a knot at one end of the casing. Set aside.

In a bowl, combine the ground chicken with 1 tablespoon of the fish sauce and half of the garlic. Mix well. Set aside to marinate for 30 minutes.

In a bowl, combine the reserved soaking liquid, chicken broth, sugar, black pepper, cayenne pepper, salt, sesame oil and the remaining 2 tablespoons fish sauce. Set aside.

Heat ¼ cup of the oil in a wok or skillet. Add the shallots, the remaining garlic and the dried shrimp and vegetable mixture and stir-fry until fragrant, about 1 minute. Add the marinated chicken and stir-fry for 2 minutes. Add the glutinous rice and stir for 1 minute. Add the sauce; toss and cook for 5 minutes over moderate heat until all of the liquid is absorbed. Remove from the heat and let cool.

Insert a sausage funnel at the open end of the sausage casing and gather the casing on the funnel tube, until you reach the knot. Stuff the sausage mixture into the casing, squeezing firmly to eliminate air pockets. Do not overstuff the casing; the rice will need room to expand during cooking. Tie the sausage at 5-inch intervals.

Bring a large pot of water to a boil. Reduce the heat to moderate and arrange the sausages in a single layer in the pot. Simmer, undisturbed, for 20 to 25 minutes (do not let the water boil or the sausages will burst). Remove the sausages and drain thoroughly on paper towels.

Heat the remaining 2 tablespoons oil in a nonstick skillet over moderate heat. Add the sausages and brown gently

Serve hot or at room temperature, with *Nuoc Cham*.

Yield: 4 to 6 servings

PORK SIMMERED IN COCONUT WATER

THIT KHO TAU

This dish was frequently served in my home, especially during hot summer days when my mother didn't feel like cooking a big meal. None of the coconut was wasted; after using the liquid in the nut, she added the coconut meat and perhaps a few hard-cooked eggs to the stew to make a wholesome meal. She liked to serve this dish with Pickled Bean Sprouts or Pickled Mustard Greens and boiled water spinach with its broth (the broth was seasoned with garlic, ginger, fresh tomatoes and *nuoc mam*).

The rind and fat are essential to this recipe; do not discard them.

■ ■ ■ ■ ■ ■ ■ ■ ■ ■ ■

Pickled Bean Sprouts (page 184) or Pickled Mustard Greens (page 189)
1½ pounds boneless fresh ham or pork shoulder with some fat and skin attached, cut into 1½-inch cubes
3 tablespoons nuoc mam (Vietnamese fish sauce)
4 shallots, thinly sliced Freshly ground black pepper
1 coconut
Sauce
1 tablespoon sugar
1 tablespoon nuoc mam (Vietnamese fish sauce)
1 tablespoon soy sauce

Prepare the Pickled Bean Sprouts or Pickled Mustard Greens. Set aside.

In a bowl, combine the ham, fish sauce, shallots and black pepper to taste. Let stand for 30 minutes.

Preheat the oven to 350°F.

Crack open a fresh coconut and pour the coconut water into a 3-quart saucepan.

Bake the coconut halves for 15 to 20 minutes, or until the shells begin to crack. Remove the coconut from the oven and let cool briefly. Place the nut pieces on a sturdy surface. Using a hammer or kitchen mallet, crack the coconut by hitting sharply on the shell; it should split apart easily. Remove the coconut meat from the shells with the point of a paring knife. Pare off the thin brown skin that clings to the white flesh. Cut the coconut meat into 2 by ¼-inch sticks.

Add ½ cup of water to the coconut water in the saucepan and bring the mixture to a boil. Add the ham and coconut meat and bring the mixture to a boil. Cook, uncovered, for 15 minutes. Reduce the heat to moderate, cover the pot and simmer for 30 minutes.

Meanwhile, prepare the sauce. Cook the sugar in a small heavy saucepan over low heat, swirling the pan constantly, until brown. It will smoke slightly. Immediately remove the pan from the heat. Stir the fish sauce and soy sauce into the caramel, being careful to guard against splattering (the mixture will bubble vigorously). Return the saucepan to low heat and gently boil, swirling the pan occasionally, until the sugar is thoroughly dissolved, about 2 minutes.

Stir the caramel sauce into the simmering stew and cook, covered, for 45 minutes longer, or until the ham and coconut pieces are very tender.

Serve with rice and Pickled Bean Sprouts or Pickled Mustard Greens.

Yield: 4 to 6 servings

GROUND PORK OMELET
CHA TRUNG

*T*his sounds like an omelet, but it is more like an egg "Fu Yung" in concept. The ground pork (or any kind of meat or seafood) is laced with beaten eggs, shaped into a cake, then fried to a golden brown. This quick, economical and delicious concoction is served as a simple dinner with pickled cabbage, sliced fresh cucumbers and a soup.

Cold leftover pork omelet makes an excellent sandwich or may be added to fried rice.

■ ■ ■ ■ ■ ■ ■ ■ ■ ■ ■

Nuoc Cham *(page 212)*
1 *pound ground pork*
1 *medium onion, chopped*
2 *scallions, finely sliced*
3 *garlic cloves, chopped*
1 *tablespoon* nuoc mam *(Vietnamese fish sauce)*
4 *eggs*
2 *tablespoons cornstarch*
Freshly ground black pepper
2 *tablespoons vegetable oil*

Prepare the *Nuoc Cham.* Set aside.

In a large mixing bowl, combine the ground pork, onion, scallions, garlic and fish sauce; mix well. Break the eggs over the mixture and combine gently. Do not beat the eggs. Add the cornstarch and ground pepper. Fold in gently.

Heat the oil in a 9-inch nonstick omelet pan or skillet over high heat. When the oil is slightly smoking, gently pour the pork mixture into the pan. Reduce the heat to moderate. Let the mixture cook without disturbing it for 3 minutes. When the edges turn brown, lift the edges of the omelet slightly with a spatula, so that the uncooked liquid gathered on top of the cake can run through to the bottom. Cook the omelet for 7 minutes longer, or until the bottom is firm and nicely browned. Slide the omelet onto a large plate; place another large plate over the omelet and invert the omelet onto it. Slide the omelet back into the skillet, uncooked side down, and cook for another 10 minutes. Transfer the omelet to a serving platter.

Cut the omelet into 2-inch squares. Serve with rice and *Nuoc Cham.*

Yield: 4 servings

BAKED CINNAMON SAUSAGE
GIO QUE

In Vietnam, this sausage is spread on large trays and baked. At the market, they are cut and sold to order. They come packed in banana leaves, which give them extra flavor.

This sausage can also be fried. Form small patties, about 2 inches in diameter, and pan-fry for about 5 minutes on each side.

■ ■ ■ ■ ■ ■ ■ ■ ■ ■ ■

2 *tablespoons* nuoc mam *(Vietnamese fish sauce)*
1 *tablespoon potato starch*
1½ *teaspoons sugar*
¼ *teaspoon freshly ground black pepper*
2 *teaspoons ground cinnamon*
1 *pound lean boneless fresh ham*
1 *ounce pork fat*

Combine the fish sauce, potato starch, sugar, black pepper, cinnamon and 1 tablespoon of water in a large bowl; mix well. Set aside.

Remove all of the fat from the fresh ham and cut into ¼-inch-thick slices. Place the meat in the marinade; toss well to coat. Cover the bowl and refrigerate for at least 4 hours, or overnight.

Before processing the meat, transfer the bowl to the freezer for 30 minutes.

Preheat the oven to 350°F. Grease an 8-inch-square baking pan. (If you don't have a small square pan, use a 9-inch-round cake pan.)

Place the partially frozen meat in a food processor and process the mixture to a very fine paste. Stop every now and then to scrape down the sides of the bowl. The paste is ready when the meat turns pinkish, is sticky and springs back to the touch. Transfer the meat paste to another bowl.

Process the pork fat to a fine paste. Add the meat paste to the processed fat and pulse briefly, only enough to blend (if you overwork the paste, it will turn into mush).

Moisten your hands with cold water. Pack the meat paste neatly into the pan, pressing down firmly with your hands to form a smooth surface. Knock the sides and bottom of the pan on a flat surface to eliminate any air bubbles.

Bake the sausage for 25 to 30 minutes, or until browned on the top. Remove the pan from the oven and allow to cool on a rack.

To serve, cut the sausage into finger-size pieces and serve warm or cold as an appetizer, in a sandwich or as part of a family meal accompanied with *Nuoc Cham,* rice or glutinous rice.

NOTE Leftover sausage can be wrapped and refrigerated for up to 1 week, or stored in the freezer for a longer period. Reheat before serving.

Yield: 4 to 6 servings

ROAST PORK, BARBECUED STYLE
XA XIU

Since this versatile barbecued pork is used in many other dishes, such as fried rice and soups, you may want to prepare a large batch and keep it on hand in the freezer. Leftover roast pork may be wrapped and refrigerated for up to 1 week; it makes great sandwiches as well.

Although this recipe calls for lean, boneless pork, many Vietnamese cooks favor the pork belly (fresh bacon, available at Asian butcher shops) for its richness and texture. If you decide to try pork belly, do not remove the skin, which, when cooked, will be much appreciated for its crispiness.

You can purchase *Xa Xiu* in many Asian markets.

■ ■ ■ ■ ■ ■ ■ ■ ■ ■

2 pounds lean boneless pork (butt, shoulder or boned fresh ham)
2 garlic cloves, chopped
½ cup chicken broth
1 teaspoon salt
¼ cup plus 1 tablespoon honey
2 tablespoons light soy sauce
1 tablespoon tomato paste
1 teaspoon five-spice powder
2 teaspoons rice wine or sherry (optional)

Cut the pork lengthwise into 1½-inch-thick strips and place in a bowl. Puncture the meat (to help tenderize it) with the point of a small knife or fork.

Combine all of the remaining ingredients in a small nonreactive saucepan. Heat, stirring, until warmed through and the honey is dissolved.

Pour the mixture over the pork and mix to coat all of the pieces. Cover and refrigerate, turning a few times, for at least 4 hours, or overnight.

Preheat the oven to 450°F. Position 2 clean racks 7 or 8 inches from each other.

Drain the pork from the marinade, reserving the marinade for basting. Place the pork strips directly on the top rack. On the rack below, place a large shallow pan half-filled with hot water. The water bath is used to catch the drippings and provide moisture during cooking. Roast for 20 minutes.

Reduce the heat to 350°F. Bake for 20 minutes longer, basting 5 or 6 times with the reserved marinade and turning the meat every 5 minutes.

Remove the meat to a rack. Cool slightly before cutting crosswise into thin slices.

Serve with plain rice as part of a family meal, or use where specified in other recipes.

Yield: 4 to 6 servings

RICE

Stuffed Crisp Rice Pancake and Nuoc Cham

RICE

*R*ice is the mainstay of the Vietnamese diet, and, therefore, the Vietnamese are very fastidious when it comes to selecting it. My mother was no exception. She bought her favorite varieties only in rice shops where customers were treated with respect and courtesy. Hot tea and candies awaited clients while they selected their rices and bargained over prices.

In Vietnam, rice comes in hundreds of varieties, differing in their characteristics: color, flavor, aroma and tenderness, as well as stickiness. The Vietnamese prefer long-grain white rice. If you are fortunate enough to find jasmin rice from Thailand, buy it. It comes in 10-pound bags in Southeast Asian groceries. The fragrant scent and tender texture of this particular variety is unsurpassed.

The most popular cooking method for rice is by absorption. In general, rice absorbs about one and one-half times its volume in water. It should be pointed out that the Vietnamese like their rice very dry and flaky; they do not wash it. Salt is never added to the rice. It is also preferable to cook rice in a thick-bottomed pot. If you own an electric rice cooker, just follow the simple directions supplied with the appliance.

■ ■ ■ ■ ■ ■ ■ ■ ■ ■ ■

Ratio of rice (for jasmin rice or other
long-grain white rice) to water:
1 cup rice   1½ cups cold water
2 cups rice   2½ cups cold water
3 cups rice   3½ cups cold water

Bring the measured water to a boil in a thick-bottomed pot over high heat. Add the rice and bring back to a boil, being careful not to let it boil over. Stir the rice with a wooden spoon. Boil vigorously for 1 minute. Reduce the heat to moderate and let the water boil until it is below the rice line and small holes or craters form on the surface. Cover, reduce the heat to as low as it will go (if using an electric stove, have a second burner preheated, then set to the lowest setting) and cook for 20 minutes. Do not lift the lid during this time or all of the steam will escape and the rice will become hard and dry. After cooking, set aside, covered, for 10 minutes before serving. Uncover, gently fluff with a fork or chopsticks. The kernels should be tender and fluffy.

N O T E If you find a crust on the bottom of the pot after the rice has been cooked, do not discard it. You may eat this very crunchy and flavorsome cracker by itself, or dunk it in meat juices or sauces, as I love to do.

Yield: 1 cup of raw rice yields 3 cups cooked rice

GLUTINOUS RICE (STICKY RICE)

XOI NEP

*B*ecause glutinous rice has no amylose, when cooked in water, the grains blend together into a dough as sticky as glue. For this reason, glutinous rice is usually steamed. In Vietnam, sticky rice is frequently served at breakfast. It can replace plain rice; in addition, it may be served with dipping sauces or simmered dishes and at special occasions, when it is combined with many other ingredients. It is also the staple food for Buddhists and vegetarians.

Instructions for two different cooking methods are given below. In both instances, soak 2 cups of glutinous rice in cold water for at least 8 hours or overnight. Rinse and drain.

■ ■ ■ ■ ■ ■ ■ ■ ■ ■ ■ ■

Steaming:

Spread the soaked rice over a dampened cheesecloth in the top of a steamer and steam for 30 to 40 minutes, sprinkling water over it from time to time. Taste while it cooks for the consistency you want, just as you would with pasta.

Boiling:

Bring 3 cups of water to a boil in a heavy-bottomed pan over high heat. Add the rice and bring back to a boil. Boil for 1 minute, taking care that the water doesn't boil over. While it is actively boiling, cover the pan with a tight lid and remove from the heat. Holding the cover tightly on the pan, drain off all of the water. Return the pan to very low heat (if using an electric stove, have a second burner preheated, then set at the lowest setting), cover and cook for 20 minutes. After cooking, set aside, covered, for 10 minutes before serving. Uncover and fluff with a fork or chopsticks.

NOTE Do not discard the crust on the bottom of the pan. Dip it in sauces, or deep-fry and eat it as a cracker.

Yield: 4 cups cooked glutinous rice

GLUTINOUS RICE
WITH MUNG BEAN PASTE
SOI VO

Glutinous rice is one of the most important staples in the vegetarian diet. This recipe shows just one way of cooking it. Other legumes and nuts most commonly paired with glutinous rice are black beans, peanuts (with skin on), fresh corn and shredded fresh coconut. Glutinous rice is usually served sprinkled with a fragrant mixture of ground roasted peanuts and sesame seeds, seasoned with sugar.

■ ■ ■ ■ ■ ■ ■ ■ ■ ■

1½ cups raw glutinous rice
½ cup dried yellow mung beans
1 teaspoon salt
¼ cup roasted peanuts (page 220), ground
2 tablespoons toasted sesame seeds (page 225), ground
1 tablespoon sugar
¼ cup peanut oil

Soak the glutinous rice and mung beans separately in water for at least 8 hours or overnight. Drain.

Steam the mung beans over high heat for 20 minutes.

Transfer the mung beans to a food processor and purée to a fine paste. Form the paste into 2 firm balls. Let stand for 20 minutes.

Grate the mung bean balls over the glutinous rice. Add the salt and stir to combine. Spread the glutinous rice over dampened cheesecloth in the top of a steamer. Steam over high heat for 45 minutes, sprinkling water over it from time to time.

Prepare the roasted peanuts and toasted sesame seeds. Just a few minutes before serving, grind the nuts and mix them with the sesame seeds and sugar in a small bowl; stir to combine.

Transfer the steamed glutinous rice to a large tray and add the oil. Rub the mixture between your hands, or fluff the mixture with chopsticks or a fork to separate the grains. Sprinkle with the peanut and sesame mix and serve hot.

Yield: 4 servings

HUE RICE
COM HUONG GIANG

*F*ragrantly seasoned, this spicy and tasty rice dish is also simple to make. Like most rice dishes, it may be served for breakfast, lunch or dinner.

■ ■ ■ ■ ■ ■ ■ ■ ■

3 cups cooked rice, cold
1 tablespoon dried shrimp (page 231)
Nuoc Cham (page 212)
1 tablespoon toasted sesame seeds (page 225), ground
1 stalk fresh lemon grass, outer leaves removed, trimmed and minced
2 shallots, sliced
2 garlic cloves, chopped
2 teaspoons sugar
2 fresh red chile peppers, seeded and chopped
4 tablespoons vegetable oil
2 scallions, sliced
1 small onion, chopped
2 tablespoons chicken broth or water
2 tablespoons nuoc mam (Vietnamese fish sauce)
Freshly ground black pepper
Coriander sprigs, for garnish

Rub the cold rice with wet hands to separate the grains. Set aside.

Soak the dried shrimp in hot water for 30 minutes. Drain.

Prepare the *Nuoc Cham* and toasted sesame seeds. Set aside.

Grind together the shrimp, lemon grass, shallots, garlic, sugar and chiles.

Heat 2 tablespoons of the oil in a wok or skillet. Add the scallions and stir-fry for 1 minute. Add the lemon grass and dried shrimp mixture and stir-fry for 5 minutes over high heat. Remove to a dish. Pour the remaining 2 tablespoons oil into the wok. Add the onion and stir-fry until translucent. Add the rice and stir-fry for 5 minutes.

Stir in the broth, fish sauce and black pepper to taste. Add the lemon grass and shrimp mixture and the toasted sesame seeds. Stir to combine well. Transfer to a heated platter.

Sprinkle with additional black pepper and garnish with the coriander sprigs. Serve with *Nuoc Cham.*

Yield: 4 servings

STUFFED CRISP RICE PANCAKE

BANH XEO

Banh Xeo, meaning "sound" pancake, aptly describes this Vietnamese-style crêpe. When poured into the skillet, the batter makes a sizzling sound. The batter can be prepared 1 day ahead, and the accompaniments can be assembled just before serving. The crêpes can be cooked and stuffed a few hours in advance, and then reheated as needed.

The use of coconut milk in this recipe is typical of southern Vietnamese specialties. Traditionally, this crêpe is prepared in a wok, but a good omelet pan is fine too. Remember to stir the rice batter well before each addition to the pan.

■ ■ ■ ■ ● ■ ■ ■ ■ ● ■

Crêpe batter
¾ *cup dried yellow mung beans*
2 *cups fresh or canned coconut milk*
1 *cup rice flour*
½ *teaspoon sugar*
½ *teaspoon salt*
¼ *teaspoon turmeric*

Accompaniments and filling
Nuoc Cham *with Shredded Carrots and Daikon (page 212)*
Vegetable Platter *(page 169)*
4 *ounces pork butt or shoulder, cut into 12 thin slices*
12 *raw medium shrimp, shelled, deveined and halved lengthwise*
1½ *tablespoons* nuoc mam *(Vietnamese fish sauce)*
4 *large garlic cloves, minced*
¼ *teaspoon sugar*
Freshly ground black pepper
2 *cups thinly sliced fresh mushrooms*
2 *cups fresh bean sprouts*
1 *large onion, thinly sliced*
¾ *cup vegetable oil*

Make the crêpe batter: Cover the mung beans with water and soak for 30 minutes. Drain. Set aside 1 cup for the filling. Place the remaining ½ cup in a blender with the coconut milk and process to a fine purée. Add the rice flour, sugar, salt and turmeric; blend well. Strain the mixture into a bowl or jar and refrigerate.

Steam the reserved mung beans for about 20 minutes, or until tender. Allow to cool. Cover and set aside.

To complete the dish: Prepare the *Nuoc Cham* and Vegetable Platter. Set aside.

In a bowl, combine the pork and shrimp with the fish sauce, garlic, sugar and black pepper to taste. Cover and refrigerate for 30 minutes.

In another bowl, combine the mushrooms, bean sprouts, onion and the cooked mung beans. To facilitate last-minute assembly, divide the mixture into 6 separate mounds on a tray.

Heat 2 tablespoons of the oil in a skillet over high heat. Add the pork and shrimp mixture and stir-fry for 2 minutes, or until the pork loses its pink color and the shrimp turn opaque. Remove to a platter.

In a wok or an 8-inch nonstick omelet pan, heat 2 tablespoons of the oil over moderately high heat. When the oil is very hot, stir the rice batter well and pour ½ cup into the wok. Quickly tilt the wok to spread the mixture into a thin pancake. Scatter 1 mound of the vegetables, 2 slices of pork and 4 pieces of shrimp on the lower half of the pancake. Reduce the heat to moderate. Cover the pan and cook for about 5 minutes, or until the bottom of the pancake is brown and crispy. Fold the pancake in half and slide it onto a platter. Keep warm in a low oven. Repeat with the remaining oil, batter and filling, making 5 more crêpes.

To serve, each diner places a piece of the rice crêpe with some filling on a lettuce leaf with selected herbs from the Vegetable Platter and strands of carrot and daikon from the dipping sauce. The bundle is rolled up, dipped in *Nuoc Cham* and eaten out of hand.

Yield: 6 servings

FRIED RICE WITH PORK, CHICKEN AND SAUSAGE

COM CHIEN THAP CAM

*O*riginally, this dish was created to use up leftover rice, bits of meat and vegetables. Here is an opportunity to use any leftover shrimp, crabmeat or Vietnamese pork sausage (*gio*) you may have on hand. The secret of *Com Chien Thap Cam* is to cook the rice a day ahead and refrigerate it overnight.

If you prefer only one ingredient, use 2 cups of pork, chicken or sausage, instead of ⅔ cups of each.

■ ■ ■ ■ ■ ■ ■ ■ ■ ■ ■

4 cups cooked rice, cold

3 eggs

¼ teaspoon salt

6 tablespoons vegetable oil, chicken fat
   or roast pork fat

4 scallions sliced

1 large onion, diced

4 garlic cloves, minced

⅔ cup diced Chinese sausage (lap xuong,
   page 235)

⅔ cup diced roast chicken

⅔ cup diced roast pork

⅔ cup diced carrots

⅔ cup sliced green beans

⅔ cup diced celery

4 shallots, sliced

2 tablespoons nuoc mam (*Vietnamese
   fish sauce*)

¼ cup soy sauce

¼ cup chicken broth or water

1 tablespoon hot chile sauce (tuong ot)
   or Tobasco

1 tablespoon sugar
   Freshly ground black pepper
   Coriander sprigs, for garnish

Before frying the rice, rub it with wet hands to separate the grains. Set aside.

In a bowl, beat the eggs with the salt.

Set a wok or large skillet over high heat and add 2 tablespoons of the oil. When the oil is hot, add the scallions and brown lightly. Add the eggs and scramble until softly set. Remove and set aside.

Swirl 2 tablespoons more oil into the wok. Add the onion and garlic and fry for 30 seconds. Add the sausage, chicken and pork and stir-fry until heated through. Add the carrots, green beans and celery and cook for 2 minutes. Remove the mixture to a bowl. Set aside.

Add the remaining 2 tablespoons oil to the wok. Add the shallots and brown lightly. Add the rice and stir-fry until heated through. Stir in the fish sauce, soy sauce, chicken broth, hot chile sauce and sugar. Stir and toss until the rice is well coated with the seasonings. Add the scrambled eggs, meats and vegetables. Stir until heated through.

Transfer the fried rice to a large heated platter. Sprinkle with black pepper and garnish with the coriander sprigs.

Yield: 6 servings

PRINCESS RICE
COM HOANG HAU

This sumptuous rice dish is usually reserved for special occasions, most notably weddings. The title is an exact translation from the Vietnamese, suggesting that it's fit for a princess's wedding.

Barbecued pork (*xa xiu*) can be purchased at most Asian markets, or you can prepare your own by following the recipe on page 129.

■ ■ ■ ■ ■ ■ ■ ■ ■ ■ ■

Pickled Carrots (page 184)
2 egg pancakes (page 219), cut into thin
    strips
1 large fresh red chile pepper
4 dried Chinese mushrooms
1 medium cucumber
1 teaspoon salt
2 tablespoons rice vinegar
2 teaspoons sugar
1 teaspoon Oriental sesame oil
1½ cups fresh or canned coconut milk
2 cups chicken broth or water
3 cups extra-long-grain rice
2 Chinese sausages (lap xuong, page
    235)
2 tablespoons vegetable oil
4 shallots, thinly sliced
4 garlic cloves, minced
4 ounces raw shrimp, peeled and
    deveined
1 tablespoon nuoc mam (Vietnamese
    fish sauce)
4 ounces fresh or canned crabmeat,
    picked over and drained
1 small onion, diced
½ cup canned straw mushrooms, drained
1½ teaspoons cornstarch
1½ teaspoons tomato paste
1 cup fresh green peas, blanched, or
    frozen peas, thawed
8 ounces barbecued pork, thinly sliced
    Coriander sprigs, for garnish

Prepare the Pickled Carrots and egg pancakes.

Use scissors to make long, uniform cuts from the tip of the chile pepper in toward the stem end (without cutting through the stem) to simulate a flower. Soak the chile in ice water.

Soak the dried mushrooms in hot water for 30 minutes. Drain, reserving ½ cup of the soaking liquid for the sauce. Remove and discard the mushroom stems; quarter the caps.

Remove the cucumber peel in alternating strips. Cut the cucumber crosswise into thin slices. Transfer to a colander, sprinkle with the salt and let stand for 15 minutes. Rinse well; drain and squeeze gently. In a small bowl, combine the cucumber, vinegar, sugar and sesame oil. Stir to blend. Set aside.

Combine the coconut milk and broth in a heavy-bottomed pot and bring to a boil over high heat. Add the rice and boil for 1 minute, stirring briefly. Cover, reduce the heat to low and cook for 20 minutes. (After cooking, the rice may sit, covered, for 30 minutes.)

Pierce the sausages with a fork. Grill or broil them for about 8 minutes, turning frequently. Remove and thinly slice.

Heat 1 tablespoon of the vegetable oil in a wok or skillet over high heat. Add the shallots and garlic and stir-fry until lightly browned. Add the shrimp and 1 teaspoon of the fish sauce. Stir-fry for 2 minutes. Add the crabmeat and cook for 1 minute longer. Remove the mixture to a dish.

Heat the remaining 1 tablespoon vegetable oil in the wok. Add the onion and stir-fry until lightly browned. Add the Chinese and straw mushrooms and stir-fry for 1 minute. Dissolve the cornstarch and tomato paste in the reserved mushroom liquid. Stir in the remaining 2 teaspoons fish sauce. Add this sauce to the vegetables in the wok and stir until the sauce is lightly thickened. Return the shrimp and crabmeat mixture to the wok, along with ½ cup of peas. Stir to combine.

Combine the rice with the remaining ½ cup peas. Mound the rice in the center of a large platter. Arrange some of the egg pancake strips, drained cucumber, sausage, pork and shrimp mixture separately in a pinwheel pattern over the top. Surround with the remaining strips of egg pancake and slices of pickled carrot. Top with the chile flower and coriander.

Yield: 6 to 8 servings

NEW YEAR'S RICE CAKE
BANH TRUNG

On New Year's Day of the lunar calendar, it is a custom for the Vietnamese to eat Rice Cake, with the hope that the new year will bring much wealth, luck and peace. One or two days before each New Year's Day, most households buy or prepare *Banh Trung* in large quantities. Such special occasions call for entire families to gather and lend a helping hand. Once the rice cakes are properly wrapped in banana leaves, they are left to cook overnight in a large barrel filled with water set over a wood fire in the backyard. All night long, people take turns checking the fire and replenishing the barrel with water. After cooking, the cakes are hung in the kitchen. They are eaten over a period of a few weeks, or they are offered as gifts to friends and relatives. Rice cakes are usually served warm or at room temperature with Vegetables in Fish Sauce (made weeks ahead) and Baked Cinnamon Sausage.

■ ■ ■ ■ ■ ■ ■ ■ ■ ■ ■

2 cups raw glutinous rice
½ cup dried yellow mung beans
2 drops green food coloring (optional)
  Baked Cinnamon Sausage (page 128)
  Vegetables in Fish Sauce (page 181)
    (optional)
4 shallots, thinly sliced
1 tablespoon nuoc mam (Vietnamese
    fish sauce)
  Freshly ground black pepper
8 ounces pork butt, cut into 2 by 2 by ½-
    inch-thick squares
For wrapping
2 sheets (14 by 16 inches) of plastic wrap
1 sheet (14 by 16 inches) of aluminum
    foil
1 banana leaf or sheet of foil (14 by
    16 inches), oiled on one side
4 lengths (24 inches long) of butcher
    string

Soak the glutinous rice and mung beans in separate bowls for at least 8 hours, or overnight. If you wish, add the green food coloring to the bowl of soaking rice. Drain and set aside.

Prepare the Baked Cinnamon Sausage and Vegetables in Fish Sauce, if using. Set aside.

In a mortar, pound the shallots to a fine paste. Stir in the fish sauce and black pepper to taste. Add the pork and mix well. Set aside to marinate for 1 hour.

Steam the mung beans for 20 minutes. Transfer to a food processor and purée to a fine paste. Form the paste into 2 firm balls. Let stand for 20 minutes. Grate the balls into a bowl and set aside.

Layer the wrapping sheets as follows: Spread 1 sheet of the plastic wrap flat on a counter. Cover with the aluminum foil. Top the foil with the banana leaf, oiled side up.

Spread 1 cup of rice on the banana leaf to form a 6-inch square. Spread half of the grated mung beans on top of the rice to form a smaller square, about 5 inches. Cover the mung beans with the pork pieces. Cover the meat with the remaining mung beans. Cover the beans with 1 cup of rice.

Bring the narrow sides of the wrapping sheets together to make a 1-inch fold, then fold once more to seal. Flatten the 1-inch fold along the package. You now have 2 open ends. Fold one end over, then stand the package on this closed end. Add ¼ cup more of glutinous rice through the open end; tap the package to expel any air holes inside. Fold the wrapping over to seal. Turn the package over. Reopen the opposite end and add the remaining ¼ cup rice, tapping again to form a neat package. Reseal that end. Using your hands, press the package into a neat square. Place the wrapped cake, with the folded side down, on the remaining sheet of plastic wrap. Seal to ensure that no water gets into the package.

Tie 2 strings alternately in each direction to form cross ties.

In a pot, place the package in cold water to cover and bring to a boil over high heat. Turn the heat to moderate, place a weight on top of the rice cake to keep it immersed in the water and cook, uncovered, for 5 hours. As the water evaporates, add more boiling water to cover the package.

When the cooking time is up, remove the package to a cake rack. Allow to cool. Remove the wrapping. Cut the rice cake into 2-inch squares. Serve with Cinnamon Sausage and Vegetables in Fish Sauce, if desired.

Yield: 4 to 6 servings

RICE AND CHICKEN CASSEROLE
COM GA

*T*his excellent rice dish is traditionally cooked in an earthen pot. A heavy pot or casserole will do.

■ ■ ■ ■ ■ ■ ■ ■ ■ ■

6 *dried Chinese mushrooms*
8 *chicken thighs (about 1 pound)*
2 *tablespoons* nuoc mam *(Vietnamese fish sauce)*
2 *tablespoons soy sauce*
½ *teaspoon sugar*
4 *garlic cloves, minced*
   Freshly ground black pepper
3 *tablespoons chicken fat or vegetable oil*
6 *shallots, finely sliced*
1 *can (15 ounces) straw mushrooms, drained*
1 *small onion, chopped*
2 *cups raw extra-long-grain rice*
2 *cups hot chicken broth*
½ *teaspoon salt*
2 *scallions, sliced*
   Coriander sprigs, for garnish

Soak the dried mushrooms in hot water for 30 minutes. Squeeze the soaked mushrooms dry, reserving ½ cup of the soaking liquid. Remove and discard the stems. Cut the mushroom caps into thin strips.

Meanwhile, bone the chicken thighs and cut the meat, with the skin, into strips, 2 inches long by ½ inch thick.

In a bowl, combine the chicken, fish sauce, 1 tablespoon of the soy sauce, the sugar, half of the garlic and black pepper to taste. Stir and set aside.

Heat 2 tablespoons of the chicken fat in a skillet. Add the shallots and stir-fry until fragrant. Add the chicken and stir-fry for 2 minutes, or until the chicken is tender. Add the mushrooms and stir-fry for 1 minute. Remove and set aside.

Heat the remaining 1 tablespoon fat in a heavy casserole. Add the onion and the remaining garlic and sauté until the onion is translucent. Add the rice and stir until it turns golden, about 5 minutes. Add the hot broth, the reserved mushroom liquid, the salt and the remaining 1 tablespoon soy sauce. Stir to combine. Cook over high heat for about 5 minutes, or until the water is just absorbed. Spread the chicken mixture over the rice. Cover, reduce the heat to low and cook for 20 minutes.

When the rice is done, stir in the scallions, mixing all of the ingredients into the rice. Transfer to a large heated platter. Sprinkle with black pepper and garnish with the coriander sprigs.

Yield: 4 to 6 servings

Noodles and Noodle Soup

Crisp-Fried Egg Noodles with Assorted Meats and Vegetables

CRISP-FRIED EGG NOODLES WITH ASSORTED MEATS AND VEGETABLES

MI XAO THAP CAM

*T*his elegant dish is usually offered at large gatherings for special occasions.

To facilitate the cooking, the egg noodles can be parboiled and fried early in the day, then kept covered on a tray, until needed. Reheat them in the oven while you do the stir-frying.

■ ■ ■ ■ ■ ■ ■ ■ ■ ■ ■

Nuoc Cham (*page 212*)
1 pound fresh thin egg noodles
   Peanut oil
12 ounces raw medium shrimp, shelled
   and deveined
12 ounces rump or flank steak
1 chicken breast, halved and boned
4 tablespoons nuoc mam (Vietnamese
   fish sauce)
1 tablespoon grated gingerroot
6 garlic cloves, chopped
2 tablespoons plus 2 teaspoons
   arrowroot or cornstarch
   Freshly ground black pepper
12 dried Chinese mushrooms
1 tablespoon dried tree ear mushrooms
½ cup chicken broth
¼ cup dry red wine (optional)
¼ cup oyster sauce
1 tablespoon soy sauce
   Vegetable oil
1 large onion, cut into slivers
½ Chinese white cabbage or Chinese
   kale, cut into 2-inch pieces
1 cup fresh snow peas, trimmed
1 large carrot, halved lengthwise and
   sliced ¼ inch thick
1 can (15 ounces) baby corn, drained
   (optional)
1 can (15 ounces) straw mushrooms,
   drained (optional)
   Coriander sprigs, for garnish

Prepare the *Nuoc Cham*. Set aside.

Drop the egg noodles into a pot of boiling water; boil for 1 minute. Rinse the noodles under cold water; drain well. Toss the noodles with a little peanut oil to prevent sticking. Line a large baking sheet with a double layer of paper towels and spread out the noodles to dry.

Halve the shrimp lengthwise. Set aside.

Cut the steak across the grain into thin 2 by 2-inch pieces. Set aside. Cut the chicken breast lengthwise into ¼-inch strips, about 3 inches long. Set aside.

In a small bowl, combine 3 tablespoons of the fish sauce, the ginger, half of the garlic, 2 tablespoons of the arrowroot and ½ teaspoon of black pepper. Stir to blend. Coat the shrimp, beef and chicken separately with the marinade. Let marinate for 30 minutes.

Soak the Chinese and tree ear mushrooms in hot water for 30 minutes. Drain, reserving ½ cup of the soaking liquid. Remove and discard the stems; cut the caps in half if they are large.

In a bowl, combine the chicken broth, reserved mushroom liquid, red wine, oyster sauce and soy sauce. Add the remaining 1 tablespoon fish sauce and the remaining 2 teaspoons arrowroot; mix well. Set the sauce aside.

Heat ½ inch of oil in a wok or skillet to 365°F. Add one-fourth of the noodles, spreading out the strands to form a flat cake. Fry until puffed and golden, about 1 minute. Turn and cook the other side for 1 minute longer. Remove the noodles from the oil with a slotted spatula to drain on paper towels; place on a large serving platter and keep warm in a 200°F oven. Continue frying until all of the noodles are used.

Heat 2 tablespoons of oil in a clean wok or skillet. When the oil is hot, fry the remaining garlic until fragrant. Add the shrimp and chicken and toss over high heat until the chicken turns white and the shrimp is opaque. Transfer to a large plate.

Heat 1 tablespoon more oil; stir-fry the beef for 1 minute. Transfer to the plate with the shrimp and chicken.

Heat 2 tablespoons more oil. Add the onion and fry until translucent. Add the Chinese cabbage, snow peas, carrot, baby corn and all the mushrooms, stir-frying for 30 seconds after each addition. Stir in the sauce and cook, stirring, until slightly thickened and the vegetables are crisp-tender. Return the shrimp, chicken and beef to the wok; mix well. Remove from the heat.

Pour the stir-fried mixture over the crispy noodles. Sprinkle with black pepper and garnish with coriander sprigs. Serve with *Nuoc Cham.*

Yield: 6 to 8 servings

Hanoi Beef and Rice-Noodle Soup

Chicken and Cellophane Noodle Soup and Shredded Cabbage and Chicken Salad

HANOI BEEF AND RICE-NOODLE SOUP

PHO BAC

All dishes in this chapter constitute a complete meal. They are consumed indiscriminately at breakfast, lunch or dinner.

This sublime recipe comes from my mother, a native of Hanoi. She always made the beef stock in large quantities—enough for at least 3 meals—and froze it in batches until needed.

In order to cut the beef into paper-thin slices, freeze the piece of meat for 30 minutes before slicing.

■ ■ ■ ■ ■ ■ ■ ■ ■ ■ ■ ■

5 pounds beef bones with marrow
5 pounds oxtails
2 pounds short rib plate, or 1 pound
  flank steak
2 large onions, unpeeled, halved and
  studded with 8 whole cloves
3 shallots, unpeeled
2 ounces fresh gingerroot, unpeeled,
  in one piece
8 star anise
1 cinnamon stick
4 medium parsnips, cut into 2-inch
  chunks
2 teaspoons salt
1 pound beef sirloin
2 scallions, thinly sliced
1 tablespoon shredded coriander
2 medium onions, sliced paper-thin
¼ cup hot chile sauce (tuong ot *or*
  sriracha *sauce)*
1 pound ¼-inch-wide dried rice sticks
  (banh pho)
½ cup nuoc mam (*Vietnamese*
  fish sauce)
Freshly ground black pepper
Accompaniments
2 cups fresh bean sprouts
2 fresh red chile peppers, sliced
2 limes, cut into wedges
1 bunch of fresh mint, separated
  into leaves
1 bunch of fresh Asian basil or regular
  fresh basil, separated into leaves

The night before, clean the bones under cold running water and soak overnight in a pot with water to cover at room temperature. (This will help loosen the impurities inside the bones. When heat is applied, these impurities are released and come to the top much faster and can be removed, therefore, producing a clear broth.)

Place the beef bones, oxtails and short rib plate in a large stockpot. Add water to cover and bring to a boil. Cook for 10 minutes. Drain. Rinse the pot and the bones.

Return the bones to the pot and add 6 quarts of water. Bring to a boil. Skim the surface to remove the foam and fat. Stir the bones in the bottom of the pot from time to time to free the impurities. Continue skimming until the foam ceases to rise. Add 3 quarts more water and bring to a boil. Skim off all of the residue that forms on the top. Turn the heat to low and simmer.

Meanwhile, char the clove-studded onions, shallots and ginger directly over a gas burner or under the broiler until they release their fragrant odors. Tie the charred vegetables, star anise and cinnamon stick in a double thickness of dampened cheesecloth. Add the spice bag, parsnips and salt to the simmering broth. Simmer for 1 hour.

Remove the short rib plates. Pull the meat away from the bones. Reserve the meat and return the bones to the pot. Simmer the broth, uncovered, for 4 to 5 hours. Keep an eye on it; as the liquid boils away, add enough fresh water to cover the bones.

Meanwhile, slice the beef sirloin against the grain into paper-thin slices, roughly 2 by 2 inches in size. Slice the reserved short rib meat paper-thin. Set aside.

In a small bowl, combine the scallions, coriander and half of the sliced onions. Place the remaining sliced onions in a small bowl and stir in the hot chile sauce. Blend well.

Soak the rice sticks in warm water for 30 minutes. Drain and set aside.

When the broth is ready, remove and discard all of the bones. Strain the broth through a strainer or colander lined with a double layer of dampened cheesecloth into a clean pot. Add the fish sauce and bring the broth to a boil. Reduce the heat and keep the broth at a bare simmer.

In another pot, bring 4 quarts of water to a boil. Drain the noodles, then drop them in the boiling water. Drain immediately. Divide the noodles among 4 large soup bowls. Top the noodles with the sliced meats. Bring the broth to a rolling boil. Ladle the broth directly over the meat in each bowl (the boiling broth will cook the raw beef instantly). Garnish with the scallion mixture and freshly ground black pepper.

Serve the onions in hot chile sauce and the accompaniments on the side. Each diner will add these ingredients as desired.

Yield: 4 servings

COLD RICE VERMICELLI
WITH SHREDDED ROAST PORK
BUN BI

The mention of rice noodles always makes me think of the appetizing, heaping bowls of *Bun Bi* sold by our next-door neighbor, a street vendor. When I was growing up in Laos, this was the kind of food I most enjoyed, either for breakfast or lunch.

■ ■ ■ ■ ■ ■ ■ ■ ■ ■ ■

1 *pound thin rice vermicelli (bun, page 223), or 4 bundles Japanese alimentary paste noodles (somen, page 223)*
2 *tablespoons roasted rice powder (page 220)*
2 *ounces dried shredded pork skin (bi kho, page 233)*
1 *teaspoon fresh galangal juice or ginger juice*
¼ *teaspoon salt*
Freshly ground black pepper
1 *pound pork loin or butt*
2 *tablespoons vegetable oil*
6 *garlic cloves, crushed*
2 *small red chile peppers, seeded*
1 *tablespoon sugar*
3 *tablespoons* nuoc mam *(Vietnamese fish sauce)*
Juice of 2 lemons
2 *cups fresh bean sprouts*
1 *tablespoon finely shredded mint*
Coriander leaves, for garnish

Prepare the noodles and roasted rice powder. Set aside.

Soak the shredded pork skin in warm water for 30 minutes. Drop the skin in a pan of boiling salted water for 15 seconds only. Immediately pour the contents into a colander and refresh with cold water; drain. In a bowl, toss the pork skin with the galangal juice. Set aside.

Sprinkle the salt and pepper over the pork loin. Place the oil in a skillet over high heat. Add the pork and brown on all sides. Cover the skillet, reduce the heat to moderately low and cook for 30 minutes, turning every 5 minutes. Two minutes before the meat is done, add two-thirds of the garlic and fry until fragrant and golden brown. Remove from the heat; discard the garlic and set the pork aside to cool.

Skim off the excess fat from the cooking juices in the pan; reserve pan juices.

Cut the roast pork into julienne and place in a large mixing bowl with the reserved pan juices.

Pound the remaining garlic, chile peppers and sugar to a very smooth paste in a mortar. Add the fish sauce and lemon juice; stir to blend. Set the dressing aside.

Sprinkle the roasted rice powder and pork skin over the roast pork. Toss well. Add the cooked noodles, bean sprouts, dressing and mint; toss well. Divide the noodle salad among 4 pasta bowls.

Garnish with the coriander leaves.

NOTE Also delicious is *Com Tam,* rice combined with just the pork mixture and the dressing, then seasoned with scallion oil and roasted rice powder.

Yield: 4 servings

CHICKEN AND CELLOPHANE NOODLE SOUP

As a young girl, I used to love going to the market on Saturdays with my mother. I was fascinated by the goings-on at the marketplace itself, but, more important, I knew we would stop at our favorite noodle shop to have a soothing bowl of *Mien Ga* for lunch. And to my mother, a meal with *Mien Ga* is never complete without a side dish of *Goi Ga,* a shredded chicken and cabbage salad and a bowl of spicy *Nuoc Cham.*

■ ■ ■ ■ ■ ■ ■ ■ ■ ■ ■ ■

8 *ounces cellophane (bean thread)*
    noodles
2 *tablespoons preserved vegetables* (tan
    xai, *page 233*)
2 *quarts chicken broth*
2 *chicken breasts, halved and boned*
8 *ounces chicken giblets*
2 *ounces fresh gingerroot, crushed*
¼ *cup* nuoc mam (*Vietnamese fish sauce*)
3 *scallions, thinly sliced*
2 *tablespoons shredded coriander*
    Freshly ground black pepper

In separate bowls, soak the cellophane noodles and preserved vegetables in warm water for 30 minutes. Drain; cut the noodles into 4-inch lengths with scissors. Squeeze the preserved vegetables to extract most of the soaking liquid. Set aside.

In a large pot, bring the chicken broth to a boil. Add the chicken breasts, giblets and ginger. As soon as the broth returns to a boil, reduce the heat to moderately low and simmer for 10 minutes. Skim off all of the residue that rises on the surface.

Remove the giblets and chicken breasts. Set aside. Remove the ginger and discard. Stir the fish sauce and the preserved vegetables into the broth. Thinly slice the giblets and shred the chicken meat by hand.

Bring the broth back to a boil. Add the cellophane noodles and cook gently for 1 minute.

To serve, remove the cellophane noodles from the broth and divide evenly among 4 large soup bowls. Top each bowl with the shredded chicken and the sliced giblets. Ladle boiling broth over all. Sprinkle with scallions, coriander and freshly ground black pepper. Serve at once as a single-dish meal, or in smaller portions as a first course.

Yield: 4 servings

SAIGON-STYLE NOODLE SOUP
HU TIEU

This so-called noodle soup is actually a "dry" noodle dish with a broth served on the side. *Hu Tieu* is a close adaptation of a popular Cambodian noodle dish; it is sometimes listed on menus in southern Vietnamese restaurants as *Hu Tieu Nam Vang,* or Cambodian-style noodles, using flat egg noodles instead of rice noodles.

Customarily, diners help themselves first to the noodles, then to a little of the broth served on the side.

■ ■ ■ ■ ■ ■ ■ ■ ■

Crisp-fried shallots (page 226)
1 pound ¼-inch-wide dried rice sticks
   (banh pho)
3 tablespoons preserved vegetables (tan
   xai, page 233)
4 chicken thighs (about 8 ounces)
8 raw medium shrimp in the shell
   (about 8 ounces)
4¼ cups chicken broth
4 pork cutlets (about 8 ounces)
8 garlic cloves, minced
1 cup sliced scallion greens
1 tablespoon nuoc mam (Vietnamese
   fish sauce)
3 tablespoons soy sauce
2 teaspoons sugar
1 teaspoon Oriental sesame oil
4 cups fresh bean sprouts
4 scallions, cut into 2-inch lengths
2 tablespoons shredded coriander
Freshly ground black pepper

Prepare the crisp-fried shallots. Reserve ½ cup plus 1 tablespoon of the oil. Soak the rice sticks and preserved vegetables separately in warm water for 30 minutes. Drain.

Combine 1 tablespoon of the preserved vegetables, the chicken thighs, shrimp, and the chicken broth in a soup pot and bring to a boil. Reduce the heat and simmer for 10 minutes. Remove the shrimp and refresh under cold water. Set aside.

Continue to simmer the broth until the chicken thighs are cooked, 10 to 15 minutes longer. Remove the chicken pieces and refresh under cold water. Set aside. Cover the soup pot and set aside.

Meanwhile, in a skillet, heat 1 tablespoon of the oil over moderate heat. Add the pork cutlets and cook on both sides until browned, about 6 minutes. Remove and allow to cool. Thinly slice the pork. Remove the chicken meat from the bones and thinly slice. Peel the shrimp and halve lengthwise. Set aside.

Heat the remaining ¼ cup oil in a skillet. Add the garlic, the remaining 2 tablespoons preserved vegetables and the scallion greens (reserve 2 tablespoons to garnish the broth); stir-fry briefly. Add the fish sauce, soy sauce, sugar, sesame oil and ¼ cup of the soup broth and bring the mixture to a boil. Remove the sauce from the heat and set aside.

Bring 3 quarts of water to a boil in a pot. Pack the bean sprouts and scallion pieces in a strainer. Dip the strainer in the boiling water for 5 seconds. Remove and refresh under cold water. Drain. Drop the rice noodles in the boiling water. Drain immediately. Rinse with cold water to remove any excess starch. Drain again.

Divide the sauce, bean sprouts, scallions and the noodles among 4 large soup bowls. Arrange the pork, chicken and shrimp over the top. Sprinkle with the fried shallots, coriander and black pepper. Reheat the broth, then ladle into 4 small soup bowls. Sprinkle with the reserved scallion greens and a dash of sesame oil.

Before eating, toss the noodles. Serve the broth on the side.

Yield: 4 servings

RICE VERMICELLI SOUP
WITH ASSORTED MEATS AND EGGS
BUN THANG

*T*hroughout Vietnam there are restaurants that specialize in noodle dishes from all over the country. The traditional favorites are Hanoi Beef and Rice-Noodle Soup (*Pho Bac*), Saigon Soup (*Hu Tieu*), Rice Vermicelli Soup with Assorted Meats and Eggs (*Bun Thang*) and Chicken and Cellophane Noodle Soup (*Mien Ga*).

This is one of my favorite noodle soups, and judging from the reactions of others, I'm not alone. Don't let the shrimp sauce turn you away; a small amount adds just the flavor balance needed.

Cut the pork sausage into julienne. Prepare the egg pancakes and noodles. Set aside.

Heat the oil in a skillet over high heat. Add the pork and brown for 1 minute on each side. Cover the skillet and reduce the heat to moderately low. Cook for 10 to 15 minutes, until the juices run clear when pierced with a fork. Set aside to cool. Cut the roast pork into julienne; set aside.

Soak the dried shrimp in warm water to cover for 30 minutes. Drain, reserving ⅔ cup of the soaking liquid for the soup.

In a large pot, combine the chicken broth, chicken breasts, half of the soaked shrimp and the reserved shrimp liquid. Bring to a boil. Skim off the residue that forms on the surface. Reduce the heat to moderately low and simmer for 10 minutes.

Remove the chicken breasts. Set aside. Continue to simmer the broth for another 15 minutes. Remove and discard the shrimp. Stir in the fish sauce and turn off the heat.

Shred the chicken meat by hand. Mince the remaining shrimp.

Divide the cooked noodles and fresh bean sprouts among 4 large soup bowls. Arrange the chopped shrimp, roast pork, pork sausage, egg strips and shredded chicken decoratively over the noodles, keeping each ingredient separate from the others. Just before serving, bring the broth to a boil. Ladle the boiling broth into the bowls. Sprinkle with the scallions, coriander and black pepper.

Serve the chiles, shrimp sauce and lime wedges at the table. Each diner can use them as seasoning as desired.

Yield: 4 servings

Steamed Rolled Ravioli, Bean Sprouts, Nuoc Cham *and Vietnamese Pork Sausage*

Egg Noodle Soup with Braised Duck

STEAMED ROLLED RAVIOLI
B A N H   C U O N

Traditionally, these silky ravioli are served for breakfast, but they can also be served as an appetizer or as a one-dish meal.

Paper-thin rice-noodle crêpes are filled with a mixture of ground pork and dried mushrooms, then rolled up as an egg roll. It is easier to make all of the rice crêpes first, and then fill them once they have cooled off. The filled ravioli can be prepared half a day in advance and served at room temperature or reheated in a steamer before serving.

Use store-bought Vietnamese pork sausage (gio, available at Vietnamese markets) for convenience or, if you prefer making your own, follow the instructions on page 116. Prepare the recipe 1 day in advance so its flavor improves with mellowing.

■ ■ ■ ■ ■ ■ ■ ■ ■ ■ ■

Accompaniments
Nuoc Cham (page 212)
Crisp-fried shallots (page 226)
1 pound fresh bean sprouts
½ cup shredded mint
½ cup shredded coriander
8 ounces Vietnamese Pork Sausage (page 116)

Filling
4 dried Chinese mushrooms
1 tablespoon dried tree ear mushrooms
8 ounces ground pork
1 tablespoon nuoc mam (Vietnamese fish sauce)
¼ teaspoon sugar
Freshly ground black pepper
2 garlic cloves, minced
2 tablespoons vegetable oil
1 small onion, chopped
2 shallots, minced
1 recipe rice-noodle crêpes (banh uot, page 224)

Prepare the *Nuoc Cham* and crisp-fried shallots. Set aside. Plunge the bean sprouts into boiling water in a pot for 30 seconds, then refresh in cold water. Drain. Combine the blanched bean sprouts with the shredded mint and coriander in a bowl. Cover and refrigerate. Cut the Vietnamese pork sausage into strips, 2½ by ½ by ¼ inch thick.

Soak the two types of mushrooms separately in hot water for 30 minutes. Drain; remove and discard the stems from the Chinese mushrooms. Mince both types of mushrooms. Set aside.

Combine the pork with the fish sauce, sugar, black pepper and half of the garlic in a bowl. Marinate for 30 minutes.

Heat the oil in a skillet over moderate heat. Add the onion, shallots and remaining garlic and sauté until fragrant, about 30 seconds. Add the pork and stir, breaking up the lumps. Cook until lightly browned, about 5 minutes. Add the mushrooms and stir-fry for a few more minutes. Remove from the heat and set aside to cool. (Everything can be prepared one day ahead up to this point. Cover and refrigerate until needed.)

Prepare the rice-noodle crêpes.

To fill, scatter 1 tablespoon of the filling in a wide vertical line about 1½ inches away from the edges of the crêpe. Fold both sides over to enclose the filling. Roll up the crêpe to make a neat cylinder. Fill all of the crêpes in this manner. Place the rolls on a dish.

You may serve the filled ravioli at room temperature or hot from a steamer.

To reheat, pour 1 inch of water into a wok or wide pot. Place a steamer rack or bamboo steamer over the water. Arrange the ravioli in a single layer on the rack. Cover and steam for 5 minutes. (Be careful—more steaming will make them mushy.)

To serve, place 5 or 6 ravioli on each plate. Top with ¼ cup blanched bean sprouts, a few strips of pork sausage and a sprinkling of crisp-fried shallots. Sprinkle generously with *Nuoc Cham*.

Yield: 4 to 6 servings (28 ravioli)

EGG NOODLE SOUP WITH BRAISED DUCK

MI VIT TIEM

A Chinese import, this dish is very popular in southern Vietnam. In Saigon's *Cho Lon* (Main Market), where numerous Chinese immigrants dwell, this specialty was offered at every corner.

Only the duck legs are used in the recipe; they can be purchased in Asian butcher shops. The braised duck can be prepared 1 day in advance and then reheated just before serving.

■ ■ ■ ■ ■ ■ ■ ■ ■ ■ ■

Marinade
2 ounces rock sugar (page 234), or 2
   tablespoons granulated sugar
¼ cup soy sauce
1 teaspoon salt
3 star anise
3 whole cloves
1 cinnamon stick
1 ounce of gingerroot, crushed
2 red chile peppers, sliced
   Dried peel from 2 oranges
½ teaspoon black peppercorns, crushed
½ teaspoon cumin seed
½ teaspoon coriander seed, crushed
½ teaspoon fennel seed or aniseed
½ teaspoon five-spice powder

Duck and soup
4 duck legs (about 2 pounds)
   Vegetable oil, for deep-frying
8 dried Chinese mushrooms
2 quarts chicken broth
2 tablespoons nuoc mam (*Vietnamese
   fish sauce*)
1 pound fresh ¼-inch-wide egg noodles
1 pound Chinese broccoli or broccoli
   rabe, cut into 2-inch sections and
   blanched
4 scallions, cut into 2-inch sections and
   blanched
   Freshly ground black pepper
   Coriander sprigs, for garnish
   Hot chile sauce (tuong ot *or* sriracha
   sauce), optional

If using rock sugar, pound or crush it to a fine powder. Place all of the marinade ingredients in a Dutch oven. Add 1 cup of water and bring the mixture to a boil. Reduce the heat and simmer for 15 minutes. Let cool slightly. Add the duck legs and turn to coat evenly. Set aside to marinate for at least 2 hours or overnight, turning occasionally

Drain the duck legs. Pour 1 inch of water into a wok or wide pot. Place a steamer rack or bamboo steamer over the water. Arrange the duck legs in a single layer on the rack. Cover and steam over high heat for 15 minutes. Remove and let cool thoroughly. Pat the duck legs dry with paper towels.

Soak the Chinese mushrooms in hot water for 30 minutes. Drain and remove the stems. Cut the caps in half if they are large.

In a wok or deep-fryer, heat 3 inches of oil to 360°F. Add 2 duck legs at a time and deep-fry until golden brown, about 5 minutes. Drain on paper towels. Fry the remaining duck legs.

In a soup pot, combine the duck legs, chicken broth, fish sauce and Chinese mushrooms. Bring to a boil. Skim the froth as it rises to the surface. Reduce the heat and simmer the mixture for about 30 minutes, or until the duck legs are tender. Remove the duck legs and keep them warm. Cover the soup and set aside.

Have a large bowl of cold water next to the pot of boiling water. Pack one fourth of the egg noodles in a shallow strainer and dip it in the boiling water for about 2 minutes; stir the noodles with a pair of chopsticks. Immediately dip the noodles in the bowl of cold water to stop the cooking. Drain briefly and transfer the noodles to an individual soup bowl. Repeat with the remaining egg noodles.

Bring the soup to a rolling boil. Meanwhile, divide the broccoli and scallions among the bowls of noodles. With a cleaver, hack each duck leg into bite-size morsels. Transfer the duck leg to each mound of noodles. Ladle the boiling broth and mushroom caps over all to cover. Sprinkle with black pepper and garnish with the coriander sprigs.

To serve, dip the duck pieces in the chile sauce, if desired.

Yield: 4 servings

Cold Rice Vermicelli with Salad and Stir-Fried Beef

Cold Rice Noodles with Shrimp

COLD RICE NOODLES WITH SHRIMP

PHO KHO TOM

*T*his noodle dish was sold by early-morning street vendors when I was a child, and I will never forget running out in the street with my own bowl to buy the first meal of the day. The vendor would fill my bowl and my sister's with this hearty noodle dish, and then we would consume it with gusto before we set off for school.

This dish will be most appreciated on hot summer days. If you are fortunate enough to find Chinese chive buds, cut them into 2-inch lengths and blanch them before adding to the noodles.

■　■　■　■　■　■　■　■　■

2 egg pancakes (page 219), cut into thin strips
½ cup roasted peanuts (page 220), ground
8 ounces dried rice sticks (banh pho, page 222)
1 fresh red chile pepper, seeded and minced
2 tablespoons sugar
¼ cup rice vinegar or distilled white vinegar
¼ cup plus 2 teaspoons nuoc mam (Vietnamese fish sauce)
3 large garlic cloves, minced
1 pound raw medium shrimp, peeled, deveined and halved lengthwise
Freshly ground black pepper
3 cups fresh bean sprouts
1 tablespoon peanut oil
2 shallots, thinly sliced
4 scallions, thinly sliced
Coriander sprigs, for garnish

Prepare the egg pancakes, roasted peanuts and dried rice sticks as instructed. Set aside.

In a bowl, combine the chile, sugar, vinegar, ¼ cup of the fish sauce and half of the garlic. Stir to blend. Set the dressing aside.

In another bowl, combine the shrimp, the remaining 2 teaspoons fish sauce, the remaining garlic and black pepper to taste. Marinate for 30 minutes.

Blanch the bean sprouts in a pot of boiling water and drain immediately. Refresh the sprouts under cold running water. Drain thoroughly.

Heat the oil in a wok or large skillet over high heat. Add the shallots and stir-fry until lightly browned. Add the shrimp mixture and cook briefly until the shrimp turn pink and curl, about 1 minute. Add the scallions and cook for 1 minute. Remove from the heat.

Place the noodles, bean sprouts, shrimp, half of the egg strips and ground peanuts in a large bowl. Drizzle the dressing over the mixture; toss well.

Transfer the noodle salad to 4 pasta bowls. Garnish with the coriander and the remaining egg strips.

Yield: 4 servings

COLD RICE VERMICELLI
WITH SALAD AND STIR-FRIED BEEF

BUN BO

*T*his southern single-dish meal is a favorite of mine; it is also the one dish that I like to introduce to friends the very first time they experience Vietnamese food. After this initiation, they are usually eager to try other Vietnamese dishes.

There is no easier or better way to entertain in the summer than with this delicious warm pasta salad. Except for the sautéed beef, which should be hot, everything else is prepared ahead of time and assembled in individual bowls. The final step is completed rapidly by stir-frying the meat and then pouring it over the noodle-salad mixture.

■ ■ ■ ■ ■ ■ ■ ■ ■ ■ ■

1 *pound thin rice vermicelli* (bun, *page 223*), *or 4 bundles Japanese alimentary paste noodles* (somen, *page 223*)
2 *recipes of* Nuoc Cham *with Carrot and Daikon (page 212)*
⅔ *cup roasted peanuts (page 220), ground*
3 *stalks fresh lemon grass, or 3 tablespoons dried lemon grass*
1½ *pounds lean beef chuck or top round*
2 *tablespoons* nuoc mam *(Vietnamese fish sauce)*
6 *garlic cloves, chopped*
3 *teaspoons curry powder*
   Freshly ground black pepper
8 *leaves of soft lettuce, thinly shredded*
½ *cup thinly shredded mint leaves*
1 *small cucumber, peeled, seeded and finely shredded*
1 *cup fresh bean sprouts*
3 *tablespoons peanut oil*
2 *small onions, thinly sliced*
   Coriander leaves, for garnish

Prepare the noodles, *Nuoc Cham* and roasted peanuts. Set aside.

If you are using fresh lemon grass, discard the outer leaves and upper half of the stalk. Cut the stalk into thin slices and finely chop. If you are using dried lemon grass, soak it in warm water for 1 hour. Drain and finely chop.

Cut the beef against the grain into thin 2 by 2-inch slices.

Combine the beef with the fish sauce, half of the garlic, 1 teaspoon of the curry powder and black pepper to taste in a bowl. Marinate for 30 minutes.

Combine the shredded lettuce, mint, cucumber and bean sprouts in a large bowl and toss well. Divide the mixed vegetables evenly among 4 pasta bowls. Top the vegetables with the cooked noodles; cover and refrigerate until ready to serve.

Heat the oil in a wok or large skillet. Add the remaining garlic and stir-fry until fragrant. Add the onions, lemon grass and the remaining 2 teaspoons curry powder; stir-fry until the onions are translucent, about 2 minutes. Add the beef to the wok and stir-fry over high heat until the beef is browned, about 1 minute. Divide the beef evenly among the 4 bowls of noodles. Top each bowl with ground roasted peanuts. Garnish with coriander leaves.

Pass the *Nuoc Cham* at the table. Diners should season their bowl of noodles with a generous amount of *Nuoc Cham* and then toss everything well before eating.

Yield: 4 servings

STIR-FRIED RICE NOODLES
WITH BEEF AND VEGETABLES

PHO XAO

*F*resh rice noodles are used for this dish, but 1 pound of dried rice sticks *(banh pho)* may be substituted. Toss the noodles with some oil just after boiling to prevent sticking, and then stir-fry as directed in the recipe.

Ideally, to sear both the noodles and the beef, a heavy cast-iron skillet should be used. Cast iron sears extremely well when hot, but it has to be smoking hot before the food is added. Be sure the ventilation fan is on.

Bok choy may be replaced by Chinese broccoli, cut into 2-inch sections, or simply use fresh spinach.

■ ■ ■ ■ ■ ■ ■ ■ ■ ■ ■ ■

1 *recipe rice-noodle crêpes (banh uot, page 224), or 2 pounds commercial fresh flat rice-noodle sheets*
 Nuoc Cham *(page 212)*
8 *ounces beef chuck or rump roast*
1 *tablespoon plus 2 teaspoons* nuoc mam *(Vietnamese fish sauce)*
¼ *teaspoon sugar*
 Freshly ground black pepper
1 *medium onion, cut into eighths and separated into segments*
4 *large bok choy leaves, cut into 2 by 1-inch strips*
4 *ounces snow peas, trimmed*
1 *medium tomato, cut into 8 wedges*
2 *scallions, trimmed and cut into 2-inch sections*
1 *tablespoon soy sauce*
3 *tablespoons oyster sauce*
5 *tablespoons peanut oil*
8 *garlic cloves, minced (about 2 tablespoons)*
 Fresh coriander sprigs, for garnish
 Fresh red chile peppers, thinly sliced

If preparing your own fresh rice-noodle sheets, proceed as instructed. Cut the sheets into ¾-inch-wide strips. Set aside. Prepare the *Nuoc Cham.* Set aside.

Slice the beef across the grain as thin as possible. Cut the slices into 2 by 1-inch strips. Combine the beef with 2 teaspoons of the fish sauce, the sugar and pepper to taste. Set aside.

Arrange the vegetables on a large platter to facilitate stir-frying. Combine the remaining 1 tablespoon fish sauce, the soy sauce and the oyster sauce in a small bowl. Set aside.

Heat a wok or large cast-iron skillet over high heat until smoking hot. Add 2 tablespoons of the peanut oil and half of the garlic; stir-fry until fragrant. Add the noodles and toss quickly until heated through, about 1 minute. Transfer the noodles to a large platter; keep warm.

In the following step it is very important that while sautéing the beef the heat be kept very high. Tilt the wok frequently into the area of highest heat to "flambé," or sear, the meat instantly; the smokier the beef, the better. If using an electric stove, turn the burner to the highest setting and sauté the beef in two batches.

Heat 1 tablespoon of the oil. When the oil is smoking, add the remaining garlic and stir-fry until aromatic. Add the beef and stir-fry for 30 seconds, until the beef is slightly pink. Remove the beef to a platter.

Heat the remaining 2 tablespoons oil. Add the onion and stir-fry until translucent and fragrant. Add the bok choy and snow peas and toss until tender but still crisp, about 2 minutes. Add the tomato, scallions and sauce mixture; toss well.

Return the beef and noodles to the wok. Stir to combine and coat the noodles and meat with the sauce. Transfer to a heated platter.

Garnish with coriander sprigs. Sprinkle with freshly ground black pepper. Serve, passing *Nuoc Cham* and chiles.

NOTE If you are fortunate enough to find Chinese chive buds, cut them into 2-inch lengths, then add to the stir-fry for more authenticity.

Yield: 4 to 6 servings

STIR-FRIED CELLOPHANE NOODLES WITH CRABMEAT

MIEN XAO CUA

*P*opular among the Vietnamese, this dish is very quick and easy to prepare. It can be served as an appetizer or as part of a meal.

■ ■ ■ ■ ■ ■ ■ ■ ■ ■ ■

4 *ounces cellophane (bean thread)*
  noodles
3 *tablespoons vegetable oil*
4 *shallots, thinly sliced*
4 *garlic cloves, chopped*
8 *ounces lump crabmeat, picked over*
½ *cup plus 2 tablespoons chicken broth*
1 *tablespoon* nuoc mam *(Vietnamese*
  fish sauce)
2 *scallions, thinly sliced*
1 *tablespoon shredded coriander*
  Freshly ground black pepper

Soak the cellophane noodles in warm water for 30 minutes. Drain and cut into 3-inch lengths.

Heat the oil in a wok or skillet over high heat. Add the shallots and garlic and sauté until the edges begin to brown.

Add the crabmeat and stir-fry for 30 seconds. Add the cellophane noodles; stir-fry for 1 minute, or until the noodles are heated through. Stir in the chicken broth and fish sauce and toss to combine. Cook until the noodles absorb most of the liquid. Add the scallions and remove from the heat.

Transfer to a serving platter. Garnish with the coriander and sprinkle with black pepper. Serve immediately.

Yield: 4 servings

CRAB DUMPLING AND RICE VERMICELLI SOUP

BUN RIEU

*I*n Vietnam, tiny freshwater crabs called *cua roc* are used in this recipe. First, they are pounded, unshelled, to a pulp and diluted with water. Then the mixture is rubbed through a fine sieve to produce a crab liquor that is essential to this soup. Finally, crab roe is added to give a pungent flavor.

This version of *Bun Rieu* can be easily made with ingredients that are readily available.

■ ■ ■ ■ ■ ■ ■ ■ ■ ■ ■ ■

*1 pound thin rice vermicelli (*bun, *page 223), or 4 bundles of Japanese alimentary paste noodles (*somen, *page 223)*
½ cup dried shrimp
2 cups warm water
8 ounces fresh or canned lump crabmeat, picked over and drained
*1 teaspoon shrimp sauce (*mam ruoc, *page 234)*
5 eggs, lightly beaten
Freshly ground black pepper
4 tablespoons vegetable oil
4 shallots, thinly sliced
4 cloves garlic, finely chopped
2 scallions, finely sliced
2 tablespoons tomato paste
*1 teaspoon chile paste (*tuong ot tuoi)
4 plum tomatoes, quartered
4 cups chicken broth or water
4 tablespoons nuoc mam *(Vietnamese fish sauce)*
1 teaspoon sugar
4 large Boston lettuce leaves, shredded
2 cups fresh bean sprouts
2 scallions, cut into 2-inch sections, shredded
½ cup mint leaves, shredded, for garnish
Coriander sprigs for garnish
1 lemon, quartered
4 chile peppers, thinly sliced
Additional shrimp sauce

Prepare the noodles. Set aside.

Soak the dried shrimp in 2 cups of warm water for 30 minutes. Drain and reserve the soaking liquid.

Using a food processor or a mortar and pestle, process or pound the shrimp until very fine. In a bowl, beat the shrimp, crabmeat, shrimp sauce, and black pepper into the eggs. Refrigerate.

In a large soup pot, heat the oil and sauté the shallots, garlic and scallions until fragrant. Add the tomato paste and chile paste; fry for 1 minute. Add the tomatoes; cook for 1 minute longer. Add the reserved soaking liquid from the shrimp, the broth, fish sauce and sugar. Bring the soup to a boil, then reduce the heat until the soup is barely simmering. Slide the crabmeat-egg mixture gently into the simmering soup. Cover the pot and simmer gently for 5 minutes, or until the mixture is slightly firm and floats on the surface. Sprinkle freshly ground black pepper over the soup.

Divide the noodles among 4 soup bowls and top each with the shredded lettuce, a few bean sprouts and the shredded scallions. Ladle the soup and the crabmeat-egg mixture over the noodles and vegetables.

Garnish with the shredded mint and coriander sprigs. Serve with the lemon wedges, chile peppers, and additional shrimp sause on the side.

Yield: 4 servings

$\mathscr{V}$EGETARIAN $\mathscr{D}$ISHES

Top: a selection of Vietnamese vegetables; bottom: Vegetarian Stir-Fry

VEGETARIAN STIR-FRY
LA HAN CHAY

This delicious stir-fry is a whole-some meal in itself.

■ ■ ■ ■ ■ ■ ■ ■ ■ ■ ■

2 *ounces cellophane (bean thread)*
   noodles
1 *tablespoon dried tree ear mushrooms*
4 *dried Chinese mushrooms*
20 *tiger lily buds*
2 *squares (8 ounces) semisoft bean curd*
   (tofu)
3 *tablespoons vegetable oil*
1 *leek, white part only, thinly sliced*
1 *small head cauliflower, broken into*
   small florets, blanched
1 *large carrot, thinly sliced*
1 *cup string beans, shredded*
½ *cup fresh or canned bamboo shoots,*
   thinly shredded
1 *cup straw mushrooms, drained*
¼ *cup soy sauce*
1 *teaspoon salt*
¼ *cup chicken broth or water*
2 *teaspoons sugar*
1 *teaspoon Oriental sesame oil*
   (optional)
   Freshly ground black pepper
   (optional)

Soak the noodles in warm water and the mushrooms and lily buds in hot water for 30 minutes. Drain. Cut the noodles into 3-inch lengths. Squeeze the tree ears until dry. Cut the Chinese mushroom caps into thin strips; discard the stems of both mushrooms. Cut away and discard the hard ends of the lily buds and tie a knot in the center of each. Cut each square of bean curd vertically into 4 equal pieces; drain thoroughly on paper towels.

Heat the oil in a wok or large skillet over moderately high heat. Brown the bean curd pieces on both sides, about 5 minutes. Remove and drain on paper towels. Cut the fried bean curd into thin strips.

Reheat the oil. Add the leek and stir-fry for 15 seconds. Add the cauliflower and carrot and stir-fry for 1 minute. Add the string beans and bamboo shoots and stir-fry for 1 minute. Add all the mushrooms, noodles, lily buds and bean curd and stir-fry for 1 minute. Stir in the soy sauce, salt, broth, sugar and sesame oil. Stir and toss until piping hot and well coated with sauce, about 2 minutes.

Serve hot, sprinkled with black pepper, if desired.

Yield: 4 to 6 servings

VEGETABLE PLATTER

DIA RAU SONG

*V*ietnamese meals include an abundance of fresh lettuce, herbs, unripe fruits and raw vegetables. These are arranged attractively on a platter and are used for wrapping cooked foods at the table, usually dipped in *Nuoc Cham* and eaten out of hand.

The following herbs, both very important to the Vietnamese, would be authentic additions to the Vegetable Platter: One is the "saw leaf herb" (*Eryngium foetidum,* or *ngo gai* in Vietnamese), a coriander relative. The other is polygonum (*P. pulchrum* or *rau ram* in Vietnamese), with pinkish stems, pointed green leaves and purplish markings. They can be found occasionally at Southeast Asian markets. If you have access to unripe mango, banana, papaya or apple and star fruit (carambola), add them to the platter. You may select or substitute the ingredients according to availability and personal taste.

■ ■ ■ ■ ■ ■ ■ ■ ■ ■

1 *large head of Boston or other soft lettuce, separated into individual leaves*
1 *bunch of scallions, cut into 2-inch lengths*
1 *cup coriander leaves*
1 *cup mint leaves*
1 *cup fresh Asian or regular basil leaves*
1 *cucumber, peeled in alternating strips, halved lengthwise and sliced thinly crosswise*
4 *ounces fresh bean sprouts*
   Pickled shallots (page 233, optional)

On a large platter, decoratively arrange all of the ingredients in separate groups. Use in recipes where required.

Yield: 4 to 6 servings

VEGETABLE SALAD

GOI CHAY

*T*his special vegetable dish features a blending of crunchy textures. It can be served with shrimp chips, glutinous rice or plain rice. If daikon is not available, substitute turnip.

■ ■ ■ ■ ■ ■ ■ ■ ■ ■

2 *egg pancakes (page 219), cut into thin strips*
1 *tablespoon toasted sesame seeds (page 225), ground*
1 *tablespoon roasted peanuts (page 220), ground*
2 *garlic cloves, minced*
1½ *teaspoons salt*
1½ *tablespoons sugar*
2 *tablespoons rice vinegar*
2 *tablespoons soy sauce*
2 *tablespoons Oriental sesame oil*
2 *ounces cellophane (bean thread) noodles*
4 *dried Chinese mushrooms*
1 *tablespoon dried tree ear mushrooms*
4 *ounces snow peas*
2 *ounces fresh or canned bamboo shoots*
1 *small carrot, peeled*
1 *small daikon, peeled*
1 *small cucumber, peeled and seeded*
1 *small green bell pepper*
1 *small red bell pepper*
2 *celery ribs*
1 *small red onion*
  Freshly ground black pepper
  Coriander sprigs, for garnish

Prepare the egg pancakes, toasted sesame seeds and roasted peanuts. Set aside.

Combine the garlic, ½ teaspoon of the salt, the sugar, vinegar, soy sauce and sesame oil in a small bowl. Stir to blend. Set the sauce aside.

Soak the cellophane noodles in warm water and the mushrooms in hot water for 30 minutes. Drain. Remove and discard the mushroom stems. Cut the mushroom caps into thin strips. Cut the noodles into 2-inch lengths.

Cut the snow peas and bamboo shoots into thin strips. Bring a pot of salted water to a boil. Immerse both vegetables and the noodles for 30 seconds; drain immediately. Refresh with cold water. Drain and dry with paper towels. Set aside.

Cut the carrot, daikon, cucumber, bell peppers, celery and red onion into thin strips and combine in a colander. Sprinkle the remaining 1 teaspoon salt over the vegetables, toss well and let stand for 30 minutes in the sink. Rinse the salt off the vegetables with cold water. Squeeze the vegetables between your hands in small batches to remove all excess liquid. Squeeze again, using paper towels (it is important that the vegetables be completely dry to ensure their crunchiness).

Combine all of the shredded vegetables with the blanched vegetables in a large salad bowl. Drizzle the sauce over the mixture. Toss well to combine.

Transfer the salad to a serving platter; sprinkle the ground nuts and black pepper over the top. Garnish with the egg strips and coriander sprigs.

Yield: 4 to 6 servings

CRISP-FRIED BEAN CURD
IN TOMATO SAUCE
DAU PHU SOT CA CHUA

This is one of the most sophisticated and tasty bean curd dishes ever invented. Some Vietnamese cooks like to add fresh bacon for extra flavor, but I find it more delicate without.

■ ■ ■ ■ ■ ■ ■ ■ ■ ■ ■

Nuoc Cham *(page 212)*
1 *pound firm bean curd (tofu)*
Peanut oil, for frying
4 *shallots, thinly sliced*
4 *garlic cloves, thinly sliced*
4 *large ripe tomatoes (about 1½ pounds), cored, peeled, seeded and diced*
2 *tablespoons* nuoc mam *(Vietnamese fish sauce)*
1 *teaspoon sugar*
½ *cup chicken broth or water*
2 *scallions, thinly sliced*
2 *tablespoons shredded coriander Freshly ground black pepper*

Prepare the *Nuoc Cham.* Set aside.

Cut the bean curd into 1-inch cubes. Drain on a double thickness of paper towels.

Pour ½ inch of oil in a skillet and set over moderate heat. Add the bean curd cubes, without crowding, and gently fry until crisp and golden brown on both sides, about 8 minutes. Remove the bean curd with a slotted spoon and drain on paper towels.

Remove all but 2 tablespoons of oil from the pan. Heat the oil over moderate heat. Add the shallots and garlic and fry until fragrant, about 1 minute. Add the tomatoes, fish sauce and sugar and cook for 1 minute. Reduce the heat to low and simmer for 15 minutes.

Add the chicken broth and bring the mixture to a boil. Return the bean curd to the pan and toss to coat evenly with the sauce. Reduce the heat to low and simmer for 5 minutes. Stir in the scallions and coriander. Transfer to a warm serving platter.

Sprinkle with black pepper to taste and serve with plain rice and *Nuoc Cham.*

NOTE For a much simpler, but no less delicious dish, substitute *Nuoc Cham* for the tomato sauce. The spiciness and tang of *Nuoc Cham* cuts the richness of the fried bean curd.

Yield: 4 servings

BRAISED BEAN CURD
DAU PHU KHO

*F*or a simple and delicious meal, serve this dish with a soup or vegetable.

■ ■ ■ ■ ■ ■ ■ ■ ■ ■ ■

1 *pound firm bean curd (tofu)*
  Vegetable oil, for deep-frying
2 *tablespoons soybean sauce (tuong,*
    page 234)
1 *tablespoon sugar*
1 *cup chicken broth or water*
¼ *teaspoon freshly ground black pepper*
1 *tablespoon Oriental sesame oil*
4 *garlic cloves, minced*

Cut the bean curd into 1-inch cubes. Drain on a double thickness of paper towels.

Pour 1 inch of oil in a skillet and set over moderately high heat. Fry the bean curd cubes, without crowding, until browned on all sides, about 8 minutes, or until crisp and golden brown. Remove the bean curd with a slotted spoon and drain on paper towels.

Combine the soybean sauce, sugar, chicken broth and black pepper in a small bowl. Stir to blend. Set the sauce aside.

Heat the sesame oil in a small saucepan. When the oil is hot, add the garlic and fry until fragrant. Stir in the sauce and bring to a boil. Add the bean curd; cover the pan and simmer over low heat, stirring occasionally, for 15 to 20 minutes.

Serve over rice, bread or noodles.

Yield: 2 servings

STUFFED TOMATOES
CA CHUA NHOI THIT

$\mathcal{T}$his colorful and tasty family-style dish is also very easy to make.

■ ■ ■ ■ ■ ■ ■ ■ ■ ■ ■

Nuoc Cham (*page 212*)
Sauce
⅓ *cup chicken broth or water*
1 *tablespoon* nuoc mam (*Vietnamese fish sauce*)
¼ *cup oyster sauce*
1 *tablespoon sugar*
1 *teaspoon tomato paste*
Tomatoes and filling
4 *large tomatoes*
2 *dried Chinese mushrooms*
1½ *teaspoons dried tree ear mushrooms*
½ *ounce cellophane (bean thread) noodles*
8 *ounces ground pork*
4 *garlic cloves, chopped*
2 *shallots, thinly sliced*
2 *scallions, thinly sliced*
¼ *teaspoon sugar*
2 *teaspoons* nuoc mam (*Vietnamese fish sauce*)
1 *egg, lightly beaten*
2 *tablespoons peanut oil*
Freshly ground black pepper

Prepare the *Nuoc Cham*. Set aside.

Combine all of the sauce ingredients in a small bowl.

Cut off the stem end of each tomato. Using a spoon, gently scoop out the pulp. Discard the tops and pulp. Dry the insides of the tomatoes with paper towels.

Soak the mushrooms in hot water and the noodles in warm water for 30 minutes. Drain well. Squeeze out the excess water from the mushrooms. Cut off the stems and discard. Mince the caps. Coarsely chop the noodles.

In a mixing bowl, combine the chopped mushrooms and noodles with the pork, half of the garlic, the shallots, scallions, sugar, fish sauce and egg. Blend with your hands; set aside to marinate for 30 minutes.

Stuff the pork mixture into the tomatoes, pressing firmly. Smooth the top into a mounded dome.

Heat the oil in a wok or skillet over moderate heat. Place the stuffed tomatoes, stuffing side down, in the hot oil. Cover the wok and fry for 5 minutes. Using a large spatula, gently turn the tomatoes (try not to break the skins), meat side up, and cook for 3 minutes longer.

Make a small space in the center of the wok and add the reserved garlic; fry until fragrant. Stir the sauce mixture and pour into the wok. Bring the sauce to a quick boil. Reduce the heat to low and simmer, covered, for 15 minutes, turning the tomatoes frequently to coat with the sauce.

The tomatoes are ready when the stuffing has absorbed half of the sauce and the tomatoes are nicely glazed. Transfer to a serving platter and sprinkle with black pepper.

Serve with plain rice and *Nuoc Cham* as part of a family meal.

Yield: 4 servings

STUFFED CABBAGE ROLLS

SU NHOI THIT HEO

This is a perfect buffet dish: It can be prepared 1 day ahead, then reheated when needed.

For a delicious soup, cook stuffed cabbage rolls in seasoned chicken broth.

■ ■ ■ ■ ■ ■ ■ ■ ■ ■

Nuoc Cham *(page 212)*
1 ounce cellophane *(bean thread)*
    noodles
3 *large dried Chinese mushrooms*
6 *dried tiger lily buds*
Filling
8 *ounces ground pork*
½ *small onion, minced*
4 *garlic cloves, minced*
2 *tablespoons* nuoc mam *(Vietnamese*
    fish sauce)
Freshly ground black pepper
Cabbage and sauce
16 *outer leaves of a white cabbage*
16 *scallion stems (green part only)*
2 *tablespoons vegetable oil*
1 *small onion, minced*
4 *garlic cloves, minced*
3 *large ripe tomatoes, cored, seeded and*
    diced
½ *teaspoon salt*
1 *teaspoon sugar*
2 *tablespoons* nuoc mam *(Vietnamese*
    fish sauce)
½ *cup chicken broth or water*
Freshly ground black pepper
Coriander sprigs, for garnish

Prepare the *Nuoc Cham*. Set aside.

Soak the noodles in warm water and the mushrooms and lily buds in hot water for 30 minutes. Drain. Remove and discard the mushroom stems. Trim and discard the hard ends of the lily buds. Coarsely chop these ingredients.

Make the filling: In a mixing bowl, combine the noodles, mushrooms, lily buds, pork, onion, garlic, fish sauce and black pepper to taste. Mix well. Set aside.

Prepare the cabbage: Drop the cabbage leaves in a large pot of boiling salted water and cook for 1 minute. Remove the cabbage leaves to a colander and refresh with cold water.

Drop the scallion stems in the boiling water and drain immediately. Refresh with cold water. Drain the cabbage leaves and scallion stems on paper towels.

Remove the tough stem end of each cabbage leaf.

Fill each cabbage leaf with 1 generous tablespoon of the filling mixture. Roll up the leaf to seal the filling. Tie a scallion stem around each roll to secure the leaf in place.

Heat the oil in a 4-quart saucepan over moderately high heat. Add the onion and garlic and stir-fry for 1 minute. Add the tomatoes and stir for 2 minutes. Stir in the salt, sugar, fish sauce and chicken broth. Reduce the heat and simmer for 5 minutes.

Add the cabbage rolls to the tomato sauce. Cover and simmer gently for 30 minutes, turning occasionally.

Sprinkle with black pepper and garnish with coriander sprigs.

Serve with rice and *Nuoc Cham*.

Yield: 4 to 6 servings

STIR-FRIED WATER SPINACH
WITH GARLIC

RAU MUONG XAO TOI

*T*he Vietnamese love water spinach for the interesting contrast in texture between the crunchy stems and the limp leaves when cooked. If it is not available, fresh spinach or watercress may be substituted.

■ ■ ■ ■ ■ ■ ■ ■ ■ ■

Nuoc Cham *(page 212)*
2 *pounds water spinach or regular spinach*
¼ *cup peanut oil*
8 *garlic cloves, minced*
1 *tablespoon* nuoc mam *(Vietnamese fish sauce)*
Freshly ground black pepper

Prepare the *Nuoc Cham.* Set aside.

Wash the spinach thoroughly. If using water spinach, pound the stems flat and cut into 2-inch sections. Keep the stems and leaves in separate mounds.

Heat the oil in a wok or large cast-iron skillet over high heat. Add the garlic and fry until fragrant. If using water spinach, add the stems first and stir-fry for 1 minute. Add the leaves and continue to stir until wilted. Add a splash of water if the greens seem too dry. Stir in the fish sauce. Transfer to a warm serving platter. Sprinkle with black pepper.

Serve as part of a meal, with *Nuoc Cham.*

Yield: 4 servings

VARIATION Add marinated beef or shrimp to this stir-fry to make a main-course dish. The beef or shrimp should be briefly stir-fried, then removed to a platter. Use the juices from the meat or shrimp instead of water when cooking the spinach. Add the meat or shrimp to the spinach only at the very end to heat through.

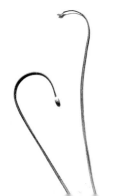

FRIED VEGETARIAN SPRING ROLLS

CHA GIO CHAY

This dish is just one example of the sophisticated cuisine Vietnamese vegetarians developed to satisfy their palate and protein requirements.

The true Buddhist vegetarian version includes neither garlic nor fish sauce and uses plain soy sauce or plum sauce for dipping, but you need not limit yourself. For more intricate flavors, try these rolls with Peanut Sauce or *Nuoc Cham* with Carrots and Daikon.

■ ■ ■ ■ ■ ■ ■ ■ ■ ■ ■

Accompaniments
Vegetable Platter (page 169)
8 ounces thin rice vermicelli (bun, page 223), or 2 bundles Japanese alimentary paste noodles (somen, page 223)
Peanut Sauce (page 211), or Nuoc Cham (page 212)

Filling
1 ounce cellophane (bean thread) noodles
1 tablespoon dried tree ear mushrooms
6 dried Chinese mushrooms
1 large carrot, finely shredded
1 large leek, white part only, chopped
6 water chestnuts, or ½ small jicama, peeled and chopped
1 pound firm bean curd (tofu), crumbled
1 cup fresh bean sprouts, coarsely chopped
6 garlic cloves, minced
3 tablespoons nuoc mam (Vietnamese fish sauce)
2 eggs
½ teaspoon freshly ground black pepper

Assembly and frying
½ cup sugar
40 small rounds of rice papers (banh trang), 6½ inches in diameter
Peanut oil, for frying

Prepare the Vegetable Platter, noodles and dipping sauce. Set aside.

Soak the noodles in warm water and the mushrooms in hot water for 30 minutes. Drain. Cut the noodles into ½-inch lengths. Remove and discard the stems from the mushrooms; squeeze to extract most of the soaking liquid. Mince all of the mushrooms.

Combine all of the filling ingredients in a large mixing bowl; blend well with your hands. Set aside.

Assemble the rolls: Fill a large bowl with 4 cups of warm water and dissolve the sugar in it.

Rice paper is quite fragile. Work with only 4 sheets at a time, keeping the remaining sheets covered with a barely damp cloth to prevent curling.

Immerse the rice paper, one sheet at a time, into the sweetened warm water. Quickly withdraw it and lay it flat on a dry towel. Do this with 4 sheets without letting them touch each other. The rice paper will become pliable within seconds.

Fold over the bottom third of each round. Put 1 generous teaspoon of filling in the center of the folded-over portion. Press it into a compact rectangle. Fold one side of the paper over the mixture, then the other side. Roll from the bottom to the top to completely enclose the filling. Continue until all of the mixture is used. (The rolls can be prepared 1 day in advance. Wrap and refrigerate.)

Fry the rolls: If possible, use 2 skillets. Pour 1 to 1½ inches of oil into each skillet and heat to 325°F. Working in batches, add some of the rolls without letting them touch, or they will stick together. Fry for 10 to 12 minutes, turning often, until golden and crisp. Remove the rolls from the oil with tongs and drain on paper towels. Keep warm in a low oven until all of the rolls are cooked.

To serve, each diner wraps a roll in a lettuce leaf along with some noodles and selected items from the Vegetable Platter and dips the package in the dipping sauce.

NOTE The fried rolls can be frozen, then thawed and reheated in a 350°F oven just to crisp and heat through.

Yield: 40 rolls

GLAZED PUMPKIN
BI NGO XAO NGOT

*T*his light, sweet vegetable dish is very popular in southern Vietnam. Easily prepared, it makes a good accompaniment to spicy dishes or just plain rice.

Look for brightly colored pumpkins with fine-grained flesh, such as sugar or cheese pumpkin, available from September through March. Butternut squash is a fine substitute, although it lacks the delicate sweet taste.

Do not discard the seeds, which are high in phosphorus. They can be dried or roasted and eaten as a snack.

■ ■ ■ ■ ■ ■ ■ ■ ■ ■ ■

2 *pounds pumpkin*
1 *tablespoon peanut oil*
6 *garlic cloves, minced*
½ *cup chicken broth or water*
1 *tablespoon* nuoc mam *(Vietnamese fish sauce)*
2 *tablespoons sugar*
   Freshly ground black pepper

Pare the rind from the pumpkin. Scoop out the seeds and fibers. Cut the flesh into 1-inch cubes.

Heat the oil in a large skillet over moderate heat. Add the garlic and fry for a few seconds without browning. Add the pumpkin and fry for 1 minute, shaking the pan to coat the cubes with oil. Add the remaining ingredients except for the black pepper and bring the mixture to a rapid boil. Cover the pan, reduce the heat to low and simmer for 20 minutes, or until the pumpkin is tender but not mushy and the sauce is reduced to about 2 tablespoons. If there is still too much liquid in the pan, reduce further by rapidly boiling the mixture, uncovered, for 1 minute.

Sprinkle with freshly ground black pepper to taste and serve at once.

Yield: 4 to 6 servings

STIR-FRIED BEAN CURD WITH LEMON GRASS ON CRISP CELLOPHANE NOODLES

DAU PHU XAO XA OT CHAY

*P*uffy noodles topped with a slightly sweet hot sauce and crisp-fried bean curd meld all the flavors in this wholesome and delicate dish.

■ ■ ■ ■ ■ ■ ■ ■ ■ ■ ■ ■

2 stalks fresh lemon grass, or 2
    tablespoons dried lemon grass
1 pound firm bean curd (tofu)
    Vegetable oil, for deep-frying
4 ounces cellophane (bean thread)
    noodles
1 can (10 ounces) straw mushrooms,
    drained with ⅔ cup of the liquid
    reserved
¼ cup hoisin sauce
2 tablespoons soy sauce
1 tablespoon plus 1 teaspoon tomato
    paste
2 red chile peppers, seeded and thinly
    sliced
2 leeks, white part only, thinly sliced
1 red bell pepper, cut into 1-inch chunks
1 green bell pepper, cut into 1-inch
    chunks
    Freshly ground black pepper
    Coriander sprigs, for garnish

If you are using fresh lemon grass, discard the outer leaves and upper half of the stalk. Cut into thin slices and finely chop. If you are using dried lemon grass, soak in warm water for 1 hour. Drain and finely chop.

Cut the bean curd into 1-inch cubes. Drain on a double thickness of paper towels.

Pour 1 inch of oil in a wok or skillet and set over moderately high heat. Fry the bean curd cubes, without crowding, until browned on all sides, about 8 minutes, or until crisp and golden brown. Remove the bean curd with a slotted spoon and drain on paper towels.

Drop about one-fourth of the cellophane noodles into the hot oil (365°F). As they puff and expand, push them down into the oil. Turn the noodles and continue to cook until the crackling stops, 15 to 20 seconds in all. Remove and drain on paper towels. Place on a serving platter and keep warm in a 200°F oven. Cook the remaining noodles in the same manner.

Combine the reserved mushroom liquid, hoisin sauce, soy sauce, tomato paste and chiles in a bowl; stir to blend. Set the sauce aside.

Remove all but 3 tablespoons of the oil from the wok. Drop in the leeks and lemon grass and stir-fry over moderately high heat for 1 minute. Add the bell peppers and stir-fry for 1 minute. Add the mushrooms and bean curd cubes and stir-fry for 1 minute longer. Stir in the sauce and bring to a boil. Stir until the sauce thickens, about 2 minutes.

Pour the mixture over the cellophane noodles. Sprinkle with black pepper and garnish with coriander sprigs.

Yield: 4 servings

VIETNAMESE POTATO PATTIES
CHA KHOAI TAY

*C*risp outside, moist inside, these potato patties are traditionally served with *Nuoc Cham* as part of a family meal. They are also ideal for cocktail parties if you use only ½ tablespoon of the mixture to form tiny pancakes. They can be cooked ahead of time, frozen, thawed and reheated in a very low oven 30 minutes prior to serving.

■ ■ ■ ■ ■ ■ ■ ■ ■ ■

Nuoc Cham *(page 212)*
2 *Idaho potatoes*
1 *teaspoon salt*
¼ *cup cornstarch*
1 *large egg, lightly beaten*
2 *scallions, minced*
½ *medium onion, minced*
3 *garlic cloves, minced*
1 *teaspoon* nuoc mam *(Vietnamese fish sauce)*
2 *teaspoons curry powder*
Freshly ground black pepper
⅔ *cup vegetable oil, for frying*

Prepare the *Nuoc Cham.* Set aside.

Peel the potatoes and remove the "eyes." Let soak in cold water to avoid discoloration; drain.

Shred the potatoes in a food processor and place in a colander. Sprinkle with the salt and mix well. Let stand in the sink for 15 minutes. Squeeze the potatoes dry and place in a mixing bowl. Add the cornstarch and mix thoroughly. Add all the remaining ingredients except the oil and mix well.

Divide the oil between two 9-inch skillets over moderately high heat. Drop the potato mixture by tablespoonfuls into the hot oil, forming individual patties about 2½ inches in diameter. The patties should not be too thick. Fry until golden brown on the bottom, about 5 minutes. Turn and cook the other side until brown and crispy. Drain on paper towels, then transfer to a serving platter.

Serve immediately with *Nuoc Cham.*

N O T E You can substitute sweet potatoes or taro root for Idaho potatoes.

Yield: 15 pancakes

VEGETABLES IN FISH SAUCE

D U A M O N

*T*his condiment is traditionally served with the New Year's Rice Cake, but it may also accompany any glutinous rice dish.

A typical combination of vegetables includes white radish (or turnip), carrots, small cucumbers, spring shallots, green papaya, whole young garlic cloves and chile peppers. In Vietnam, these vegetables are first dried in the sun for a couple of days, then covered with a fish sauce and sugar mixture and left to pickle over a period of 2 to 3 weeks.

■ ■ ■ ■ ■ ■ ■ ■ ■ ■ ■ ■

¾ *cup plus 2 tablespoons* nuoc mam
    (Vietnamese fish sauce)
¼ *cup plus 1 tablespoon sugar*
 1 *large turnip*
 2 *medium carrots*
 1 *tablespoon salt*
12 *small shallots, peeled*
12 *whole garlic cloves, peeled*
12 *fresh red chile peppers*

Preheat the oven to 200°F.

Combine the fish sauce, sugar and 1½ cups of water in a small saucepan. Bring to a boil and boil for 2 minutes over high heat. Cool thoroughly.

Peel the turnip and carrots and cut into sticks ½ by ½ by 1½ inches long. Rub the vegetables with the salt; let stand 30 minutes in the sink. Rinse under cold running water to remove all the salt. Squeeze out the water and pat dry.

Spread the turnip and carrot sticks on a baking sheet or roasting pan. Place in the oven and leave the door ajar. Let dry out for about 2 hours, turning the vegetables every 30 minutes. The vegetables are ready when they have shrunk by two-thirds. Remove from the oven and allow to cool thoroughly.

Place the dried turnip and carrot sticks in the bottom of a 1-quart Mason jar. Layer the shallots, garlic and chiles on top. Pour the fish sauce-sugar mixture over the vegetables and close the jar tightly. Refrigerate. After 2 weeks, the vegetables are ready. They can be eaten at once or refrigerated for several months.

Drain before serving.

N O T E It is very important to let the boiled liquid and the vegetables cool before combining. The cooling prevents the vegetables from fermenting.

Yield: 2 cups

STIR-FRIED LONG BEANS WITH SHRIMP

DAU DUA XAO TOM

*C*hoose skinny, firm pods with a dark green color; they are considerably tastier and crispier than the lighter green ones (which are flabby and stringy). If long beans are unavailable, substitute green beans or cauliflower.

■ ■ ■ ■ ■ ■ ■ ■ ■ ■ ■ ■

Nuoc Cham *(page 212)*
1 *pound raw shrimp, shelled, deveined and halved lengthwise*
1 *tablespoon* nuoc mam *(Vietnamese fish sauce)*
6 *garlic cloves, minced*
¾ *teaspoon sugar*
Freshly ground black pepper
4 *tablespoons vegetable oil*
1 *large onion, cut into thin slivers*
1 *pound long beans (page 229), trimmed and cut into 2-inch lengths*
¼ *cup soy sauce*
½ *teaspoon salt*
4 *scallions, cut into 2-inch lengths*

Prepare the *Nuoc Cham.* Set aside.

In a bowl, combine the shrimp, fish sauce, half of the garlic, ¼ teaspoon of the sugar and black pepper to taste. Set aside to marinate for 30 minutes.

In a wok or large skillet, heat 2 tablespoons of the oil over high heat. Add the remaining garlic and fry until fragrant. Add the marinated shrimp and toss with the garlic until the shrimp turn pink, about 1 minute. Remove to a platter.

Add the remaining 2 tablespoons oil to the wok. When hot, add the onion and stir-fry over medium heat until lightly caramelized. Add the long beans and toss with the onion for 1 minute. Stir in the soy sauce, salt, the remaining ½ teaspoon sugar and ¼ cup of water. Cook over moderately high heat for 5 minutes, or until the beans are crisp-tender. Add the shrimp and scallions to the wok; toss everything together and remove to a serving platter.

Sprinkle with black pepper. Serve with rice and *Nuoc Cham.*

Yield: 4 servings

PICKLED BEAN SPROUTS
DUA GIA

*T*his is usually served with a simmered dish of meat or fish during hot summer days.

■ ■ ■ ■ ■ ■ ■ ■ ■ ■ ■ ■

1 pound fresh bean sprouts
1 bunch of scallions, cut into 2-inch-long sections
1 tablespoon salt
½ cup distilled white vinegar

Mix the bean sprouts and scallions in a large bowl.

Combine the salt, vinegar and 4 cups of water in a small saucepan. Bring to a boil. Cool until warm to the touch. Pour the brine over the bean sprout mixture. Marinate for at least 1 hour, or until ready to serve. Drain before serving.

NOTE Pickled Bean Sprouts are best served the same day they are made. They will not stand longer marinating since sogginess will affect their texture.

Yield: 4 to 6 servings

PICKLED CARROTS
CAROT CHUA

*T*hese pickles are often served as an accompaniment to grilled foods that are wrapped in lettuce and herbs at the table. You may also substitute daikon, radish, turnip, cucumber, garlic, etc.

■ ■ ■ ■ ■ ■ ■ ■ ■ ■ ■ ■

3 carrots
½ cup rice vinegar
1 tablespoon sugar
¼ teaspoon salt

Peel the carrots; cut crosswise into ⅛-inch rounds.

Combine the vinegar, sugar, salt and ½ cup of water in a small saucepan. Bring to a boil. Remove and let cool to room temperature.

Add the carrot rounds to the mixture and marinate for at least 1 hour. Drain the carrots before using.

Pickled carrots can be stored in a covered jar and refrigerated for 2 to 3 weeks.

NOTE For a more appealing presentation, you can try carving the carrots into decorative shapes before slicing.

Yield: 2 cups

STUFFED BEAN CURD
DAU HU NHOI

This centuries-old recipe is a Vietnamese adaptation of a well-known Hakka dish (there was a mass emigration to northern Vietnam by both Cantonese and Hakkas in the seventeenth century).

■ ■ ■ ■ ■ ■ ■ ■ ■ ■ ■

Nuoc Cham (*page 212*)
Sauce
⅓ *cup chicken broth or water*
1 *tablespoon* nuoc mam *(Vietnamese fish sauce)*
¼ *cup oyster sauce*
1 *tablespoon sugar*
1 *teaspoon tomato paste*
   Filling
2 *dried Chinese mushrooms*
4 *ounces raw shrimp, shelled and deveined*
4 *garlic cloves, chopped*
4 *ounces ground pork*
2 *shallots, thinly sliced*
¼ *teaspoon sugar*
2 *teaspoons* nuoc mam *(Vietnamese fish sauce)*
   Freshly ground black pepper
2 *pounds firm bean curd (tofu)*
⅓ *cup cornstarch, for dusting*
2 *tablespoons peanut oil*

Prepare the *Nuoc Cham.* Set aside.

Combine the chicken broth, fish sauce, oyster sauce, sugar and tomato paste in a bowl. Stir to blend. Set the sauce aside.

Prepare the filling: Soak the mushrooms in hot water for 30 minutes. Drain well and squeeze out any excess water. Remove and discard the mushroom stems; mince the caps.

Process or mash the shrimp to a fine paste.

In a mixing bowl, combine the chopped mushrooms and shrimp paste with half of the garlic, the pork, shallots, sugar, fish sauce and pepper. Mix well with your hands to blend. Set aside to marinate for 30 minutes.

Cut the bean curd into 2 by 4-inch rectangles about ½ inch thick. Dry thoroughly on a double layer of paper towels. Line up the bean curd slices on a flat worktop and sprinkle with cornstarch. Divide and spread the filling over each piece of tofu. Sprinkle the filling with cornstarch.

Now, build double-deck sandwiches by pressing 2 pieces of the tofu together. Press slightly with the palm of your hands to secure the filling. Carefully remove any excess filling from the edges.

Heat the oil in a skillet over moderate heat. Place the bean curd pieces in the oil and brown each side for 1 minute. Reduce the heat to low, cover the pan and cook, turning from time to time, for 15 minutes.

Make some space in the middle of the skillet and add the remaining garlic. Fry until fragrant. Pour in the sauce mixture and let the mixture come to a boil. Cook for 5 minutes longer, or until the sauce becomes thick and shiny. Turn the bean curd in the sauce to coat.

Serve with rice and *Nuoc Cham.*

Yield: 4 servings

STIR-FRIED PICKLED BAMBOO SHOOTS WITH FRESH BACON
MANG CHUA XAO HEO

*M*y mother learned this dish from one of her best friends, a native of Hue. The fresh bacon gives a rich and delicious flavor to the slightly pickled bamboo shoots. Fresh bacon (pork belly) can be found at butcher shops in Chinatown.

The pickled bamboo shoots come preserved in salt in a plastic package. They are available at Vietnamese or Chinese grocery stores.

■ ■ ■ ■ ■ ■ ■ ■ ■ ■

Nuoc Cham (*page 212*)
1 pound pickled bamboo shoots (page 228)
8 ounces fresh bacon (pork belly)
2 tablespoons nuoc mam (*Vietnamese fish sauce*)
4 garlic cloves, chopped
  Freshly ground black pepper
2 tablespoons peanut oil
4 shallots, thinly sliced

Prepare the *Nuoc Cham.* Set aside.

Soak the pickled bamboo shoots for about 1 hour, with several changes of water to remove the salt. Drain the bamboo shoots; squeeze dry. Set aside.

Cut the fresh bacon into slices 1 by 2 by ¼-inch thick. Combine the meat with 1 tablespoon of the fish sauce, half of the garlic and black pepper to taste. Mix well. Let stand for 30 minutes.

Heat the oil in a skillet or wok over moderately high heat. Add the bacon and stir-fry for 5 minutes, or until browned. Remove the fresh bacon with a slotted spoon to a platter.

Add the shallots and the remaining garlic to the skillet and fry for a few seconds. Add the bamboo shoots and stir-fry for about 3 minutes, or until well coated with oil and heated through. Add the remaining 1 tablespoon fish sauce and the cooked bacon. Stir to blend and cook for 1 minute longer.

Transfer the mixture to a warm platter. Sprinkle with black pepper. Serve with rice and the *Nuoc Cham.*

Yield: 4 servings

STIR-FRY OF CHARRED EGGPLANT WITH SPICY SWEET-AND-SOUR SAUCE
CA TIM NUONG XAO DAM OT

This is one of my favorite eggplant dishes. The grilled eggplant yields a delicious smoky and nutty flavor, further enhanced by garlic and fresh basil. Choose small but firm eggplants for this purpose; the Japanese variety is preferred.

■ ■ ■ ■ ■ ■ ■ ■ ■ ■ ■

1½ *teaspoons sugar*
2 *tablespoons distilled white vinegar*
1 *tablespoon* nuoc mam *(Vietnamese fish sauce)*
2 *large red chile peppers, seeded and shredded*
2 *pounds firm eggplants*
3 *tablespoons peanut oil*
8 *garlic cloves, crushed*
¼ *cup shredded fresh Asian or regular basil*
Freshly ground black pepper

Combine the sugar, vinegar, fish sauce and chiles in a small bowl. Set the sauce aside.

Prick the eggplants with a fork. Grill over medium coals or hot gas flames, turning until the flesh is soft and the skins charred, about 4 minutes. If using an electric stove, place the eggplants directly on the burners. Remove to a rack and allow to cool. Peel and discard the charred skin. Cut the eggplants into strips, 2½ inches long by ½ inch wide.

Heat the oil in a wok or large skillet until very hot. Add the garlic and stir-fry for a few seconds. Add the eggplants and sauté for 2 minutes. Add the sauce and sauté for 1 minute, tossing to coat the eggplants with the sauce. Add the basil and remove from the heat.

Transfer to a warm serving platter. Sprinkle with black pepper and serve with rice as part of a family meal.

Yield: 4 servings

BRAISED BAMBOO SHOOTS
MANG KHO CHAY

Another important vegetable in vegetarian cooking is the bamboo shoot. Fat, round, ivory winter bamboo shoots, which yield a tender yet crunchy flesh, are used for this recipe.

One good brand, Ma Ling, come from the Republic of China and is available at most Asian markets. There is no substitute for winter bamboo shoots; sliced bamboo shoots are not suitable for this recipe.

■ ■ ■ ■ ■ ■ ■ ■ ■ ■ ■

1 *pound whole winter bamboo shoots*
1 *tablespoon vegetable oil*
¼ *cup soy sauce*
½ *cup chicken broth or water*
1 *tablespoon sugar*
1 *teaspoon Oriental sesame oil*

Cut the bamboo shoots lengthwise into pieces ½ inch wide and 2½ inches long.

In a saucepan, heat the vegetable oil until it smokes. Add the bamboo shoots and stir-fry for 1 minute. Stir in the soy sauce, broth and sugar. Bring the mixture to a boil. Reduce the heat to low, cover the pan and simmer for 1 hour, or until the shoots are tender but still crunchy. Add the sesame oil and mix well.

Serve hot, with the sauce drizzled over rice.

NOTE Soaked and squeezed dry, Chinese mushroom caps may be added when stir-frying the bamboo shoots. Use the soaking liquid from the mushrooms in place of the broth or water.

Yield: 4 servings

PICKLED MUSTARD GREENS
DUA CAI

*M*ustard greens are also known as mustard cabbage. In Vietnam, Pickled Mustard Greens are often served with Pork Simmered in Coconut Water. You may use other varieties of cabbage or serve with different simmered foods.

In contrast to pickled bean sprouts, pickled cabbage withstands longer marinating. A true brine contains just water and salt, and the pickling process could take up to a week in hot weather. To reduce the marinating time to a couple of days, I have decreased the amount of salt and added extra vinegar.

Before cooking or serving, rinse the vegetable well in water. During cooking, season it with a pinch of sugar to offset the acidity. Once pickled, the cabbage has the color of a pickled green olive, becomes crunchy and develops a sour tang.

■ ■ ■ ■ ■ ■ ■ ■ ■ ■ ■

1 pound mustard greens
1 bunch of scallions, cut into 2-inch long sections
1 tablespoon salt
½ cup rice vinegar or distilled white vinegar

Cut the mustard greens crosswise into pieces ½ inch wide and 2 inches long.

Combine the scallions with the greens in a large bowl.

Mix the salt, vinegar and 4 cups of water in a saucepan. Bring to a boil. Cool until warm to the touch. Pour the brine over the vegetables. Place a small plate or dish on top of the vegetables to weigh them down and keep them immersed in the pickling solution.

Let stand at room temperature for 2 or 3 days, or until the cabbage turns yellowish and tastes sour. Drain before serving.

Yield: 4 to 6 servings

$\mathscr{D}$ESSERTS

Sweet Rice Dumplings with Ginger Syrup

SWEET RICE DUMPLINGS WITH GINGER SYRUP
BANH TROI NUOC

In Vietnam, it's customary to eat dumplings on the third day of the Third Lunar Month, during which it is forbidden to light a fire in the kitchen. On this day, cold food (prepared the day before) is consumed, including these little round sweet rice dumplings. A poet, Ho-Xuan-Huong, wrote this famous quatrain. She described *Banh Troi* while making an analogy to her adventurous, yet pure and dignified private life:

My body is white and my destiny round,
I float and sink, water and mountain
Hard or soft, I depend on the skills of the
person who kneads me
Despite everything, I always keep a
consistent heart.

Serve this unusual and delicious dessert after a light meal. It must be eaten at room temperature for the ginger to develop its full flavor. The heat of the ginger nicely counterbalances the sweet syrup.

■ ■ ■ ■ ■ ■ ■ ■ ■ ■ ■ ■

Ginger syrup
1 *ounce fresh gingerroot, crushed*
1 *cup sugar*
1½ *cups hot water*
Filling
¼ *cup dried yellow mung beans (page 233)*
1½ *tablespoons sugar*
¼ *cup plus 2 tablespoons toasted sesame seeds (page 225)*
Dough
2 *cups glutinous rice flour*
¾ *cup boiling water*

Make the ginger syrup: Cook the ginger and sugar in a small heavy saucepan over low heat, swirling the pan constantly, until the sugar browns. It will smoke slightly. Immediately stir the hot water into the caramel, being careful to guard against splattering (the mixture will bubble vigorously). Boil the mixture, swirling the pan occasionally, until the sugar is thoroughly dissolved, about 3 minutes.

Remove from the heat and set aside to steep in a cool place. When the syrup is completely cooled, strain and discard the ginger. (The syrup can be prepared several days ahead. Cover and refrigerate. Reheat when needed.)

Make the filling: Soak the mung beans in warm water for 30 minutes; drain. Steam over high heat for 20 minutes. Transfer to a food processor; add the sugar and purée to a fine paste. Refrigerate until the mixture firms up, about 20 minutes.

Prepare the sesame seeds; reserve 2 tablespoons for garnish. In a mortar, pound or process the remaining sesame seeds to a paste.

Combine the sesame paste and mung bean paste; blend well. Pick up the combined paste by teaspoonfuls and roll to form small marble-size balls. Repeat until all the paste is used; there will be about 16 balls. Set aside.

Make the dough: Place the glutinous rice flour in a mixing bowl. Add the boiling water to the bowl. Working quickly, use chopsticks or a fork to stir the mixture until it forms a sticky dough. Cover the dough and let stand for 5 minutes, or until cool enough to handle.

Dust a work surface with flour and knead the dough for 3 minutes, or until soft and smooth.

Divide the dough into 2 equal parts. Roll each part by hand into a rope that is about 10 inches long and 1 inch in diameter. Cut each rope into 10 equal portions. Roll each portion into a ball. Work with 1 ball at a time; keep the others covered with a damp cloth.

Use the palm of your hand to flatten a dough ball into a 2½-inch disk. Place 1 mung bean ball in the center; gather the edges around the filling and pinch to seal. Roll the filled dough into a round ball between the palms of your hands. Repeat until all of the mung bean balls are used.

Divide the remaining 4 portions of dough into 16 pieces, then roll each of them between the palms of your hands to form small marble-size balls. Cover and set aside.

Bring a large pot of water to a boil. Add the filled dumplings and cook for 2 minutes over moderate heat. Add the smaller dumplings and cook for another 3 minutes, until they rise to the surface. Drain the dumplings in a colander.

Reheat the ginger syrup over low heat in a large pot. Add the drained dumplings to the syrup and let simmer for 2 minutes. Set aside to cool.

Serve each guest 4 large dumplings and 4 small dumplings, along with the ginger syrup, in individual dessert cups or bowls. Sprinkle with the reserved toasted sesame seeds.

Yield: 4 servings

Coconut Tartlets and Candied Coconut

Sesame Cookies

COCONUT TARTLETS
BANH DUA NUONG

These toothsome little tarts, with a buttery sweet soft crust, are my favorites. The crust is similar to the French *pâte sucrée* but has the consistency of a rich sugar cookie dough, which virtually melts in your mouth.

If you don't have tartlet pans, use small brioche pans or a 9-inch tart pan.

■ ■ ■ ■ ■ ■ ■ ■ ■ ■ ■

Dough
¼ cup vegetable shortening, or
    4 tablespoons (½ stick) softened
    butter, cut into pieces
2 tablespoons sugar
1 egg yolk
½ teaspoon vanilla extract
¾ cup all-purpose flour, sifted
¼ teaspoon baking powder

Filling
2 cups grated fresh coconut (page 226)
2 tablespoons sugar
4 tablespoons (½ stick) softened butter,
    cut into pieces
1 egg yolk
2 tablespoons heavy cream
½ teaspoon vanilla extract

Glaze
1 egg yolk
1 tablespoon butter, melted and cooled

Preheat the oven to 350°F.

Make the dough: In a mixing bowl, beat the shortening and sugar until creamy and fluffy. Stir in the egg yolk and vanilla; mix to combine. Add the flour and baking powder and mix well. Knead the dough until smooth.

Divide the dough into 6 portions. Place each piece of dough in a 3-inch tartlet pan and press to line the mold. Refrigerate until ready to use.

Make the filling: Prepare the grated fresh coconut as directed. Combine the coconut, sugar and butter in a mixing bowl. (Omit the sugar if using canned or packaged sweetened coconut shreds.) Knead to form a soft mixture. Add the egg yolk, cream and vanilla; blend well with your hands to form a smooth, soft paste.

Divide the mixture into 6 portions. Fill each tartlet with one portion of the coconut mixture; smooth the top. Place the tartlets on a cookie sheet.

Make the glaze: Beat the egg yolk lightly. Stir in the melted butter.

Bake the tartlets for 15 minutes. Brush the surface and crust edges of the tartlets with the glaze. Return to the oven and bake for 5 minutes longer.

Turn the oven to broil. Run the tartlets under the broiler and broil until the glaze becomes shiny and the crust and coconut turn golden, about 30 seconds.

Cool the tartlets slightly before unmolding.

Serve warm or cold.

Yield: Six 3-inch tartlets

SESAME COOKIES
BANH ME

A close cousin of the popular Chinese almond cookies, this Vietnamese version is much lighter and more flavorsome. They are a delightful treat with hot tea.

■ ■ ■ ■ ■ ■ ■ ■ ■ ■ ■

¾ cup toasted sesame seeds (page 225)
2¼ cups all-purpose flour, sifted
1 teaspoon baking powder
½ teaspoon baking soda
1½ cups vegetable shortening
1 cup sugar
2 whole eggs
1 teaspoon vanilla extract
All-purpose flour, for dusting
1 egg yolk mixed with 1 teaspoon water

Preheat the oven to 350°F. Line 2 cookie sheets with parchment paper.

Prepare the sesame seeds. Reserve ¼ cup to garnish the cookies; coarsely grind the remaining seeds.

Combine the ground sesame seeds, sifted flour, baking powder and baking soda in a bowl.

In a mixing bowl, cream the shortening and sugar until fluffy. Add the eggs, one at a time, and beat until smooth after each addition. Add the vanilla and stir to combine. Add the dry ingredients to the creamed mixture, a little at a time, and mix until well combined. The dough will be moist and pull away from the sides of the bowl.

Dust a work surface with about ¼ cup flour. Knead the dough to form a smooth ball. To shape each cookie, roll 1 tablespoon of dough into a ball. Press lightly with the palm of your hand to form a 1½-inch round. Place the cookies 2 inches apart on the baking sheets; freeze for 20 minutes.

Brush the cookies with the egg wash. Press the reserved sesame seeds into the dough. Bake for 15 to 20 minutes, or until lightly browned. Remove and allow to cool. Store in an airtight cookie tin for up to 2 weeks.

Yield: 50 cookies

ICED JELLY, LOTUS SEED AND MUNG BEAN DESSERT

CHE HOT SEN THAT TRANH

This sweet confection, flavored with coconut, is cooling on a hot day. It is often described as "rainbow drink" *(che ba mau)* in Vietnamese restaurants; however, lotus seeds are usually replaced by black beans or black-eyed peas.

■ ■ ■ ■ ■ ■ ■ ■ ■ ■ ■

½ *cup dried lotus seeds (page 232) (see Note)*
½ *cup dried yellow mung beans (page 233)*
1 *stick (¼ ounce) agar-agar (page 231)*
3 *tablespoons sugar*
½ *teaspoon vanilla extract, or a few drops of jasmine or rose water*
  Few drops red or green food coloring (optional)
  Syrup
1 *cup sugar*
1 *cup fresh or canned coconut milk (page 227)*
1 *teaspoon potato starch*
1 *teaspoon vanilla extract*

Soak the dried lotus seeds in warm water for at least 2 hours or overnight. Do the same for the mung beans. Drain.

Place the lotus seeds and mung beans separately into 2 pots of water to cover. Bring to a boil. Reduce the heat to moderate and cook until they are very tender but not mushy, about 15 minutes for the beans, and 50 minutes for the lotus seeds. As the water evaporates, add more boiling water to cover the seeds. Drain. Set aside.

In a saucepan, soak the agar-agar in 1 cup of hot water for 30 minutes. Add the sugar and bring to a boil. Reduce the heat and simmer, stirring frequently, for 10 minutes. Stir in the vanilla and food coloring. Pour the mixture into a 9-inch-square baking pan. Chill the mixture until firm.

Make the syrup: If using fresh coconut milk, prepare it as directed on page 227. Combine the sugar, coconut milk, potato starch and 1¾ cups of water in a saucepan. Bring to a boil. Reduce the heat and simmer for 10 minutes. Stir in the vanilla. Remove from the heat and let cool thoroughly.

Shred the jellied agar-agar with a knife or hand grater into long strands.

To assemble the dessert, half-fill 4 milk-shake glasses with crushed ice. Layer on top some lotus seeds, mung beans and jellied agar-agar strands. Pour the coconut-flavored syrup over all. Serve with a spoon and straw.

NOTE As a shortcut, substitute 1 cup of drained canned lotus seeds, which are ready to serve. One cup of diced grass jelly (page 232) may be substituted for the jellied agar-agar.

Yield: 4 servings

BLACK-EYED PEAS AND SWEET RICE IN COCONUT MILK

CHE DAU TRANG

*T*he baking soda reduces the cooking time of the beans and tenderizes them at the same time, so keep an eye on the beans while they cook; they will be done in no time.

■ ■ ■ ■ ■ ■ ■ ■ ■ ■

1 cup fresh or canned coconut milk (page 227)
⅓ cup raw glutinous or sweet rice
½ cup dried black-eyed peas
¼ teaspoon baking soda
½ cup sugar
1 teaspoon vanilla extract

If using fresh coconut milk, prepare it as directed on page 227.

Soak the glutinous rice and black-eyed peas separately in warm water for at least 2 hours. Drain.

Cover the beans with 3 cups of water in a saucepan. Add the baking soda. Bring to a boil. Reduce the heat to moderate and simmer the beans for 10 minutes, or until just tender. Refresh with cold water and drain.

Bring 2 cups of water to a boil in a saucepan. Add the glutinous rice and boil for 5 minutes. Stir in the sugar and vanilla. Add the cooked beans and simmer for 5 minutes longer. Set aside to cool slightly.

Divide the bean-rice mixture among 4 dessert bowls. Drizzle about ¼ cup of the coconut milk on top of each. Serve warm.

NOTE For a richer taste, float a tablespoon or two of unsweetened coconut cream on top of this sweet soup.

Yield: 4 servings

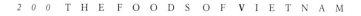

Gypsum powder is a chemical agent used to coagulate soybean milk, it is available in Asian pharmacies.

The jellied bean curd should be served thinly sliced. To do so, cut off the lid of a 4-inch can (that of a coffee tin is ideal) and run it across the top of the curd, gently slicing out thin layers.

■ ■ ■ ■ ■ ■ ■ ■ ■ ■ ■ ■

Curd
½ cup dried soybeans
¼ cup rice flour
1 teaspoon gypsum powder (page 232), dissolved in 1 teaspoon cold water in a small bowl

Syrup
1 ounce piece of fresh gingerroot, crushed
1 cup sugar
1½ cups hot water

Soak the soybeans for at least 8 hours or overnight. Drain.

Set a fine-mesh strainer lined with a linen or fine muslin dish towel over a 5-quart pot.

In a blender, purée the soybeans with 2½ cups of water. Pour the mixture into the strainer. Gather the cloth and squeeze the milk into the pot. Return the soybean pulp to the blender. Add 2½ cups of water and blend again; squeeze as before.

In a bowl, dilute the rice flour with 2 cups of water. Add to the soybean milk in the pot. Bring the mixture to a boil over moderately high heat. Stir continuously, with a circular motion, so the liquid does not burn or stick to the pot. When steam appears and the milk starts to foam, keep stirring for about 3 more minutes, being careful it doesn't boil over. Turn off the heat.

Ladle ¼ cup of the hot milk into the gypsum powder in the bowl. Stir quickly to mix. Immediately pour the mixture back into the pot; stir once. Cover the pot with a tight lid; let stand undisturbed. The milk will jell in about 30 minutes.

While the curd is setting, make the syrup: Place the ginger and sugar in a small saucepan. Cook over low heat, watching carefully to prevent burning and scorching. Shake and swirl the pan over the heat until the sugar becomes liquid and caramel colored, about 3 minutes. It will smoke lightly. Immediately add the hot water, being careful to guard against splattering. Swirl the pan until the mixture is blended.

Return the pan to moderate heat and cook, swirling, until the mixture boils and the sugar is thoroughly dissolved, about 3 minutes. Remove from the heat and set aside to steep.

When the syrup is completely cooled, strain and discard the ginger. If any water has collected on the surface of the curd, spoon it off.

To serve, run a can lid across the top of the jellied mixture, slicing out thin rounds of curd. Place the curd in individual bowls or dessert cups. Ladle about ¼ cup of the ginger syrup over each serving.

Serve hot, at room temperature or cold.

Yield: 4 servings

FRIED STUFFED BANANAS
CHUOI CHIEN

In France, there isn't one Vietnamese restaurant that doesn't offer fried bananas. They are generally served flambéed, a method dear to the French and adopted by the Vietnamese.

To make fried bananas more interesting, I like to stuff them with pistachio or hazelnut paste (available at specialty stores) and flambé them with rice wine. The result is a heavenly dessert as is, but it may also be served with ice cream.

■ ■ ■ ■ ■ ■ ■ ■ ■ ■ ■ ■

⅔ cup all-purpose flour, sifted
¼ cup cornstarch, sifted
2 teaspoons sugar
  Pinch of salt
1 teaspoon baking powder
1 tablespoon vegetable oil
4 large ripe but firm bananas
¼ cup pistachio or hazelnut paste
  Vegetable oil, for deep-frying
  Cornstarch, for coating
½ cup rice wine or rum
  Confectioners' sugar

Combine the flour, cornstarch, sugar, salt and baking powder in a large bowl. Make a well in the center and gradually add ⅔ cup plus 1 tablespoon water, mixing well to make a smooth batter. Add the vegetable oil and stir until smooth. Refrigerate the batter for at least 1 hour.

Peel the bananas and halve crosswise. Split each half lengthwise and stuff with ½ tablespoon of the pistachio paste. Take care to stuff banana pieces neatly so the paste will not fall out during cooking.

Heat 2 inches of oil in a wok or heavy deep skillet to 375°F. Dredge the bananas in cornstarch; shake off any excess. Dip the stuffed bananas, a few at a time, in the batter. Carefully add a few pieces at a time to the hot oil. Fry, turning once, for 3 to 4 minutes, or until golden brown and crisp. Drain on paper towels. Transfer to a flameproof dish.

Place the liquor in a deep ladle and heat gently over moderate flame to ignite. Pour the liquor over the banana fritters. Using a fork and spoon, turn each fritter to coat with the flaming liquor.

Sprinkle the bananas with sifted confectioners' sugar and serve.

Yield: 4 servings

CANDIED COCONUT

MUT DUA

*A*lthough this candy can be store-bought, most Vietnamese cooks enjoy making a variety of candied fruits and vegetables on festive occasions, such as the Lunar New Year, and for family and special visitors. Other popular candied fruits and vegetables include ginger, lotus seeds, persimmon, sweet potato, tamarind and winter melon.

Traditionally, a wide copper pot is used in preparing this delicacy. If you don't have one, use a wide heavy-bottomed pan.

Select a fresh coconut. The amount of liquid in it determines its freshness, so shake the coconut to ensure that it is heavy and contains a lot of liquid.

■ ■ ■ ■ ■ ■ ■ ■ ■ ■

1 *medium coconut*
1 *cup sugar*
1 *teaspoon vanilla extract*

Preheat the oven to 350°F.

Pierce the "eyes" of the coconut with a screwdriver or ice pick. Drain the clear, sweet liquid (coconut water) into a bowl to be used as a drink or frozen for future use in recipes such as Pork Simmered in Coconut Water (page 125).

Bake the drained coconut for 15 to 20 minutes, or until the shell begins to crack. Remove from the oven and let cool briefly. Place the nut on a sturdy surface. Using a hammer or kitchen mallet, crack the nut in half by hitting sharply on the middle of the coconut. The shell will split apart easily. Remove the coconut meat from the shell with the point of a paring knife. Pare off the thin brown skin that clings to the white flesh.

Pack the coconut meat in the feed tube of a food processor fitted with a thin slicer blade. Slice, using firm pressure.

Bring a large pot of water to a boil. Add the coconut and boil for 5 minutes. Drain; refresh with cold water and dry on paper towels.

Place the sugar and 1½ tablespoons of water in a large heavy-bottomed pot or copper kettle. Set the pot over moderate heat to melt the sugar, about 3 minutes. Stir in the vanilla. Add the coconut. Cook, stirring constantly with a wooden spoon, over moderately low heat until all of the water evaporates and the sugar crystallizes and becomes dry, about 30 minutes. Remove and allow to cool.

Serve with tea or coffee. Candied coconut can be stored in a glass jar or cookie tin kept at room temperature for up to 1 month.

Yield: about 3 cups

LYCHEE AND GINGER ICE

DA VAI, GUNG

This light and flavorful tropical ice is a welcome finale to a rich meal. You may also serve it as a palate cleanser between the courses of a fancy dinner.

■ ■ ■ ■ ■ ■ ■ ■ ■ ■ ■

1 can (11 ounces) lychees in heavy syrup
½ ounce fresh gingerroot, peeled and grated

Combine the lychees and syrup, the ginger and ⅔ cup of water in a blender or food processor and blend to a fine purée.

Pour the puréed mixture in a 9-inch square baking pan. Cover and freeze until firm, about 3 hours.

Break the iced mixture into chunks and process again until just slushy. Return to the pan and freeze until solid.

Allow the mixture to soften slightly, about 5 minutes, before scooping into chilled dessert cups or champagne glasses.

Serve, garnished with mint leaves, lychees and a light, crisp cookie, if desired.

Yield: 4 servings

COCONUT FLAN WITH CARAMEL
BANH DUA CA RA MEN

*T*his is the ultimate coconut dessert —an adaptation of the classic *crème renversée,* or *flan au caramel.* The technique used is distinctively French but the flavors are all Vietnamese.

This custard is at its best when prepared a day in advance and refrigerated so the flavors can mellow. If you just can't wait, you might try the Vietnamese method of rapid cooling for dishes such as this: place a small scoop of shaved ice on top of each custard before serving!

■ ■ ■ ■ ■ ■ ■ ■ ■ ■ ■

Caramel
¼ cup sugar
¼ cup hot water
Custard
1 cup fresh or canned coconut milk (page 227)
1 cup milk
¼ cup sugar
4 eggs
1 teaspoon vanilla extract

Preheat the oven to 325°F.

Make the caramel: Cook the sugar in a small heavy saucepan over low heat, swirling the pan constantly, until brown. Stir the hot water into the caramel, being careful to guard against splattering (the mixture will bubble vigorously). Boil the mixture, swirling the pan occasionally, until the sugar is thoroughly dissolved, about 2 minutes.

Pour the caramel syrup into a 1-quart soufflé dish or five 4-ounce ramekins. Tilt the molds to coat all of the surfaces with the caramel.

Make the custard: If using fresh coconut milk, prepare it as directed on page 227. Combine the coconut milk, milk and sugar in a medium saucepan over low heat. Scald until the sugar dissolves completely. Remove from the heat.

In a large bowl, whisk the eggs and vanilla. Gradually whisk the hot coconut milk mixture into the eggs, blending thoroughly.

Strain the custard through a fine sieve into a bowl. Carefully pour into the caramel-lined soufflé dish or ramekins.

Line a large roasting pan with 2 layers of paper towels (see Note). Put the soufflé dish in the roasting pan and add hot water to reach halfway up the side of the dish. Bake in the center of the oven for 50 minutes (30 minutes if using ramekins), or until a knife inserted in the center comes out clean. Be careful not to let the water boil; do not disturb the custard while baking. This is the only "secret" to producing a smooth and velvety custard.

Remove the soufflé dish immediately from the hot water. Allow to cool in a cold-water bath. Chill thoroughly.

To serve, run a knife around the edge of the custard and turn out onto dessert plates. Serve with shaved ice or whipped cream, if desired.

NOTE The paper towels in the roasting pan serve a twofold purpose: First, they allow the hot water to circulate under the soufflé dish while baking to distribute the heat evenly; second, if using small ramekins, it stabilizes them and keeps them from moving around while baking.

Yield: 5 servings

BANANAS IN COCONUT MILK

CHE CHUOI

$\mathcal{T}$his simple yet satisfying dessert is very popular in Vietnam. Since most Vietnamese do not eat dessert right after a meal, this sweet soup is often served as a snack late in the afternoon. As young kids, my sister and I most enjoyed that time of day, when our mother would treat us to sweet soups bought from a street vendor.

This dessert is at its best when served warm.

■ ■ ■ ■ ■ ■ ■ ■ ■ ■ ■

3 cups fresh or canned coconut milk
   (page 227)
2 tablespoons toasted sesame seeds (page
   225)
¼ cup very small tapioca pearls (page
   236)
⅓ cup sugar
4 large, ripe but firm bananas

If using fresh coconut milk, prepare it as directed on page 227. Prepare the toasted sesame seeds. Set aside.

Cover the tapioca pearls with warm water in a bowl and set aside to soak for 20 minutes. Drain.

Combine the coconut milk, sugar and ⅔ cup of water in a 3-quart saucepan. Bring to a boil, taking care that the liquid does not boil over. Reduce the heat to low and simmer.

Peel the bananas and cut into 2-inch lengths. Add the banana pieces and drained tapioca pearls to the coconut milk mixture in the saucepan. Partially cover the pan and let simmer for 10 to 15 minutes, or until the tapioca pearls are clear.

Ladle the banana-coconut milk mixture into individual serving bowls. Sprinkle the toasted sesame seeds on top. Serve hot or warm.

NOTE For a richer taste, the Vietnamese like to float a tablespoon or two of unsweetened coconut cream on top of this dessert.

Yield: 4 to 6 servings

SWEET RICE WINE

*R*ice is so important in Vietnam that it is consumed in a great many ways. Sweet rice wine is one good example. A crushed yeast ball, a little water, flour and sugar are combined with steamed glutinous rice. The mixture is allowed to stand until a sweet wine develops.

■ ■ ■ ■ ■ ■ ■ ■ ■ ■ ■

1 cup raw glutinous rice
½ yeast ball (page 235), crushed
1 teaspoon all-purpose flour
¼ cup sugar

Soak the rice for 8 hours or overnight. Drain; rinse and drain again.

Spread the rice over dampened cheesecloth in the top of a steamer and steam for 20 minutes. Rinse the rice with warm water to remove the excess starch. Transfer to a mixing bowl.

Combine the yeast ball with the flour and stir into the rice. Transfer the rice to a glass jar or some other nonmetal container.

In a saucepan, bring ½ cup of water and the sugar to a boil. Reduce the heat and simmer for 10 minutes. Set aside to cool.

Pour the syrup into the jar over the rice; stir to combine. Cover the jar loosely, wrap completely in a paper towel or foil to prevent any light from entering and position it in a warm place for 5 to 7 days. Refrigerate for up to 1 month.

To serve, ladle the mixture into small glasses or dessert cups.

Yield: 2½ cups

Sauces

PEANUT SAUCE
NUOC LEO

*T*his delicious sauce originated in the central region and is used as a dip for many dishes in this book. Usually, *tuong,* a fermented soybean sauce, and glutinous rice are used to produce this sauce.

After several experiments, I ended up with this variation where *tuong* and glutinous rice are replaced by hoisin sauce and peanut butter, ingredients that are more readily available.

■ ■ ■ ■ ■ ■ ■ ■ ■ ■ ■

¼ *cup roasted peanuts (page 220),*
ground
1 *tablespoon peanut oil*
3 *garlic cloves, minced*
1 *teaspoon chile paste* (tuong ot tuoi)
1 *tablespoon tomato paste*
½ *cup chicken broth or water*
½ *teaspoon sugar*
2 *tablespoons peanut butter*
¼ *cup hoisin sauce*
1 *fresh red chile pepper, seeded and*
thinly sliced

Prepare the roasted peanuts. Set aside.

Heat the oil in a small saucepan. When the oil is hot, add the garlic, chile paste and tomato paste. Fry until the garlic is golden brown, about 30 seconds. Add the broth, sugar, peanut butter and hoisin sauce and whisk to dissolve the peanut butter. Bring to a boil. Reduce the heat and simmer for 3 minutes.

Divide the sauce among individual dipping bowls and garnish with the ground peanuts and sliced chile. Serve warm or at room temperature.

Yield: About 1 cup

QUICK PEANUT SAUCE

*T*his is my "lazy" version of *Nuoc Leo* sauce.

■ ■ ■ ■ ■ ■ ■ ■ ■ ■ ■

¼ *cup hoisin sauce*
¼ *cup chicken broth or water*
1 *tablespoon* nuoc mam *(Vietnamese fish sauce) or soy sauce*
2 *tablespoons store-bought dry-roasted unsalted peanuts, ground*
1 *fresh red chile pepper, seeded and thinly sliced*

Combine the hoisin sauce, chicken broth and fish sauce in a small bowl. Stir well to blend.

Divide the sauce among individual dipping bowls. Garnish with the ground peanuts and sliced chile.

NOTE When serving this sauce with Buddhist vegetarian dishes, use water and soy sauce instead of broth and fish sauce.

Yield: ⅔ cup

SPICY FISH SAUCE
NUOC CHAM

Of all the sauces, *Nuoc Cham* is perhaps the most indispensable at the Vietnamese table, where it serves somewhat the same function as salt and pepper do in the West. It is a delightfully tangy, piquant seasoning. Like most Vietnamese sauces, it includes *nuoc mam,* or fish sauce. *Nuoc mam* gives a well-defined personality to Vietnamese food; it is what makes Vietnamese food uniquely Vietnamese.

■ ■ ■ ■ ■ ■ ■ ■ ■ ■ ■

2 small garlic cloves, crushed
1 small fresh red chile pepper, seeded
  and minced
2 tablespoons sugar
2 tablespoons fresh lime or lemon juice
¼ cup rice vinegar
¼ cup nuoc mam *(Vietnamese fish sauce)*

Combine the garlic, chile and sugar in a mortar. Pound with a pestle to a fine paste.

Add the lime juice, vinegar, fish sauce and ¼ cup of water. Stir to blend.

Alternatively, combine all the ingredients in a blender or food processor and process for 30 seconds, or until the sugar dissolves.

NOTE If you wish to make additional sauce and have it handy, do as follows: Place the sugar, vinegar and water in a saucepan and bring the mixture to a boil. Remove from the heat and let cool.

Add the lime juice and fish sauce. This sauce may be stored in a tightly closed bottle or jar and refrigerated for 2 or 3 months. Each time you need *Nuoc Cham,* just crush some fresh chiles and garlic and add as much sauce as needed.

Yield: 1 cup

VARIATION Some people like to garnish this sauce with shredded carrots and daikon (or white turnip). This can also serve as a quick substitute for pickled carrots when they are indicated in a recipe.

Nuoc Cham with Shredded Carrot and Daikon

1 small carrot, shredded
1 small daikon or turnip, peeled and
  shredded
1 teaspoon sugar
1 cup Nuoc Cham

Toss the carrot and daikon shreds with the sugar in a small bowl. Let stand for 15 minutes to soften the vegetables.

Add the *Nuoc Cham* to the softened vegetables and stir.

Yield: 1½ cups

GINGER DIPPING SAUCE

NUOC CHAM GUNG

𝒯his pungent dipping sauce, flavored with *nuoc mam* and ginger, makes a superb accompaniment for Boiled Duck with Ginger Rice Soup. You may also use it as a dip for freshly shucked oysters or steamed mussels.

■ ■ ■ ■ ■ ■ ■ ■ ■ ■ ■

2 *garlic cloves, crushed*
1½ *tablespoons sugar*
1 *fresh red chile pepper, seeded and minced*
1 *tablespoon grated fresh gingerroot*
3 *tablespoons fresh lime or lemon juice*
3½ *tablespoons* nuoc mam *(Vietnamese fish sauce)*

Combine the garlic, sugar, chile and ginger in a small bowl or mortar. Crush the mixture to a paste.

Add the lime juice and fish sauce and stir to blend.

Yield: ½ cup

SWEET-AND-SOUR DIPPING SAUCE
SOT CHUA NGOT

*T*his sauce accompanies beautifully fried fish and seafood, especially Shrimp Fritters.

If you plan to serve this sauce to accompany other hors d'oeuvres at a buffet, double or triple the recipe. Cool the sauce completely, then refrigerate it in a covered jar until needed; it will keep for up to 1 month. Reheat before using; it is at its best when served warm, not piping hot.

■ ■ ■ ■ ■ ■ ■ ■ ■ ■ ■

¼ *cup sugar*
¼ *cup distilled white vinegar*
¼ *cup chicken broth or water*
¼ *teaspoon chile sauce or Tabasco sauce*
2 *tablespoons soy sauce*
2 *tablespoons* nuoc mam *(Vietnamese fish sauce)*
1 *tablespoon tomato paste*
1 *tablespoon cornstarch*
1 *teaspoon grated fresh gingerroot*
1 *tablespoon vegetable oil*
2 *garlic cloves, chopped very fine*

In a small bowl, combine all of the ingredients except the oil and garlic. Stir until the cornstarch is well dissolved.

Heat the oil in a small saucepan over moderate heat. When the oil is hot, add the garlic and fry until golden, about 15 seconds. Stir the sauce mixture and immediately pour into the saucepan. Cook over moderate heat, stirring, until thickened, about 5 minutes. Serve warm.

Yield: 1 cup

TAMARIND DIPPING SAUCE
NUOC CHAM ME

*A*n unusual, delightful dipping sauce best suited to steamed or boiled seafood.

■ ■ ■ ■ ■ ■ ■ ■ ■ ■ ■

2 *ounces lump tamarind, or*
  2 *tablespoons tamarind concentrate*
½ *cup boiling water*
1 *tablespoon* nuoc mam *(Vietnamese fish sauce)*
½ *teaspoon sugar*
1 *fresh red chile pepper, seeded and minced*

Cover the lump tamarind with the boiling water and let soak for 15 minutes, or until the tamarind is soft. Force the tamarind through a fine sieve into a small bowl. If tamarind concentrate is used, dilute it with only ¼ cup warm water.

Stir in the fish sauce and sugar. Mix well to dissolve the sugar.

Divide the sauce among small individual serving bowls. Sprinkle the minced chile on top.

Yield: ½ cup

SOYBEAN AND GINGER SAUCE
NUOC TUONG

This is a variation of the Ginger Dipping Sauce that uses *tuong*, or fermented soybean sauce (see Appendix). Although this sauce is served exclusively with Vietnamese Roast Beef in this book, you may try it with other roast or boiled meats or as a dip for simply cooked vegetables.

■ ■ ■ ■ ■ ■ ■ ■ ■ ■ ■

2 garlic cloves, crushed
1 fresh red chile pepper
1 tablespoon plus 1 teaspoon sugar
1 tablespoon grated fresh gingerroot
¼ cup fresh lemon juice
¼ cup tuong (fermented soybean sauce)
1 tablespoon nuoc mam (Vietnamese fish sauce)

Pound the garlic, chile, sugar and ginger to a fine paste in a small bowl.

Add the lemon juice, *tuong*, fish sauce and ¼ cup of water. Stir well to blend.

Yield: ⅔ cup

SHRIMP SAUCE
MAM TOM

Also called *mam ruoc*, this shrimp sauce base is the favorite condiment in the central region. It is used a flavoring agent in almost everything, from soups, broths and salads to meats. As a dipping sauce, it is mainly served with boiled or steamed meats and seafood. Shrimp sauce is so pungent that it is never offered in restaurants in the West.

■ ■ ■ ■ ■ ■ ■ ■ ■ ■ ■

2 large garlic cloves, crushed
1 fresh red chile pepper, seeded
2 tablespoons sugar
2 tablespoons mam tom (shrimp sauce)
¼ cup plus 2 tablespoons fresh lemon juice
2 tablespoons nuoc mam (Vietnamese fish sauce)

Combine the garlic, chile and sugar in a mortar and pound to a fine paste.

Add the shrimp sauce and lemon juice; stir to blend. Add the fish sauce and 2 tablespoons of water. Mix well.

Yield: about 1 cup

ANCHOVY AND PINEAPPLE SAUCE
MAM NEM

*T*his is by far the most intricate of sauces in the Vietnamese culinary repertoire. What makes it so special is the use of a condiment called *mam nem,* prepared from ground fresh anchovies and salt and fermented over a period of time. It can become dangerously addictive.

Traditionally, *mam nem* is served as a dipping sauce for barbecued or fried fish. In general, it goes well with grilled foods. It is an essential sauce for Beef Fondue with Vinegar.

Use only fresh pineapple and remember to shake the bottle of anchovy sauce thoroughly before using. Anchovy cream may be substituted.

■ ■ ■ ■ ■ ■ ■ ■ ■ ■ ■

1 *cup minced fresh pineapple*
3 *tablespoons* mam nem *(anchovy sauce)*
2 *garlic cloves, crushed*
1 *fresh red chile pepper, seeded*
1 *tablespoon sugar*
3 *tablespoons fresh lemon juice*
1½ *teaspoons rice vinegar or distilled white vinegar*
3 *tablespoons* nuoc mam *(Vietnamese fish sauce)*

Over a bowl, squeeze the pineapple between your hands to extract as much juice as possible. Combine the pulp and juice and set aside.

Into a bowl, strain the anchovy sauce through a very fine sieve, pressing on the solids with a spoon to extract all of the liquid. Discard the solids.

Pound or crush the garlic, chile and sugar to a fine paste in a bowl. Stir in the pineapple mixture, strained anchovy sauce, lemon juice, vinegar and fish sauce. Stir to blend.

Yield: 1⅓ cups

VARIATION If you are unable to find *mam nem* sauce, here is a variation of the above recipe, using canned anchovies. Add pineapple, if desired.

2 *garlic cloves, crushed*
1 *fresh red chile pepper, seeded*
2 *tablespoons sugar*
2 *cans (2 ounces each) flat anchovies, drained*
¼ *cup* nuoc mam *(Vietnamese fish sauce)*
¼ *cup fresh lemon juice*
2 *tablespoons pineapple juice or water*

Combine the garlic, chile and sugar in a mortar and pound to a fine paste. Add the anchovies and mash to a very smooth paste.

Stir in the fish sauce, lemon juice and pineapple juice. Mix well.

Yield: about 1 cup

CARAMEL SAUCE
NUOC DUONG THANG

*W*idely used in Vietnamese cooking, this sauce is essential in simmered dishes. Its main function is to enhance the flavor of some foods, but it also can be added to dishes where a glazed appearance is desired.

Most cooks like to keep large quantities of this sauce on hand, but I would rather prepare some as I need it, for top freshness and flavor. It is easy and quick to prepare. The only rule to remember when preparing this sauce is to turn off the smoke alarm and open all windows, as the sauce will smoke heavily, with a pungent smell.

■ ■ ■ ■ ■ ■ ■ ■ ■ ■ ■

⅓ *cup sugar*
¼ *cup* nuoc mam *(Vietnamese fish sauce)*
 4 *shallots, thinly sliced*
   Freshly ground black pepper

Cook the sugar in a small heavy saucepan over low heat, swirling the pan constantly, until brown. It will smoke slightly. Immediately remove the pan from the heat and stir the fish sauce into the caramel, being careful to guard against splattering (the mixture will bubble vigorously).

Return the mixture to low heat and gently boil, swirling the pan occasionally, until the sugar is completely dissolved, about 3 minutes. Add the shallots and ground pepper to taste; stir to combine.

Use in recipes where required.

NOTE Cool this sauce thoroughly before using. If cold food is added to a caramel sauce that is hot, the sugar will harden instantly and you'll end up with a dish full of candy chips.

Yield: ⅓ cup

APPENDIX

CHICKEN BROTH
NUOC DUNG GA

*T*his chicken broth is the foundation for a number of soups and sauces. In order to obtain a rich broth, it is best to use an old fowl such as a stewing hen, adding to it whatever quantity of chicken bones or parts you may have on hand.

■ ■ ■ ■ ■ ■ ■ ■ ■ ■ ■ ■

1 stewing hen (about 5 pounds)
2 pounds chicken bones
4 quarts cold water
1 ounce fresh gingerroot, crushed
2 teaspoons salt

Cut the hen into 6 or 8 pieces, discarding the fat. Rinse the hen and bones with cold water, then place in a stockpot or large kettle with the water and crushed ginger; bring to a boil. Skim the surface until foam stops forming, about 10 minutes. Reduce the heat to low and simmer for 2 hours (to ensure a clear broth, it is very important that the liquid doesn't boil but merely simmers).

Remove and discard the hen and chicken bones. Add the salt. Set aside to cool. Strain the broth through a very fine sieve or chinois lined with dampened cheesecloth into a bowl. Pour the clear broth into glass containers. Refrigerate for up to 1 week, or freeze for future use. Remove any fat that congeals on top before using.

Yield: 3 quarts

EGG PANCAKES
TRUNG TRANG

*T*hese egg pancakes are important components of numerous Vietnamese recipes, mostly salads and rice dishes. They are used not only as garnish but also for added flavor and texture.

A good nonstick omelet pan is essential to make these delicate egg pancakes. Halve this recipe when only 1 egg pancake is required.

■ ■ ■ ■ ■ ■ ■ ■ ■ ■ ■ ■

2 eggs
¼ teaspoon nuoc mam *(Vietnamese fish sauce)*
Freshly ground black pepper
Vegetable oil

Beat together the eggs, fish sauce, pepper to taste and ½ teaspoon of water in a bowl.

Brush the bottom of a 9-inch nonstick omelet pan with some of the oil. Place over moderate heat until hot. Pour in ¼ cup of the egg mixture and immediately tilt the pan to spread the egg evenly over the bottom. The egg pancake should be very thin and crêpe-like. Cook until the egg is set, about 30 seconds. Turn and cook on the other side for 15 seconds longer. Transfer the egg pancake to a plate or cutting board. Repeat with the remaining egg mixture. Allow to cool.

Use the pancakes whole, or roll them into a cylinder and cut crosswise into thin strips.

Yield: 2 egg pancakes

ROASTED RICE POWDER
THINH

*R*oasted rice powder is used as a flavoring and binding agent in various recipes throughout this book. It is necessary to soak the rice first in order to obtain a deep golden color after roasting. Soaking also makes the rice easier to grind.

■ ■ ■ ■ ■ ■ ■ ■ ■ ■ ■

⅓ *cup raw glutinous rice*

Soak the glutinous rice in warm water for 1 hour. Drain.

Place the rice in a small skillet over moderate heat. Toast the rice, stirring constantly with chopsticks or a wooden spoon, until deep golden brown, about 15 minutes.

Transfer the roasted rice to a spice grinder or blender and process to a fine powder (the powder should resemble sawdust). Sift the ground rice through a very fine sieve into a bowl. Discard the grainy bits. Store the rice powder in a tightly covered jar in your refrigerator and use as needed. It will keep for up to 3 months.

Yield: ⅓ cup

ROASTED PEANUTS
DAU PHONG RANG

*U*se shelled and skinned unsalted peanuts for this purpose. Cook a small amount at a time and use shortly after they are roasted to preserve their flavor. Amounts are specified in recipes using roasted peanuts.

■ ■ ■ ■ ■ ■ ■ ■ ■ ■ ■

Place the peanuts in a skillet over moderate heat and cook, stirring constantly, until the nuts turn golden brown, about 5 minutes. Allow to cool. Pound in a mortar with a pestle or process in a spice grinder until the peanuts are a bit chunky.

NOTE Store-bought dry-roasted unsalted peanuts may be substituted in recipes calling for roasted peanuts.

SHRIMP CHIPS

BANH PHONG TOM

*S*hrimp chips are easy and fun to cook. They are usually served with drinks as an hors d'oeuvre or used as a "scoop" for eating salads. When deep-fried, they swell within seconds of entering the oil to double or triple their original size.

Shrimp chips are sold by the box and resemble dehydrated potato chips (see page 234). The method for cooking shrimp chips follows. Recipes in this book calling for shrimp chips will specify amounts.

Dried shrimp chips
Vegetable oil, for frying

In a wok or small heavy saucepan, heat 2 inches of oil to 350°F. Add 2 or 3 chips at a time (1 at a time if large). Keep them immersed in the oil with a chopstick or slotted spoon until puffy, 10 to 15 seconds; immediately turn over and cook on the other side for 10 to 15 seconds longer. Remove and drain on paper towels.

These feather-light crackers can be served immediately or stored at room temperature in an airtight plastic container for up to 4 days. If they get soggy, open the container lid and let the chips "breathe" for awhile, until they become crispy again.

NOTE If the chips start browning too fast, reduce the heat and wait until the oil cools down a bit before adding the next chip. Otherwise, you will have crackers that are burned and not sufficiently puffed.

DRIED RICE STICKS
BANH PHO

One bag (1 pound) of dried rice sticks will feed 4 to 6 people. When cooked, rice noodles should remain *al dente,* or *au point* in French. After the preliminary soaking, the noodles will soften instantly in boiling water, so be careful not to overcook. If they are not going to be used right away, toss them lightly with oil, cover and keep at room temperature until needed.

■ ■ ■ ■ ■ ■ ■ ■ ■ ■ ■

Soak the rice sticks in warm water for 30 minutes. Drain. Bring 4 quarts of water to a boil in a large pot. Drop in the noodles. With a pair of chopsticks, lift and separate the noodle strands to prevent clumping. As soon as the water returns to a boil, drain immediately in a colander. Refresh the noodles under cold running water, fluffing them with the chopsticks to remove all excess starch. Drain thoroughly before using.

EXTRA-THIN RICE VERMICELLI
BANH HOI

Half a bag (½ pound or 4 squares) will serve 4 to 6 people.

Try to steam these noodles as close to serving time as possible, in order to keep them warm and moist. When *banh hoi* is required in a recipe, always garnish it with these 3 flavorings: scallion oil, crisp-fried shallots and ground roasted peanuts.

■ ■ ■ ■ ■ ■ ■ ■ ■ ■ ■

Line a steamer rack with damp cheesecloth. Dip *banh hoi* squares quickly in warm water, then arrange them in a single layer on the cheesecloth. Cover and steam for 5 minutes. From time to time during the steaming, sprinkle the noodles with water. Transfer to a plate.

To serve, drizzle scallion oil (including scallion bits) over the top. Sprinkle with fried shallots and ground roasted peanuts.

THIN RICE VERMICELLI
BUN

In Vietnam, the art of noodle making is learned by the most skilled cooks. *Bun* and various other noodles are made fresh by noodle specialists and sold daily, wrapped in banana leaves. In the West, we must make do with the dried variety. You may also try *somen* (Japanese alimentary paste noodles), which I find superior to rice vermicelli.

One bag (1 pound) of *bun* will serve 4 to 8 people, depending on whether the noodles are served as a side dish or as a main dish. For best results, cook these noodles a few hours ahead of time, cover and keep at room temperature or refrigerate until needed.

■ ■ ■ ■ ■ ■ ■ ■ ■ ■ ■

Soak the rice vermicelli in warm water for 15 to 20 minutes. Drain. Bring 4 quarts of water to a boil in a large pot. Drop in the noodles. With a pair of chopsticks, lift and separate the strands to prevent clumping. Boil the noodles for no more than 2 or 3 minutes. Test after 2 minutes so you will know when they are just *al dente.*

Drain in a colander and rinse well with cold running water so that no excess starch remains on the noodles. Drain thoroughly before using.

JAPANESE ALIMENTARY PASTE NOODLES
SOMEN

Somen is the best substitute when *bun* (thin rice vermicelli) is not available. *Somen* is a very fine wheat flour noodle that comes in a 1-pound package divided into 4 ribbon-tied bundles. The thinner the noodle, the better.

Four bundles (1 pound) of *somen* will serve 4 to 8 people, depending on whether they are served as a main dish or as an accompaniment to a grilled dish.

■ ■ ■ ■ ■ ■ ■ ■ ■ ■ ■

To cook 1 pound of *somen,* bring 4 quarts of water and 1 tablespoon salt to a boil in a large pot. Break each bundle in half and drop the noodles in the fast boiling water; cook briefly for no more than 1 or 2 minutes, depending on the thickness of the strands. With chopsticks, lift and separate the noodles to prevent clumping. Test after 1 minute so you will know when they are *al dente.* Drain in a colander. Rinse well with cold running water so that no excess starch remains on the noodles. Drain well before using.

Somen can be cooked a few hours beforehand. To prevent the cooked noodles from drying out, cover with plastic wrap and refrigerate until needed.

RICE-NOODLE SHEETS OR CRÊPES

BANH UOT

*R*ice-noodle sheets (*sha he fen* in Chinese) are commercially sold folded and bagged in plastic. They do not refrigerate or freeze well and, therefore, have to be kept at room temperature and consumed the same day. Making fresh noodles from scratch can also be a lot of fun.

These wet noodle sheets are usually cut up into ¾-inch strands for soups and stir-fries.

When a recipe calls for rice noodle crêpes, use 2 tablespoons of batter instead of ½ cup.

1 *cup rice flour*
½ *cup cornstarch*
½ *cup potato starch*
½ *teaspoon salt*
¼ *cup vegetable oil*

Combine all of the ingredients with 3 cups of cold water in a large mixing bowl. Blend well with a wire whisk. Let the batter rest for 30 minutes.

Generously oil a large baking sheet and set it next to the stove, along with a small bowl of vegetable oil and a brush.

Brush an 8-inch nonstick omelet pan with oil and set over low heat for 3 minutes. Stir the batter very well. Pour ½ cup (or 2 tablespoons for crêpes) of the batter into the pan. Tilt the pan and swirl to distribute the batter evenly. Cover the pan with a tight lid and steam for 5 minutes (2 minutes for the crêpes), or until the rice sheet looks bubbly.

Remove the lid without allowing the condensed water to drip onto the rice sheet. Loosen the edges of the rice sheet with the tip of a spatula; slide the rice sheet onto the oiled baking sheet. Allow the rice sheet to cool slightly before turning it a few times to coat both sides with oil. Transfer the cooled rice sheet to an oiled plate. Make sure that the baking sheet is generously oiled before placing another rice sheet on it.

Continue making rice sheets, taking care to whisk the batter thoroughly each time before adding it to the pan. Also allow each noodle sheet to cool thoroughly before stacking the next; otherwise they will stick together. Rice sheets may be prepared early in the day, covered with plastic wrap and kept at room temperature until ready to use.

NOTE To make this recipe work use fairly low heat and make sure that the pan is brushed with oil and heated for 15 seconds before adding each batch of well-stirred batter. To speed up the preparation time of this recipe, use 2 omelet pans at a time; while one rice sheet is being steamed, use the other pan to start the next sheet and so on until all the batter is used.

Yield: 7 noodle sheets (2 pounds), or about 28 paper-thin crêpes

TOASTED SESAME SEEDS
ME RANG

*L*ike peanuts, sesame seeds should be consumed shortly after they are toasted. Amounts are specified in recipes using toasted sesame seeds. Use raw, hulled white sesame seeds.

■ ■ ■ ■ ■ ■ ■ ■ ■ ■ ■

Place the sesame seeds in a skillet over moderate heat and cook, stirring constantly, until golden brown, about 3 minutes. Cool. Use as specified in the recipe.

To grind sesame seeds, process in a spice grinder or pound in a mortar with a pestle. Do not reduce sesame seeds to a powder; they should still retain a grainy texture.

NOTE When ground sesame seed is specified in a recipe, you can toast the seeds ahead of time. Grind them only a few minutes before using to best conserve the flavor.

SCALLION OIL
HANH LA PHI

*M*any Vietnamese dishes require this delicate scallion-flavored oil. Brushed over noodles, barbecued meats, vegetables or breads, it complements each item.

■ ■ ■ ■ ■ ■ ■ ■ ■ ■ ■

¼ cup peanut oil
2 scallions, finely sliced

Heat the oil in a small saucepan until hot but not smoking, about 300°F. Remove the pan from the heat and add the sliced scallions. Let the mixture steep at room temperature until completely cooled.

This oil mixture will keep stored in a tightly covered jar at room temperature for 1 week.

Yield: ¼ cup

CRISP-FRIED SHALLOTS
HANH KHO PHI

This is an important ingredient in many dishes throughout this book. Use as specified in recipes.

■ ■ ■ ■ ■ ■ ■ ■ ■ ■ ■

½ cup vegetable oil
½ cup thinly sliced shallots

Heat the oil in a small saucepan until hot but not smoking, about 300°F. Add the shallots and fry over moderate heat until crispy and golden brown, about 5 minutes. Do not overcook. Immediately remove the shallots with a slotted spoon and drain on paper towels. Reserve the oil for another use.

NOTE Cooked this way, shallots can be stored in a tightly covered jar on the kitchen shelf for up to 1 month.

Yield: about ⅓ cup

GRATED FRESH COCONUT

Grated fresh coconut is sometimes available in the frozen-food section at Asian markets. If you use canned or packaged coconut, try to get the type that is moist-packed and, preferably, unsweetened.

Grated coconut can be made easily at home, using a food processor or hand grater. Select a coconut that feels heavy and sounds full of water when shaken.

Preheat the oven to 350°F.

Pierce the "eyes" of the coconut with a screwdriver or ice pick. Drain the clear, sweet liquid (coconut water) into a bowl to be used as a drink or frozen for future use in recipes such as Pork Simmered in Coconut Water (page 125).

Bake the drained coconut for about 15 minutes, or until the shell begins to crack. Remove the coconut from the oven and let cool briefly.

Place the coconut on a sturdy surface. Using a hammer or kitchen mallet, crack the shell by hitting sharply on the middle of the coconut. The shell will split apart easily.

Remove the coconut meat from the shell with the point of a paring knife. Pare off the thin brown skin that clings to the white flesh. Shred the coconut in a food processor fitted with the shredding disk.

Yield: 2 cups

COCONUT MILK

NUOC COT DUA

■ ■ ■ ■ ■ ■ ■ ■ ■ ■ ■

2 medium coconuts, shelled, meat grated
5 cups boiling milk

Place the grated coconut in a food processor fitted with the steel blade. Add half of the boiling milk and blend until the coconut meat is finely ground (you may have to do this in small batches if you have a small food processor). Let steep for 30 minutes.

Pour the liquid through a fine sieve, lined with a thin kitchen towel or dampened cheesecloth, into a large bowl. Gather the edges of the towel together and squeeze out as much of the liquid as possible. Repeat the process with the same coconut meat and the remaining boiling milk to make a second pressing. Discard the coconut meat. Combine the two extractions. Refrigerate until needed.

As the coconut milk cools, coconut cream will rise to the top. This can be spooned off to use in desserts, or simply reblended into the milk. Stir to blend before each use.

NOTE Since coconut milk is highly perishable, refrigerate it for no longer than 3 days. For longer storage, freeze it in ice-cube trays, then store, wrapped in plastic bags. Before using, heat the coconut milk until completely melted. Two cubes equal ¼ cup.

If using dried, shredded, unsweetened coconut (desiccated coconut), use 2 cups hot half-and-half for every ½ pound dried coconut.

If fresh or dried coconut is unavailable, for every cup of coconut milk needed, use 1 cup of half-reduced heavy cream to ½ teaspoon of coconut extract.

Yield: about 4 cups

BASIC TOOLS AND EQUIPMENT

The traditional Vietnamese kitchen is a simple affair; it has far less equipment and tools than one in the West. With a wok, a cleaver, a chopping block and a mortar and pestle, a Vietnamese cook can work wonders with whatever ingredients he or she is given.

Therefore, for you to prepare the dishes described in this book, there's no need to invest in a whole new set of cooking utensils. Your kitchen probably already has everything you need. A skillet can be used in place of a wok. A food processor, blender or spice grinder can replace a mortar and pestle and will also make your work easier.

These basic serving pieces should be enough to give your table a Vietnamese accent: rice bowls, small saucers for dipping sauces, Asian soup bowls (for noodle soups and salads), chopsticks and porcelain spoons (porcelain is preferred because it does not absorb heat as metal does). All are usually available at Asian markets.

COOKING METHODS

Besides boiling, deep-frying, stir-frying, steaming and roasting, two very strong Vietnamese culinary traditions are grilling over charcoal and simmering in a plain or spicy caramel sauce.

Before cooking, cut-up meats are generally marinated with spices and Vietnamese fish sauce (*nuoc mam*) for thirty minutes or more. The purpose of this preseasoning is to enhance the taste of the food as well as to preserve the vitamins and protein content in the meat, while retaining its tenderness and delicacy.

The French term *mise-en-place* aptly describes the preparation steps needed before the final assembly of a recipe. Its literal meaning implies that all ingredients must be in a ready-to-cook state before the actual cooking takes place. For most Vietnamese dishes, more time is spent over the cutting board than over the stove. Any dehydrated foodstuffs, such as dried mushrooms or cellophane noodles, must be reconstituted well in advance of cooking. Vegetables, meats, fish and seasonings must be cut into the appropriate size and shape for each dish. All the ingredients should be made ready and kept easily accessible. A complete *mise-en-place* is essential as the cooking time of most dishes (especially stir-fries) is very short, with little time available to do last-minute preparation.

Items marked with an asterisk are essential ingredients to keep in your cupboard, refrigerator or freezer for Vietnamese meals.

FRESH VEGETABLES

Asian eggplant *(ca tim)* Also known as Chinese eggplant, this long, thin, seedless lavender variety has a sweet flavor and no hint of bitterness. Small firm ones are considered the best. Unlike Western eggplant, they do not require peeling, salting or rinsing.

Bamboo shoots *(mang)* Bamboo shoots fall into 2 categories: winter and spring. Winter shoots are best ("Na Ling" or "Companion" brands preferred); they are dug up from the cracked earth before the shoots grow to any length or size, making them extra-tender and tasty. Spring shoots are larger and more stringy. In Asian markets, look for bamboo shoots that are kept in large plastic tubs; although they are also processed, they do not have a tinned taste (like the canned ones).

Pickled or "sour" bamboo shoots (*mang chua*) are fresh shoots preserved in brine. They are sold shredded or sliced in vacuum-packed plastic bags. Use for stir-fries and hearty soups.

Bean curd/tofu *(dau hu)* Known in the U.S. as tofu, the pressed bean curd of the soybean has all the essential amino acids, is low in calories and is totally without cholesterol. It is flavorless but blends beautifully with other ingredients. You can do absolutely anything with bean curd: deep-fry, sauté, steam, bake, simmer, broil or purée. It comes in 3 textures: soft—added to soups or steamed dishes where cooking time is brief; semi-soft—used in stir-fries; and firm—for stuffing and deep-frying.

If bean curd is not to be used the same day, it should be put in a container with water to cover and then refrigerated. Replace the water each day. Cared for in this way, bean curd will keep for a week or longer. It is available in supermarkets or Asian markets.

Bean sprouts *(gia)* Mung bean sprouts, the most widely available variety, can be found almost anywhere. Never use canned bean sprouts; they don't have the crunchy texture that is their main characteristic. You can also grow your own from dried mung beans. They are eaten raw, added to soups or stir-fried. They will keep, covered with water, in the refrigerator for up to 3 days. In preparing fresh bean sprouts, keep in mind that they are mostly water. When stir-frying bean sprouts, do it quickly over very high heat, or they will release water and thin out the sauce.

Chinese cabbage, flowering *(cai xanh)* Distinguished by its yellow flowers and by its firm, small-stemmed stalks and crisp green leaves, this variety is considered the best of Chinese cabbages and is much prized by Vietnamese cooks. The taste is pleasant and mild and the texture tender but crisp. These stems must be peeled. Substitute Italian broccoli rabe *(rapini)*.

Chinese cabbage, Swatow mustard *(cai tau)* Also known as mustard greens, this vegetable resembles head lettuce in size and shape but differs in that the leaves wrapping the heart are thick stalks. This variety has a particularly sharp flavor, adding a wonderful clean taste when combined with other ingredients. However, after parboiling, the stalks become tender and succulent and the assertive flavor gets milder. Cut the stems into strips before cooking.

Pickled or "sour" mustard greens *(cai chua)* are the young tender hearts of mustard green cabbage preserved in brine. They are sold vacuum-packed in plastic bags. Use for stir-fries and soups.

Chinese flowering chives *(hoa he)* These are the thin, stiff flowering stems from Chinese chives. They are distinguished by a single, conical bulb at the tip of each stem. Sold fresh by the bunch, the stalks are tender and mild to eat. Select young stems with small, hard, tight flower heads; those with open flowers are considered fibrous and too old to eat. Refrigerate, wrapped in a plastic bag, for up to 3 or 4 days. Cut the flower and stem into 2-inch lengths and discard the bottom inch or so. Use in soups, salads, stir-fries or wherever an onion flavor is desired.

Chinese kale/broccoli *(cai lan)* This vegetable is distinguished from the other cabbages by clusters of white flowers and white haze on the leaves. It has smooth, round stems that are tender, succulent and flavorful. The stems must be peeled. Stir-frying enhances most of the good points of this vegetable. Substitute Western kale.

Daikon *(cu cai trang)* Also known as Asian white radish, this root is distinguished by its large cylindrical size (similar to a carrot), with smooth skin and whitish color. The flesh is crisp, juicy and mildly pungent and absorbs the flavors of soups and stews. It is also consumed raw in salads or pickled. Substitute white turnip.

Jicama *(cu dau)* Jicama is a brown-skinned root vegetable resembling a turnip. The crisp, delicious white flesh tastes like a cross between a juicy pear, a crunchy water chestnut and a starchy potato. It must be peeled and may be eaten raw in salads or cooked. Jicama is available in Southeast Asian and Caribbean greengrocers as well as many supermarkets.

Long beans *(dau dua)* As the name suggests, these beans can measure up to 2 feet in length. They are called "chopstick beans" in Vietnamese. These long beans are the immature pods of dry black-eyed peas. Select thin, dark, firm pods; the smaller the pods, the younger and more tender they are. They are available from Chinese greengrocers or at some Caribbean markets in the autumn. This vegetable is mostly enjoyed for its crunchy texture. Wash and cut into 2-inch lengths. Substitute string beans or tiny French green beans *(haricots verts)*.

Taro root *(khoai mon)* This oval-shaped tuber is distinguished by its brown, hairy skin with encircling rings. The flesh may vary from white to cream-colored, and is often speckled with purple. It tastes like bland potato with a very smooth, creamy texture. Vietnamese cooks use this starchy root the same way you would potato or sweet potato. Usually, small peeled chunks are steamed and added to a stew or sweet pudding.

Water spinach (rau muong) This aquatic plant may be considered Vietnam's national vegetable. It is not a relative of the Western spinach but is used in much the same way. It thrives in swamps but grows equally well on dry land. It has hollow stems and light green arrowhead-shaped leaves. It is prized by Vietnamese cooks for its outstanding contrast in texture between crunchy stems and limp leaves with a mild taste like spinach, when cooked. It is sold by the bunch at Chinese and Vietnamese greengrocers. Soak in water and wash thoroughly before using. To use, cut into 2-inch lengths and discard the stalk's bottom inch or so. It is good for stir-fries and soups. The stalks may be finely shredded, soaked in cold water to curl and then added raw to salads. Substitute regular spinach.

HERBS, GRASS AND SEASONINGS

Asian basil (rau que) This tropical anise-flavored basil, with purple stems and flowers, is available only at Vietnamese and Thai markets. Also known as Thai basil, this herb is exceptionally flavorful. It is a prerequisite for flavoring *Pho,* a famous beef and noodle soup. Substitute purple basil or regular sweet basil.

Carambola (khe) Also called star fruit, carambola is a deeply ribbed, yellow-green tropical fruit that is ovoid in shape. Sliced, it yields star-shaped pieces that are beautiful for garnishing. Traditionally, the unripe, sour fruit is eaten raw in salads. In seasoning soups, it may replace tamarind.

*Chiles (ot) Vietnamese cooks use two basic varieties of chiles. First, there's the large, elongated red or green chile, resembling the Italian pickling pepper. It is mildly hot and used sliced or whole, for garnishing. It is available in Asian markets, Caribbean greengrocers and some supermarkets. The second type is a tiny, fiery hot pepper called "bird" pepper, used for seasoning. Usually, these green and red chiles are mixed in small plastic bags and sold in Vietnamese and Thai markets. Refrigerate or freeze, wrapped in a plastic bag. Substitute fresh cayenne peppers or *serrano* chile pepper, the kind used in Mexican salsas.

Chinese chives (he) These long, flat green chives resemble large blades of grass. The flavor is reminiscent of garlic as well as onion. They are a common ingredient of the Vietnamese Vegetable Platter and Fresh Spring Rolls. They may be used as you would Western chives. Chinese chives are sold by the bunch. Refrigerate, wrapped in a plastic bag, for up to 3 days.

*Fresh coriander (rau ngo/mui) Also known as cilantro or Chinese parsley. The leafy green herb, resembling flat-leafed parsley, is highly scented, with a tart and refreshing taste. It is a prerequisite in Vietnamese cookery; without it, Vietnamese food will not be authentic. Refrigerate, wrapped in a moist paper towel, in a plastic bag. Like most fresh herbs, coriander should be added to a hot dish at the very end, since heat dissipates the flavor.

*Gingerroot (gung) Always use fresh ginger when you can; powdered ginger is a very poor substitute. Fresh gingerroot is available in Asian markets, Caribbean greengrocers and in most supermarkets. Select young rhizomes that are sweeter and more tender than older ginger, identified by large hair or fibers protruding from the root. Ginger can be frozen or refrigerated for months. Contrary to popular belief, it is not necessary to peel ginger; the skin contains the vitamins. Ginger is used for both its aromatic and chemical effects. It is added to fish, seafood and organ meats, not only to mask or remove objectionable odors, but to lend a subtle piquancy to the dish as well.

*Lemon grass (xa) Also called citronella root, lemon grass is an aromatic tropical grass that characterizes Vietnamese and Thai cuisine. Only the bulb-like base of the stalk is used to impart a compelling balm-like flavor to food. It isn't always available fresh, so when you find some, buy a few bunches. Cut the bulb portion up to the place where the leaves begin to branch, discarding the loose leaves. Freeze, wrapped in a plastic bag. When needed, peel off a layer of the tough outer leaves to disclose a white underlayer; crush lightly before slicing or chopping to release more flavor.

Dried lemon grass is lemon grass that has been shredded and dried. Soak in warm water for 1 hour and then chop before adding to recipes.

Sugar cane *(mia)* Sugar cane is a tall tropical grass, having a fat, jointed stalk resembling bamboo. It is cultivated widely in Vietnam as a food crop and as a source of sugar. The juicy yellow flesh is spongy and stringy. In Vietnam, the pressed juice from the canes is served as a soft drink in the summer. Mulled with ginger, it becomes a hot beverage for the winter. It is sold fresh at Caribbean greengrocers and Asian markets but is more readily available canned. Fresh sugar cane requires peeling.

*Tropical mint *(bac-ha)* Of the numerous Asian mint species, the round-leafed mint, a tropical variety of spearmint, is the one most commonly used by Vietnamese cooks. This fragrant herb is an integral part of Vietnamese salads, especially in the traditional Vegetable Platter (page 169). Refrigerate, wrapped in a moist paper towel, in a plastic bag.

SUNDRIES AND FLAVORINGS

Most of the following ingredients have a long shelf life if kept very dry in tightly covered containers, preferably out of the sun.

Agar-agar *(thach-hoa)* Agar-agar is a gelatin derived from refined seaweed. It is available in 2 forms: packages of two 10-inch-long rectangular sticks (*kanten* in Japanese), or 2- to 4-ounce packages of 14-inch translucent strands that resemble crinkled strips of cellophane. It is widely used in Southeast Asian cooking for molded jellied sweets, as it sets without refrigeration in temperatures up to 100° F. To use agar-agar, soak it in warm water for 30 minutes. Squeeze the pieces dry. Add to cold water in a saucepan (as a general rule, ½ stick of *kanten* or ⅔ ounce of agar-agar will thicken 4 cups liquid) and simmer until the agar-agar dissolves completely. Add sugar or other ingredients and heat again just to a boil. Pour into a mold or dish and refrigerate until set.

*Anchovy sauce *(mam nem)* A blend of fermented anchovies and salt, this sauce comes bottled and has to be diluted and seasoned to make the traditional *Mam Nem* sauce (page 216). It is available in Vietnamese and Thai groceries; the best brand is labeled "Saigon's *Mam Nem*." Store it in the refrigerator after opening.

Substitute canned anchovies or anchovy paste, mixed with a little water.

Banana leaves *(la chuoi)* In Vietnam, banana leaves are used to wrap foods for steaming or to enfold food for carrying. The food is served in the leaf, but the leaf is not eaten. It is sold fresh or frozen in 1-pound packages in Latin American and Asian markets. To use, thaw (if the leaves are frozen), then dip the leaves briefly in boiling water to make them pliable. Usually, an overwrapping of foil is necessary to prevent water from seeping into the food. Store unprepared leaves in the freezer. Substitute *Ti* leaves (available fresh at florists) or foil.

Chile paste *(tuong ot tuoi)* A fiery hot mixture of mashed fresh red chiles, garlic, salt and soybean oil. Do not confuse this product with the Chinese hot bean paste. Look for "Huy Fong" brand. It is used as a table condiment and seasoning for sauces and stir-fries. Substitute mashed fresh chile pepper.

*Chile sauce *(lak kiu chuong/tuong ot)* Also known as Sriracha hot chile sauce. This bottled, thick, fiery Louisiana-style hot sauce is made from ground fresh chile peppers, garlic, sugar, salt and vinegar. It is used as a table condiment and seasoning in soups and salads. Substitute *Sambal oeleck* or Tabasco.

*Coconut milk *(nuoc dua)* Coconut milk is the chief ingredient used in preparing Vietnamese curries and sweets. It is the liquid wrung from grated and soaked coconut meat. The clear and flavorsome juice inside the hard shell is called coconut water; it is mainly used as a soft drink or as a tenderizing agent in stews and fondues. It is much easier to buy canned or frozen coconut milk, available in Asian and Caribbean markets, than to make your own. However, a recipe is provided on page 227. Do not confuse coconut milk with coconut cream, a heavy, sweetened coconut product often used in Latin-American cooking. Only unsweetened coconut milk is used in this book.

*Curry paste *(tuong ca-ri)* This chile oil-based curry paste is more pungent and spicier than curry powder. It is usually combined with curry powder to give a dish an assertive flavor. The best brands are "Daw Sen" and "Golden Bell," sold at Indian and Chinese groceries.

*Dried shrimp (*tom kho*) These are shelled, dried and salted shrimp with a pungent flavor, used in small quantities to season certain dishes, especially soups and stir-fries (it is not a substitute for fresh shrimp. The larger in size and darker pink in color, the better the quality and the higher the price will be. Soak in warm water for 30 minutes or longer before cooking. Reserve the intensely flavorful soaking liquid; it will give a delightful lift to soups and sauces.

*Fish sauce (*nuoc mam*) *Nuoc mam* is like Thai *nam pla* but stronger. This thin, brownish sauce is obtained by fermenting salted fresh anchovies. It is a prerequisite in Vietnamese cuisine. "Squid" and "Ruang Ton" brands are widely available, bottled, in Asian markets and some supermarkets.

*Five-spice powder (*huong-liu*) This fragrant, reddish brown powder is a blend of ground star anise, fennel or anise seed, clove, cinnamon and Sichuan peppercorns. It is used to flavor barbecued meats and stews. If possible, buy it in small amounts as it is very strong and a little goes a long way. It keeps indefinitely in a covered jar.

Flower water/essences (*nuoc hoa*) In Vietnam, flower waters and essences are often used to flavor sweet drinks and desserts. Most popular are jasmine, grapefruit and orange-blossom water. They are produced by distilling the fresh petals of these flowers. You may substitute flower essences, but they are more concentrated; use only a few drops. Flower waters and essences are sold in Asian or Indian markets, liquor stores and pharmacies.

Galangal (*rieng*) Also know as *laos*, its Indonesian name, galangal resembles ginger but has zebra-like markings and pink shoots. If it is unavailable, substitute fresh ginger juice or ground galangal. Dried galangal is used only in soups and stews; soak before using. It is sold in Vietnamese and Thai stores.

*Glutinous rice (*gao nep*) Also called "sweet rice," or "sticky rice." There are 2 types of glutinous rice: the Chinese and Japanese short-grained type and the longer-grained Thai variety, which is favored by the Vietnamese. This rice has a soft, sticky texture with a slightly sweet flavor when cooked. Stuffed with mung bean paste and fresh bacon, it becomes rice cake (*Banh Trung*), a New Year's favorite. It is available at Vietnamese and Thai markets. Substitute Japanese *moki* rice. For cooking instructions, see page 133.

Grass jelly (*thach-den*) Also known as *Xinh-Xao* or *Liangfen* agar jelly in Chinese. Prepared from seaweed and cornstarch, this black jelly tastes and smells faintly of iodine. It is sold in cans at Asian markets. Drain and dice or shred the jelly before adding it to soybean milk or sweet drinks made of simple syrup, coconut milk, crushed ice and a few drops of jasmine water.

Gypsum (*thach-cao*) Chemically known as calcined calcium sulfate, gypsum is also called plaster of Paris or plaster stone. This chemical agent has been used by the Chinese as a coagulant for bean curd for over a thousand years. It is sold at Chinese pharmacies.

*Hoisin sauce Hoisin sauce is a sweet, piquant brown paste made from soybeans, red beans, sugar, garlic, vinegar, chile, sesame oil and flour. Vietnamese cooks often mix it with broth, fresh chile pepper and ground peanuts to make a dip. It is also used as a barbecue sauce for meat and poultry. Available in cans or jars, different brands have slightly different flavors; "Koon Chun" is a slightly spicier brand. Refrigerate after opening.

Lily buds (*hoa hien/kim cham*) Also called "golden needles," these are the buds of a special type of lily (*Hemerocallis fulva*). The pale gold, 2- to 3-inch-long dried buds are often used in combination with tree ears and cellophane noodles to add texture to stir-fries, soups and stuffings. Soak them in warm water for 30 minutes, then remove the hard stems before cooking.

Lotus seeds (*hat sen*) These seeds of the lotus plant resemble large, round peanuts. In Vietnam, where very fresh, young lotus seeds are available, they are eaten raw, used in stews, soups (especially in vegetarian cooking and sweet confections). They also may be mashed into a paste and used as a filling for Moon Cakes. Canned and dried lotus seeds are sold in Chinese markets. Canned lotus seeds need no preparation, while the dried ones must be soaked in water overnight and then boiled until tender.

*Mung beans, yellow (*dau xanh*) Green mung beans are normally used to grow bean sprouts. Husked, green mung beans become yellow mung beans. Yellow mung beans are often used in preparing starchy dishes and sweets. They are sold in Asian and Indian markets as "peeled split mung beans." Look for "Cock" or "Summit" brands.

*Mushrooms, Chinese black (*nam huong*) These dried mushrooms are sold in 8-ounce packages at Asian markets. They are expensive buy highly esteemed for their distinct, robust flavor and succulent texture. There are different varieties but the best are *fah goo* (in Chinese): They have thick caps, 1 to 2 inches in diameter, and are light brown in color with prominent white cracks on their surface. Generally, they are very fragrant. Dried mushrooms require soaking. Strain and save the soaking liquid to add flavor to stocks and sauces. Though fresh or dried Japanese shiitake mushrooms are not as flavorful, they may replace Chinese mushrooms.

*Mushrooms, straw (*nam rom*) Attractive umbrella-shaped caps with a yellowish brown color distinguish these mild-flavored mushrooms. They are also known as "paddy straw" mushrooms because they grow on straw and rice husks. Considered a delicacy, they are added to soup and stir-fries. Straw mushrooms are available "peeled," in cans, at most Asian markets and at some supermarkets. Substitute canned button mushrooms.

*Mushrooms, tree ears (*nam meo/moc nhi*) Also called cloud ears or wood ears. The "ear" designation of these black, chip-like fungi refers to their convoluted shape, reminiscent of a human ear. The best tree ear mushrooms are the very tiny, wrinkled and bark-like specimens that often are mislabeled as "dried vegetables." When soaked in water, they expand to four or five times their original size and become jelly-like and translucent but stay crisp. They are mainly used to add texture to stir-fries, stuffings and vegetarian dishes.

Oyster sauce (*dao han*) Oyster sauce is a thick, richly flavored slightly sweet, salty brown sauce made from oyster extract, soy sauce, sugar and vinegar. The flavor of different brands varies considerably; one of the best is "Panda" brand. It is sold bottled in Asian stores and most supermarkets. It is mainly used to season stir-fries.

*Peanuts (*dau phong*) Peanuts are an important ingredient in Vietnamese cooking. Raw peanuts are preferred because they are usually roasted and ground just before serving to release their intense nutty flavor. Peeled raw peanuts are sold in Asian markets. Peanuts are used for texture and flavor in dipping sauces and as garnish for cooked food. For roasting instructions, see page 220. Substitute dry roasted, unsalted peanuts.

*Pickled shallots (*cu kieu chua*) These are the very young, tender bulbs of scallions (spring onions, packed in vinegar, sugar and salt. They are used as a condiment to accompany grilled foods and noodle dishes or added as seasoning to sweet-and-sour dishes. Pickled shallots, sometimes called pickled leeks, are sold in jars or cans in Asian stores. The best quality comes in a jar; look for "Mee Chun, Champion" brand. Drain before using.

*Pork skin, dried shredded (*bi heo kho*) These are sold only in Vietnamese markets. Look for "Viet My" or "Golden Dragon" brands.

*Preserved vegetables (*tan xai*) Called *chong choy* in Chinese, this condiment is a mix of cured bits of Chinese cabbage and seasonings. It is sold in small crocks at Chinese markets. Extremely pungent, it is used only in small amounts to add flavor to soups and noodle dishes. As it is quite sandy, be sure to rinse thoroughly before using.

*Rice papers, dried (*banh trang*) These round, translucent, brittle sheets are made of rice flour, water and salt and are sold in Asian markets. Their cross-hatch pattern comes from being dried on bamboo trays. They are essential in preparing the national dish *Cha Gio*. They come in various sizes of round and triangular shapes. The round papers are used for spring rolls, while the triangular ones are used at the table to wrap grilled foods. Store, sealed in a plastic bag, in a cupboard. Soften, a sheet at a time, in warm water until flexible and ready to use. There is no substitute. Chinese egg-roll wrappers will not do; they are too thick.

*Rice powder, roasted *(thinh)* A prerequisite in Vietnamese cooking, this traditional flavoring may be bought in Vietnamese groceries or can be easily prepared at home; see the instructions on page 220.

*Rice vinegar (*giam gao*) I use rice vinegar instead of white vinegar in numerous recipes for its mild, sweeter taste. Sold in Asian markets and supermarkets, the Japanese varieties "Marukan" and "Chikyu-uma" are excellent.

*Rock sugar *(duong phen)* Also called "rock candy" or "yellow rock sugar," the name aptly describes the sweetener that looks like a crystallized rock. It is made from white sugar, brown sugar and honey and, therefore, is much sweeter than regular sugar. It is sold in 1-pound bags in Chinese groceries. Store in the refrigerator. Cover the lumps with a cloth, then crush into a powder using a mallet or hammer. It is used to season Vietnamese sausages and meatballs. Substitute white sugar.

*Sesame oil *(dau me)* The Oriental type of sesame oil is a rich-flavored, amber-colored oil obtained from pressed roasted sesame seeds. A dash or two is added to marinades or at the last moment of cooking to flavor certain dishes. Do not confuse this type of oil with the cold-pressed, unroasted sesame oil sold in health food stores, which is insipid in flavor. Look for "Kadoya" brand. Store in a cool, dark place to slow rancidity.

*Sesame seeds (*me*) Sesame seeds are sold hulled or unhulled in Asian markets, health food stores and supermarkets. Hulled white sesame seeds are preferred. A day-to-day ingredient in Vietnam, toasted and crushed sesame seeds are used to flavor dipping sauces and marinades or to coat sweets and other foods. After roasting, they lose flavor rapidly, so be sure to toast them as close to serving time as possible. For instructions on toasting sesame seeds, see page 225.

*Shrimp chips (*banh phong tom*) Labeled as "prawn crackers" or *kroepoek* (in Indonesian), these dried, reddish pink chips are made from ground shrimp, tapioca starch and egg whites. They are popularly eaten in Vietnam as a snack or as an accompaniment to salads. They are sold in 2 sizes: small and large. Small chips are usually tastier; look for "Pigeon" brand, packed in 8-ounce boxes. Shrimp chips must be deep-fried before serving. As their Vietnamese name indicates (literally, puffed shrimp chips, they swell to triple their size as soon as they hit the hot oil. For instructions on cooking shrimp chips, see page 221. Store tightly sealed in a plastic bag.

*Shrimp sauce *(mam tom/mam ruoc)* This very pungent product is made from pounded, salted fermented shrimp. It is grayish pink and sold in bottles or jars at Vietnamese and Chinese grocery stores; "Lee Kum Kee" brand is excellent, but try to obtain "Mam Ruoc Bao Giao Thao," the best Vietnamese product on the market. In Vietnam, shrimp paste is commonly used to flavor soups, salads, dipping sauces, fried rice and dishes containing pork or beef. Do not confuse with Thai dried shrimp paste. Substitute anchovy paste.

Soybeans, dried *(dau nanh)* Soybeans are the edible dried seeds of the Glycine Soja plant. Used in the production of bean curd (tofu), they are the main ingredients in preparing soybean milk and jellied bean curd. They are sold in Asian groceries.

*Soybean sauce *(tuong)* Soybean sauce is a traditional light brown sauce prepared from a soybean product in which the ground beans are mixed with water, roasted rice powder and salt. It is sold, bottled, only in Vietnamese groceries. Do not confuse soybean sauce with the saltier, thicker Chinese ground bean paste. Vietnamese vegetarians commonly utilize this sauce. Substitute yellow bean sauce, diluted with a little water.

*Soy sauce *(si dau)* Where soy sauce is required in this cookbook, Japanese "Kikkoman" or "light" soy sauce should be used. It is lighter in color and different in taste and saltiness from regular Chinese soy sauce, which is dark and stains food black.

*Star anise (*hoi huong*) Star anise the dried pod of an exotic tree of the *Magnoliaceaes* family, native to

China. Mainly grown in the Lang-Son region (north Vietnam), this bark-like spice has cloves that resemble an eight-pointed star. Not related to aniseed, it yields a strong licorice flavor and is used to enhance soups and stews. When chewed, it sweetens the breath and aids digestion. Sold in Asian markets and spice shops. Substitute anise seed.

*Tamarind *(me chua)* Tamarind is a sour-tasting fruit with shelled pods that contain seeds. It is usually added in liquid form to flavor soups, and this is obtained by soaking and straining the pulp of the pod. The pulp is sold, soft-dried, in 8-ounce blocks. "Erawan" brand is excellent. Store in an airtight container at room temperature; it will keep indefinitely. Substitute lemon juice or vinegar with a touch of sugar.

*Turmeric *(bot nghe)* Turmeric is the ground powder of a rhizome of the ginger family. Deep yellow in color, this spice is used primarily as a dye. It is sold in the spice section of all supermarkets.

Yeast ball *(men)* *Men* is also known as "wine ball," an Oriental dry yeast used in making rice wine. It is sold in Vietnamese and Chinese food stores or pharmacies. Relatively small, this round, grayish ball is usually sold in pairs, wrapped in a tiny plastic bag; ask for it.

MEATS AND SAUSAGES

*Chinese sausage *(lap xuong)* Chinese sausages may be made from pork, duck liver or beef, but pork is most popular. These dried, red, sweet sausages (*lop chong* in Cantonese) are sold, hung by the strings, in Chinese meat markets or in 1-pound packages in Asian groceries. Blanch before cooking (to make the sausage less fatty). An easy, delicious way to cook this sausage is to place it directly on top of rice as it cooks in a pot.

*Vietnamese pork sausage, boiled *(gio)* This savory sausage is a very important ingredient in Vietnamese cuisine. It is sold, wrapped in banana leaves and aluminum foil, only in Vietnamese groceries. Keep some on hand in your freezer.

NOODLES

*Cellophane noodles *(mien/bun tau)* Also called bean threads or mung bean vermicelli. Cellophane noodles are not really noodles but rather a vegetable product made from mung bean starch. They are used primarily for their texture in soups and stuffings. Soak in warm water for 30 minutes, then cut into shorter lengths before cooking. If they are to be deep-fried, cook them straight from the package (they will puff dramatically in hot oil), then use as a nest for stir-fries. They are sold in 1-pound or 2-ounce packages in Asian stores and some supermarkets.

*Egg noodles *(mi)* In areas with a substantial Asian population, egg noodles are sold dried, in packages, or fresh in the refrigerated sections of Chinese markets. Two basic varieties are used in this book: the long, extra-thin Cantonese-style egg noodle strands called *don mein,* often swirled into a nest, used for deep-frying, and the broader egg noodles called *fu don mein,* about ¼ inch wide and flat, used in soups. Fresh egg noodles are preferable. Do not confuse them with "chow mein noodles." Store in plastic bags in the freezer for months or in the refrigerator for 3 or 4 days.

*Rice sticks *(banh pho)* Also called "dried rice sticks." Rice sticks are flat thin noodles made from rice flour and water; they are available dried in 1-pound packages in most Asian markets. There are 3 sizes to choose from: wide, medium and narrow strands. The wide variety is used primarily in stir-fries, although some people like to use it in soups. The medium size is most popular; it is used in the traditional soup *pho,* in cold or warm noodle salads and stir-fries. The narrow size is more suitable for noodle soups. For cooking information, see page 222.

*Rice vermicelli, thin *(bun)* Called *Mai fun* in Chinese. These thin, brittle, white rice noodles are dried in 8-inch looped skeins. They are packaged in layers and sold in Asian markets. Look for "Double Swallow" or "Mount Elephant" brand. *Bun* are used in soups and noodle salads and are served cold at the table as an accompaniment to grilled or curried dishes. The best substitute is Japanese alimentary paste noodles or *somen.* For cooking information, see page 223.

*Rice vermicelli, extra-thin *(banh hoi)* As *bun* above, *banh hoi* is a rice noodle variety as fine as hair, possibly the thinnest of all noodles. They are packed, dried, in 1-pound packages, containing 8 individual portions swirled into a square cake. Look for "Summit" brand. *Banh hoi* are so thin they need almost no cooking. They are used primarily as an accompaniment to grilled foods. For cooking information, see page 222.

Somen (Japanese alimentary paste noodles) Delicate thin white noodles made from wheat flour, *somen* resembles the traditional *bun* (rice vermicelli) of Vietnam in texture and flavor. Even after cooking, *somen* stays moist at room temperature or refrigerated. It comes in 1-pound boxes with 5 individual bundles tied by a black ribbon. For cooking information, see page 223.

FLOURS AND THICKENERS

Potato starch (bot khoai) Potato starch is added to meatballs and pâtés as a binder, yielding a slightly crunchy texture. Potato starch is available in the kosher foods department of supermarkets and in Asian markets.

Rice flour (bot gao/bot te) This is a type of flour made from long-grain rice. Do not confuse it with glutinous rice flour, which is made from sweet rice; the two are not interchangeable. Rice flour is the basis for many rice noodle dishes and sweets. "Erawan" and "Tienley" are two excellent brands. It is sold in 1-pound bags in Asian markets.

Rice flour, glutinous or sweet (bot nep) Glutinous or sweet rice flour is made from glutinous rice. It is used to make sweet confections. Look for "Erawan" or "Peacock" brand in Asian markets or for *mochiko* in Japanese stores.

Tapioca starch/flour (bot nang) This is the starch of the cassava root. A very important ingredient in preparing fresh noodle wrappers, it gives them a translucent sheen and chewiness.

Tapioca pearls (bot bing-bang) These are granules made from the starch of the cassava root. Pearl tapioca is used mainly as a thickener and texture ingredient in certain soups and sweet puddings. It is available in Asian groceries and many supermarkets, packed in 8-ounce bags.

Anzen Japanese Foods and Imports, 736 Northeast Union Ave., Portland, OR 97232, Tel: 503/233-5111.

Aphrodisia Products, Inc., 282 Bleecker St., New York, NY 10014, Tel: 212/989-6440.

Asian Food Market, 217 Summit Ave., Jersey City, NJ 07306, Tel: 201/333-7254.

Bangkok Market, 4757 Melrose Ave., Los Angeles, CA 90029, Tel: 213/662-9705.

De Wildt Imports, Inc., R.D. #3, Bangor, PA 18013, Tel: 215/588-0600.

Far East Trading Co., 2835 N. Western Ave., Chicago, IL 60618, Tel: 312/486-5800.

Haig's Delicacies, 642 Clement St., San Francisco, CA 94118, Tel: 415/752-6283.

Jung's Oriental Food Store, 1140 E. 9th St., Des Moines, IA 50316, Tel: 515/266-3891.

Kam Kuo Food Products, 7 Mott St., New York, NY 10013, Tel: 212/349-3097.

Kam Man Food Products, 200 Canal St., New York, NY 10013, Tel: 212/571-0330.

Montana Mercantile, 1500 Montana Ave., Santa Monica, CA 90403, Tel: 213/451-1418.

Oriental Food Market and Cooking School, 2801 West Howard Street, Chicago, IL 60645, Tel: 312/274-2826.

Pacific Mercantile Grocery, 1925 Lawrence St., Denver, CO 80202, Tel: 303/295-0293.

Southeastern Food Supplies, 400 NE 67th St., Miami, FL 33138, Tel: 305/758-1432.

Star Market, 3349 N. Clark St., Chicago, IL 60657, Tel: 312/472-0599.

Super Asian Market, 2719 Wilson Blvd., Arlington, VA 22201, Tel: 703/527-0777.

Uwajimaya, 519 Sixth Ave. S., Seattle, WA 98104, Tel: 206/624-6248.

Vietnam House, 242 Farmington Ave., Hartford, CT 06105, Tel: 203/524-0010.

Prop Credits

Dishes by **Richard Bennett** for Great Barrington Pottery, Housatonic, Mass.: pages 18, 22, 23, 31, 43, 50, 66, 71, 91, 127, 190.

Dishes by **Marek Cecula** for Tiffany, Fifth Ave., New York, N.Y.: page 86.

Painted backgrounds by **Betsy Davis,** New York, N.Y.: pages 18, 58, 66, 71, 86, 127, 158, 162, 175.

Dishes courtesy **Gordon Foster,** 1322 Third Ave., New York, N.Y.: pages 27, 95, 118, 155, 194, 207.

Dishes by **Pascal Golay** for Contemporary Porcelain Gallery, 105 Sullivan St., New York, N.Y.: pages 46, 175.

Plates and bowl by **Paul Hoff** for Contemporary Porcelain Gallery, 105 Sullivan St., New York, N.Y.: page 74.

Plates by **Dan Levy** for Contemporary Porcelain Gallery, 105 Sullivan St., New York, N.Y.: page 75.

Plates courtesy **Frank McIntosh** at Henri Bendel, West 57th St., New York, N.Y.: pages 38, 98, 110, 130, 142, 146 (napkin), 162, 183.

Bowl by **Lyn Riccardo** for Contemporary Porcelain Gallery, 105 Sullivan St., New York, N.Y.: page 146.

Plates by **Patricia Glave Roninger** for Contemporary Porcelain Gallery, 105 Sullivan St., New York, N.Y.: pages 158, 159.

Glasses from New Glass for Gallery Nillson, 138 Wooster St., New York, N.Y.: page 199.

Platters courtesy Terrafirma, West 25th St., New York, N.Y.: page 79.

Conversions

LIQUID MEASURES

FLUID OUNCES	U.S. MEASURES	IMPERIAL MEASURES	MILLILITERS	FLUID OUNCES	U.S. MEASURES	IMPERIAL MEASURES	MILLILITERS
	1 TSP	1 TSP	5	12	1½ CUPS OR ¾ PINT		240
¼	2 TSP	1 DESSERT SPOON	7	15		¾ PINT	420
½	1 TBS	1 TBS	15	16	2 CUPS OR 1 PINT		450
1	2 TBS	2 TBS	28	18	2¼ CUPS		500, ½ LITER
2	¼ CUP	4 TBS	56				
4	½ CUP OR ¼ PINT		110	20	2½ CUPS	1 PINT	560
				24	3 CUPS OR 1½ PINTS		675
5		¼ PINT OR 1 GILL	140	25		1¼ PINTS	700
6	¾ CUP		170	27	3½ CUPS		750
8	1 CUP OR ½ PINT		225	30	3¾ CUPS	1½ PINTS	840
				32	4 CUPS OR 2 PINTS OR 1 QUART		900
9			250, ¼ LITER	35		1¾ PINTS	980
10	1¼ CUPS	½ PINT	280	36	4½ CUPS		1000, 1 LITER

SOLID MEASURES

U.S. AND IMPERIAL MEASURES		METRIC MEASURES		U.S. AND IMPERIAL MEASURES		METRIC MEASURES	
OUNCES	POUNDS	GRAMS	KILOS	OUNCES	POUNDS	GRAMS	KILOS
1		28		18		500	½
2		56		20	1¼	560	
3½		100		24	1½	675	
4	¼	112		27		750	¾
5		140		28	1¾	780	
6		168		32	2	900	
8	½	225		36	2¼	1000	1
9		250	¼	40	2½	1100	
12	¾	340		48	3	1350	
16	1	450		54		1500	1½

OVEN TEMPERATURE EQUIVALENTS

FAHRENHEIT	GAS MARK	CELSIUS	HEAT OF OVEN	FAHRENHEIT	GAS MARK	CELSIUS	HEAT OF OVEN
225	¼	107	VERY COOL	375	5	190	FAIRLY HOT
250	½	121	VERY COOL	400	6	204	FAIRLY HOT
275	1	135	COOL	425	7	218	HOT
300	2	148	COOL	450	8	232	VERY HOT
325	3	163	MODERATE	475	9	246	VERY HOT
350	4	177	MODERATE				

INDEX

Page numbers in **boldface** indicate photographs

Designed by Rita Marshall
Composed in Serlio and Simocini Garamond
by Dix Type Inc., Syracuse, NY 13220
Printed and bound by Toppan Printing Company
Tokyo, Japan